Arnold Wesker

CASEBOOKS ON MODERN DRAMATISTS
VOLUME 17
GARLAND REFERENCE LIBRARY OF THE HUMANITIES
VOLUME 1672

CASEBOOKS ON MODERN DRAMATISTS
KIMBALL KING, *General Editor*

Arnold Wesker
A Casebook

Edited by
Reade W. Dornan

Garland Publishing, Inc.
A member of the Taylor & Francis Group
New York and London
1998

Library of Congress Cataloging-in-Publication Data

Wesker, Arnold, 1932–
    Arnold Wesker : a casebook / edited by Reade W. Dornan.
        p.   cm. — (Garland reference library of the humanities ; vol.
1672. Casebooks on modern dramatists ; vol. 17)
    Includes index.
    ISBN 0-8153-1178-8 (alk. paper)
    1. Wesker, Arnold, 1932– —Criticism and interpretation.
I. Dornan, Reade W.   II. Title.   III. Series: Garland reference
library of the humanities ; vol. 1672.   IV. Series: Garland
reference library of the humanities.   Casebooks on modern dramatists ;
vol. 1672.
PR6073.E75Z53   1998
822'.914—dc21   98-5256
                                                                     CIP

Cover photograph of Arnold Wesker by Dusty Wesker.

Printed on acid-free, 250-year-life paper
Manufactured in the United States of America

To David—with love and gratitude

Table of Contents

General Editor's Note

While Arnold Wesker and Harold Pinter were both raised in the London Jewish community, Wesker has made far greater use of Jewish traditions and attitudes in his plays. Furthermore, he has created a more truly proletarian drama than any of his contemporaries. The poor are taken seriously in his works and possess a dignity and determination that contrasts sharply with traditional portrayals of the English working class—the good-natured, ineffectual, congenitally lazy stereotypes that have existed for centuries in English literature. Wesker's characters are not humorless. The music hall humor and crude humor that Stoppard and Pinter have also employed successfully in sophisticated dramas is present in Wesker, too. Still, the emphasis of his plays is on a hard-won survival in a caste system. His most famous plays form a trilogy: *Chicken Soup, Roots,* and *I'm Talking about Jerusalem.* A major presence in English drama, Wesker is read by all serious British students preparing for their "A levels." He continues to write vigorously for the stage and other cultural projects.

The editor of this Casebook, Reade Dornan, was attracted to Wesker's work through the attention that the Centre 42 movement brought to arts for the people. Her book, *Arnold Wesker Revisited,* explores that history in light of Wesker's total corpus. Dornan has also written articles on John McGrath, Caryl Churchill, contemporary women playwrights, and Omaha Magic Theatre. Her most recent research has been on the Theatre-in-Education movements in Britain and the United States. In this volume she surveys the achievements of a British literary giant.

Kimball King

Acknowledgments

Above all, I would like to thank the contributors who contributed articles without adequate compensation. I hope they feel some satisfaction from participating in a project that assembled the best of the Weskerian scholars and brought in very high quality work. I am especially grateful for their patience and good nature.

Thanks to Arnold Wesker, who, despite his busy schedule, gave me advice when I needed it. His gentle encouragement kept me focussed.

My appreciation also goes to Kimball King, Phyllis Korper, and Gary Konas at Garland for their forbearance and support. Without their perserverence, the casebook would never have come to completion.

And finally, I would like to thank *Modern Drama* (vol. 29, June 1986: 185–206) for allowing us to reprint "Wesker and Utopia in the Sixties" by Heiner Zimmermann in revised form, and *The New Review* (Feb. 1975) for allowing us to reprint a slightly altered "Profile 10: Arnold Wesker" by Margaret Drabble.

Introduction
Reade Dornan

Why Wesker?

For those of us living far from London and outside the British Empire, Arnold Wesker is an ideal playwright to study. Most of his plays are in print (Penguin); a seven-volume set is accessible to those of us who cannot purchase theatre tickets to productions across the waters. Since most of his works are mounted in England's regions or in Europe and quite a number of the more recent plays have not seen production at all, even Britons may have trouble seeing the plays. Most of us have therefore become readers of Wesker's works rather than theatre patrons. In that sense, we are all front row critics—of the texts.

Penguin's decision to publish a multi-volume set of the plays reflects Wesker's ongoing broad appeal to theatre audiences in diverse cultures worldwide. Universal themes of political disillusionment, failed family relationships, intense love affairs, and frustration in the workplace speak to audiences in Denmark, Malaysia, Canada, Norway, Cuba, Japan, Italy, India, Poland, Sweden, Germany, France, and the United States wherever readers appreciate the weight of ordinary experience. There have been translations of these plays in many more countries than I can name. Indeed, at least one of Wesker's plays has been in production somewhere in the world just about every day since the early 1970s.

It is in the schools that Wesker's plays most often retain their currency. For many years, *Shylock* and plays from the *Trilogy* appeared as staples on the exam lists in Britain, Italy, and France. What often appeals to students is his stubborn defense of the individual. Refusing to be influenced by the political trends like many leftist causes of his time, Wesker has championed the cause of stubborn heroes against ideologies and popular movements that drown alternative voices. His individualism goes beyond the normal British tolerance for eccentricity, in that he will defend individuals whose political values are abhorrent even to himself. Wesker has repeatedly written letters on behalf of such groups as Cuban rebels, Palestinian protestors, and the IRA.

Wesker's vehement stand against the movement of "political correct-ness" is yet another example. Although a member of a religious mi-nority that is threatened around the world, he nevertheless battles the right of racists to speak out nonviolently even if they brutally de-nounce Jews. Wesker would rather mock racist terms than suppress the hatred that often festers and later erupts into a more violent form.

Wesker's independent spirit is embraced by today's young people, weary and wary of politics of all sorts. Students sense he is one of them—idealistic, somewhat reactionary, and aloof. He is popular among teachers as well. It's the educator in Wesker that raises his stock among many academics. Like them, he is a staunch proponent of open and accessible education. In his earliest years as a playwright, in the 1958 "Let Battle Commence!," he declared optimistically, "I want to teach. I want to write my plays not only for the class of people who acknowledge plays to be a legitimate form of expression, but for those to whom the phrase "form of expression" may mean nothing whatso-ever. It is the bus driver, the housewife, the miner and the Teddy Boy to whom I should like to address myself" (96). He was driven by a need to explain to Mr. Smith—unemployed, bored, and abusive of his family—what it was all about, and so he wrote plays to change the world around him. Believing that works of art are transformative, he vowed to give his working-class neighbors "tools for living." He urged other artists to do the same: "We must pick up our poems, our plays and films, tuck them under our arms and go out to the public and do battle with them" (98). The Centre 42 movement, he believed, might be one instrument for reaching and educating working-class audi-ences. Critics in the 60s were rightfully scornful of his naive paternal-ism, but many teachers felt they understood the spirit in which these remarks were made.

What Wesker quickly discovered during those early years was that to be effective, education entails more than merely exposing his audi-ences to art's power. What he belatedly realized is that educators can-not teach directly; they can only facilitate learning. Understanding comes first through experience, and only then does the work of art bear significance. With that eventual revelation, he suggested in his lecture "Words—a Definition of Experience" a course for schools in which students would explore words beyond the dictionary's defini-tions by learning about a few key terms such as "freedom" and "re-sponsibility" or "reason" or "culture" or "conscience" in the context of their experiences. A deeper understanding of these words would then become part of the child's "survival kit" to identify the dynamics of human experience enough to comprehend "what is being done to one, and what one is doing to others." In his autobiography, Wesker told this story about his son Lindsay Joe who misunderstood the insults of taunting bullies and was subsequently punched by one of them. Wesker wrote, "Words contain within them concepts of human behaviour. He was not equipped with such words." On the face of it, this addition to the syllabus in the form of a vocabulary lesson appears limited in application, but as Richard Appignanesi points out in his Afterword to *Words as Definitions of Experience*, Wesker's ideas reflect the practice of Paulo Freire's education for *Cultural Action for Freedom*, which also discusses the possibility of using a list of "generative words" (6) in reading. Both Wesker and Freire argue that education begins with a critical awareness of human interaction, and both believe in the educational process as a first line of defense against oppression.

Freire would add, however, that true freedom is a *cultural literacy* which promotes a critical consciousness of the political, socio-cultural, economic, and historical dimensions. Freire was always moving the student toward a self-awareness and action through a collective consciousness, whereas Wesker is more interested in simply nurturing individual awareness. However, like Freire, Wesker seeks a more open, self-aware and non-violent society even though he is not as acutely interested in social justice, or empowerment, or critical inquiry as Freire.

Wesker's drive to educate rises largely out of his dread of racism and a need to preach religious tolerance. Education for him is the only effective foil against the bigot. In his autobiography he writes, "Like most Jews, I'm manic about the need for education and the value of knowledge. We fear ignorance as a cesspit breeding inferiority complexes out of which creeps hatred of what is unknown, mob violence against what is different" (*Dare* 110).

He has therefore continued to maintain an almost blind faith in the ability of theatre to teach generosity and understanding. *Shylock* (1976), for example, attempts to elicit sympathy for the Jew, sympathy that would not have served Shakespeare's ends, by exemplifying the Jewish "reverence for the power of the intellect." *When God Wanted a Son* (1986) brings out the dynamics of a marriage strained by the differences between a Jew and a gentile. And three of Wesker's more recent plays tell us about Jewish history: *Badenheim, 1939,* a 1987 play based on Aharon Appelfeld's novel about Jews shortly before they are shipped to a concentration camp; *Beorhtel's Hill,* a 1989 commissioned work pleading for tolerance for recent immigrants; and *Blood Libel,* a 1991 adaptation of a twelfth-century trial in which Jews are blamed for the rape and death of a child.

Wesker's drive to educate is somewhat ironic, since he is largely self-taught. He was seven years old when World War II began in 1939. Although he left London only briefly during the bombing in 1940, his attendance at school during the war was not entirely business as usual. These were formative years in his education lost to political upheaval. By his own account in *As Much as I Dare,* they were lost to the sorts of things that capture a boy's imagination more than spelling or grammar—iron bunks in the London Underground, escapades in the bombed warehouses, and flirtations with young girls. Wesker failed his eleven plus exam in 1943 and went on to Upton House Central School to learn clerical work. Although he was good at math, he was quite sure that he would never be fit for the tasks of a clerk/ bookkeeper. When the V2 doodlebugs began dropping on England in September 1944, his parents arranged for his evacuation to South Wales where Wesker spent his twelfth and thirteenth years. After he returned to London, he remained in school only three more years until he was sixteen.

A lack of formal education at the post-secondary level was not an obstacle to his becoming a reader and spending the rest of his life as a writer, so he takes pride in being a successful autodidact. Still, he wishes he had been pushed by his parents to attain a university education. Evidence for this is the large number of teachers in his plays. No other profession comes up as often. There is the absent high school teacher of *Yardsale* as well as the college professors of *One More Ride on the Merry-Go-Round* and *Lady Othello.* They are joined by Ronnie, who wants nothing more than to teach, and several men of erudition and letters—Shylock, Joshua in *When God Wanted a Son,* Manfred in *The Friends,* Thomas of Monmouth in *Blood Libel,* and Montcrief and Vincent in *Three Women Talking.* Many are characters with whom Wesker identifies one way or another. He admires none more than Shylock, a learned man with a classical education that guides neophytes through the "sacred" books, treasures containing ideas seminal to Western thought. Like his Shylock, Wesker is a "hoarder of other men's genius" in the books he buys and cherishes, even though he knows that he's not as analytic as many readers; "I read, listen, converse, but I'm not blessed with the ease of erudition. I shall always feel like a novice, a convert, an alien. Neither clarity nor power of thought comes easily to me, sometimes not at all." He adds wryly, "...there are certain people I sense not to engage with, I smell their learning, their feats of memory, their fluency, their power to marshal argument, as dogs smell one another knowing they can trot or not trot alongside them (*Dare* 110).

Wesker must have therefore had mixed feelings when he was invited to direct *The Wedding Feast* at Denison University in Granville, Ohio, as the first of their Jonathan R. Reynolds Playwrights-in-Residence and to teach two classes as a visiting lecturer. One was a course in Wesker's works, co-taught with Jon Farris, and the other was a course in playwriting. The position as resident playwright was similar to a visiting lectureship which he held at the University of Colorado summer writers' conference in 1974. Paul Levitt's article in this volume details this wonderful story. During Wesker's 1995 fall semester at Denison he discovered once again how well he worked with students and how much he liked being around them. Although he admires the world of learning, he concedes that he is more content to live in his Welsh mountain home and write plays, "I would have a hard time being a professor [full time]," he confessed to me in a brief exchange (December 7, 1995).

That admission is something of a reversal for Wesker who at one time wanted nothing more than to use playwriting as device for indoctrination. When Wesker was young and arrogant, he believed that he could use his plays to "undermine people's existing values and impose [his] own on them" ("Let Battle Commence!" 99). A wiser, more humble Wesker would not consider that objective today. Still, he believes in the power of language to humanize. Poised at the keyboard of his laptop, he assumes his role as a teacher in many arenas as he fires off letters to the editor, writes essays for publication, and shapes a plays for production. He willingly converses on a variety of subjects that include politics, playwriting, directing the theatre. Wesker loves nothing more than an "authentic dialogue." Like Ronnie in the *Trilogy*, he strives to build bridges by exchanging ideas and understanding. His quest for ideas includes more than an erudite discussion among the learned, because he willingly talks about family relationships, male and female entanglements, and the mistakes we make as human beings. His informal classroom thus combines theatre, personal experience, and human interaction. Somewhere in that unconventional approach is his unspoken and solemn entreaty to practice forbearance toward others for the sake of those points we share in common—our need to be loved, the inclination in all of us to failure, and the sorrow of our losses.

The Purpose and Scope of This Casebook

The primary goal of this casebook is to provide a dialogic forum for readers of Wesker's works across the world. Contributors from Italy, Germany, India, Great Britain, and the United States provide critical analyses of almost all the works. Their essays, often referring to the ideas of one another, enable a rich exploration and cross fertilization from multiple perspectives. Good examples of this diversity are the three articles here on how Wesker's political positions changed over time. Keith Gore of Great Britain reassesses Wesker's works for our time, arguing that they have outlived the worn-out political labels belonging to the "kitchen sink" drama and the ideology of the Angry Young Men through their enduring characters endowed with universal qualities. As evidence, he offers a thorough reading of *Chicken Soup with Barley*. Kevin Asman, a doctoral student at Michigan State University, offers a socialist reading of *Roots*, demonstrating once again that Wesker's brand of William Morris socialism has a wide appeal. And Heiner O. Zimmermann from Heidelberg reads the ideology of Wesker's plays through utopian theory, comprehensively tracing shifts in Wesker's political philosophy. Zimmermann sees a yearning for the totalizing ideas of utopia in the early plays, a major shift after *Their Very Own and Golden City* towards disillusionment, and a more enlightened recognition that "a utopia of plurality" has succeeded the totalizing vision of the 60s liberal humanists.

Four essays by friends and colleagues of Wesker contribute valuable biographical material. Margaret Drabble's "Arnold Wesker," originally written in the 70's and reprinted here, is an affectionate and frank vignette of Arnold Wesker in earlier times. Describing Wesker at the apex of his early career and at the beginning of his financial and professional difficulties, she assesses his place in British theatre, examines a few of his plays, and offers us a revealing glimpse into his character as a Jew, a family man, and a writer. Though twenty years old, her observations are so incisive that her remarks hold true today.

In a discussion of *Their Very Own and Golden City*, Clive Barker recalls those pregnant moments in the early 70s when he and Wesker and many others were trying to make Centre 42 a viable enterprise. Centre 42 was the exciting vision of a handful of socialists in the early 60s; among them were Clive Barker and John McGrath, who hoped to form a cooperative for working-class artists—musicians, writers, performers—to showcase works for the people. It would not only provide a forum but also a network for communally minded artists. Wesker joined them in 1960 and eventually co-directed Centre 42 with Clive Barker—Wesker was its Artistic Director, and Barker was its Technical Director. Their most immediate duties were to raise ongoing financial support for Centre 42 and to mount festivals that would play in small towns outside London as non-elitist entertainment in regions where there was little opportunity for first-rate live performances. Their excitement was infectious, and it led to well-attended festivals, but their ability to meet operational expenses was disappointing. Centre 42 closed its doors in 1970. Barker reflects on their ideals in the early years and that bittersweet time at the end.

Fellow playwright and longstanding friend of Wesker, Paul Levitt records personal anecdotes about the part he played in the inception of several Wesker plays. Wesker is indebted to the University of Colorado Professor Levitt and student Lois Buehler, whose suggestions for the adaptation of Shakespeare's *Merchant of Venice* form the basis of the play originally called *The Merchant* and now titled *Shylock*. The play's idea came from Buehler's research on the treatment of the Jews in Renaissance Italy. Not as well known is Levitt's role in suggesting material for *Caritas* and *Blood Libel* (earlier entitled *William of Norwich*). These are stories which he recalls for us here.

Turning to the autobiographical elements in Wesker's plays, Alessandra Marzola finds the medium of radio ideal for *Yardsale*, a play that provides Wesker with the vehicle he needs to express his personal disappointment in the public which has abandoned him. Marzola argues that the radio play breaks from the semiotic architecture of theatre by taking full advantage of its monologic form. Marzola points to linguistic fragments woven into brief sketches as emblems of the scraps and discards of the garage sale and the salvage of

Stephanie's broken marriage. Stephanie's hurt acts as a metaphor for
Wesker's drop in popularity.

Continuing the dialogue, three contributors situate Wesker's plays
in a variety of theatrical movements. Kimball King establishes the
American context for *The Kitchen*, linking it particularly to the modernist plays written in Europe and the United States in the 50s and
60s. King explains that Wesker added to the canon by blending naturalism and realism with psychological portrayals and ideological content. Margaret Rose sketches a short history of the one-person and
monologic plays which predate Wesker's one-woman plays. Wesker's
contribution to the popular tradition of one-person plays dating back
to the eighteenth century is his development of women characters
out of a male sensibility. Meenakshi Ponnuswami draws a continuous
line in history from the New Left writing of Arnold Wesker to the
Newer Left plays of the 70s by political playwrights such as David
Edgar, Howard Brenton, and Caryl Churchill. She finds surprising
similarity between the two groups in their ideology and approach,
and she concludes that the weakness of both groups lies in the need
for a more inclusive definition of the popular arts for the working
classes.

Assuming a variety of critical stances including a social-historical
reading, a reader-response approach, and biographical and structur-
alist readings, our contributors open conversations which we all may
draw on to take to other communities with an extended understanding of Wesker's theatre.

After laying out the basic theories of theatre translation, Rossana
Bonadei wrestles with the difficulties of translating *Whatever Happened to Betty Lemon?* from English to Italian. Bound by linguistic
and cultural limitations, Bonadei finds that some aspects of theatre,
namely comedy, are never fully translated. Out of the German Re-
public, Peter Müller uses Bakhtin's concept of monologue and dialogue to explore the interplay between audience and character in the
monoplays as well as those with multiple characters. Müller accounts
for the lack of communication between characters and their emotional isolation from one another.

Three articles explore Wesker's characters. Glenda Leeming reads
across the plays to look at Wesker's treatment of women and concludes that he is in tune with the notion that all marginalized peoples,
including women, are somehow culturally conditioned. Because of

his Jewish upbringing and awareness of antisemitism, he is sensitive to the treatment of the "Other" by the dominant culture. Angela Locatelli sees a strong Lukacsian realism throughout all the one-woman plays. Using closely defined semiotic terms, Locatelli explains how Wesker's stage directions expand the traditional sense of realism to shape full characters and recognize the growing importance of women. Martin Priestman wrestles with the puzzle of Pip Thompson in a character study of *Chips with Everything*. Pip rejects the working-class conscripts, and yet he also rebels against the officers in his unit. Priestman helps us understand the historical and cultural conditions that made Pip's form of rebellion problematic for both the officers and the men in the ranks.

A reading that invokes Jewish history and tradition adds an important dimension to this volume. As though answering Zimmermann's discussion about totalizing utopias, Robert F. Gross examines *The Old Ones* for what it tells us about Wesker as an artist of fragments. He argues that, although Wesker's discussions of chaos and dissolution might suggest a postmodern center that does not hold, his plays actually reveal a romantic yearning for cohesion. Examining the fragmentary structure of the play, the fragmented relationships, the numerous biblical references and pieces of the Jewish tradition, Gross concludes that the fragments point collectively to mythic themes of creation and a quest for wholeness.

Two essays refer to the critical reception of Wesker's plays. Robert Wilcher situates *The Four Seasons* directly in the midst of Wesker's harshest critics of the 60s, who had preferred a naturalistic language in the socialist tradition of Clifford Odets but found, instead, a stylized dialogue that was almost poetic in its composition. Their disappointment in *The Four Seasons* marked one of the rejections of his plays by London audiences. Wilcher convincingly defends Wesker's choice of language by drawing links from the dialogue to both the structure of the play and an interpretation of it. His close reading also underscores how carefully Wesker must have selected his words. And finally, an old friend and fellow director, Robert Skloot, sums up Wesker's career by identifying the tension between the individual and the collective as a key aspect of his life and works. Skloot praises the generous spirit that informs the best of Wesker's plays. They contain those moments of tension when the playwright overrides his own feisty individualism to reach out and add to our sense of community.

Skloot identifies the weakest moments of the plays as those when the larger themes of *civitas* and justice lose ground to set pieces and light humor that adds very little to an understanding of ourselves.

Since the anticipated audience of this collection is academic, spanning the interests of both students and faculty, each contributor has avoided highly theoretical discussion. All the plays are mentioned in one way or another, and most of the plays are discussed at great length to aid the reader who has not read the full corpus of Wesker's work. One last note: the parenthetical numbers in this volume refer to the most recent Penguin edition of the plays by volume and page. For example, (2:31) would be Volume 2, page 31.

༄

Chronology

1932   Arnold Wesker was born May 24 in Stepney, East London, son of Joseph Wesker, tailor, and Leah (née Cecile Leah Perlmutter). Has one sister, Della, born 1926.

1936–1948 Evacuated to various places in England and Wales during the war. Attended Upton House Central School in Hackney, East London from 1943–1948.

1948–1952 Accepted by Royal Academy of Dramatic Art but did not attend for lack of money. Went to work as a pastry cook, furniture maker, bookseller's assistant, plumber's mate, and spent two years' national service in the Royal Air Force.

1957   *The Kitchen* was written.

1958   *Chicken Soup* opened at the Belgrade, Coventry, and transferred to London's Royal Court Theatre. It was awarded an Arts Council grant of £300, which Wesker used to marry Doreen (Dusty) Bicker.

1959   *Roots* opened at the Belgrade Theatre. Later it played at the Royal Court Theatre and in the West End with Joan Plowright. His first son, Lindsay Joe, was born.

1960   *I'm Talking About Jerusalem* opened as part of the *Trilogy* at the Royal Court.

1961   *The Kitchen* opened at the Belgrade and transferred to the Royal Court. Film version was also released. His daughter, Tanya Jo, was born.

1962   *Chips with Everything* opened at the Royal Court and was voted Best Play of 1962 and played successfully in the West End. His second son, Daniel, was born.

1963   *Menace* aired on BBC television. *Chips with Everything* opened on Broadway.

1964   *Their Very Own and Golden City* was awarded the Italian Premio Marzotto prize of £3,000 and later premiered at Belgian National Theatre.

1965   *The Four Seasons* premiered at the Belgrade Theatre, Coventry and was transferred to the West End.

1966   *Their Very Own and Golden City* opened at the Royal Court.

1970   *The Friends* premiered at the Roundhouse. Wesker resigned as its Artistic Director in December. *Fears of Fragmentation*, an essay collection, was published.

1971   Short-story collection *Six Sundays in January* was published.

1972   *The Journalists* is written but not performed because of an actors' revolt. *The Old Ones* opened at the Royal Court.

1974   *The Wedding Feast* premiered in Stockholm, Sweden, at the Stadtsteater. Its British premiere was at the Leeds Playhouse in 1977. Short-story collection *Love Letters on Blue Paper* was published.

1976   Television production of *Love Letters on Blue Paper*. Premiere of *The Merchant* (now called *Shylock*) in Stockholm.

1977   Zero Mostel died suddenly in previews of *The Merchant. One More Ride on the Merry-Go-Round* is written but not performed until 1985 at the Phoenix Arts in Leicester. The English version of *Shylock* premiered on Broadway but did not open in England until 1978 when it played in Birmingham.

1978   *Said the Old Man to the Young Man*, a collection of short stories, was published.

1979   *Chicken Soup with Barley* won a gold medal in Spain for best foreign play.

1980   Film script, *Lady Othello*, was written.

1981   *Caritas* opened at the Cottesloe National Theatre. *The Journalists* premiered in Wilhelmshaven, Germany.

1982   *Four Portraits—Of Mothers* premiered in Tokyo. Its first UK performance was at Edinburgh Festival in 1984, and its first London performance took place at the Half Moon theater in 1987.

1983   *Annie Wobbler* first heard as a radio play on Suddeutscher Rundfunk (Germany). It played in London in 1984 at the Fortune Theatre.

1984   *Yardsale* was first broadcast by BBC Radio 3. It was first staged in 1985 at the Edinburgh Festival.

1985 Essay collection, *Distinctions*, was published.

1986 *When God Wanted a Son* was written.

1987 *Yardsale* and *Whatever Happened to Betty Lemon?* played together for the first time at the Lyric Theatre Studio, Hammersmith. *Badenheim 1939* was adapted from an Appelfeld novel. *Lady Othello* was adapted as a play.

1988 Wesker wrote *The Mistress* and *Beorhtel's Hill*, a community play that celebrated the fortieth anniversary of Basildon, a New Town in England. *Caritas* was adapted into an opera libretto.

1990 *Three Women Talking* was written. It premiered at the Northlight Theatre in Chicago in 1992.

1991 *The Mistress* premiered in Rome, Teatro Flaiano. Its world premiere was at the Teatro Petrach, Arezzo, Italy.

1992 *Letter to a Daughter* premiered in Seoul, Korea. *Wild Spring* was written. *Blood Libel* (originally named *William of Norwich*) was adapted from an historical account by Thomas of Monmouth for a theater opening in Norwich.

1993 The *Trilogy* was mounted as a co-production among eighteen theaters in France.

1994 Autobiography, *As Much as I Dare*, was published.

1997 *Break my Heart*, a 30-minute play commissioned by the Sherman Theatre, Cardiff and Harlech T.V. *Denial* was completed. *The Birth of Shylock and the Death of Zero Mostel (Diary of a Play)* published.

1998 *The King's Daughters* was published. Premiere of *Letter to a Daughter* (rev.), Edinburgh Festival.

I. The Politics in Arnold Wesker's Plays

The Trilogy, Forty Years On
Keith Gore

There is a great temptation to see Arnold Wesker as a dramatic author belonging to a particularly exciting period in the English theatre, but a period which now belongs firmly to the past. The view is ill-founded, as the highly successful London revival of *The Kitchen* early in 1994 clearly showed: the fact that the Royal Court Theatre should be fully booked well in advance is surprising when one considers that, in practice, theatre managements, as well as theatre critics, have often been inclined to write Wesker off, even more than some of his contemporaries. No doubt personal reasons come into play, in that Wesker's reputation as a very demanding author has in itself tended to create resistances. What is perhaps more important, however, is that the theatre is, and always has been, subject to certain dictates of fashion. Wesker, like others of his theatrical generation, was taken up with enthusiasm as representative of a new departure for the theatre in the London of the post-War years. Here, it was thought, was a series of young authors, unmarked by the solidly middle-class structure of the theatre which had come through from pre-War England. The various labels which were attached to them are evidence of this response. References, for example, to "kitchen-sink drama" carried with them resonances of populism, related to the notion that the kitchen is one of the places where the working class is to be found, and indeed could be seen to live, if the evidence of John Osborne's *Look Back in Anger*, with the kitchen sink firmly installed on the stage, could be taken as in some way typical. Theatre-goers were all of a sudden confronted with a series of so-called "Angry Young Men," part of a generation dissatisfied with the social and economic conditions of the world and only too ready to express their dissatisfaction with a degree of bitterness and radical thought.

Labels have their usefulness in that they make it possible to situate authors with respect to each other as well as in the broader context of theatrical, literary, or artistic life in general. Like readers of novels, those who go to the theatre have an impression of knowing what they are buying when the label they see attached to the product at any rate appears to carry some kind of guarantee of quality or interest. Such labels can even be exploited by the authors in question as a means of promoting or selling their goods to the public. Nevertheless, the dangers are considerable if only because labels, in the long run, lead to lassitude: "Not *another* kitchen-sink drama!" That is characteristic, of course, of the dangers of being involved in a fashion, bearing in mind that fashion, in the strict sense (when applied to the clothes women wear, for example) is something which by definition demands the new: how could any lady of fashion ever consider making an appearance in one of last year's dresses? On a more serious level, the fashion phenomenon means that dramatic authors, like others, become trapped in a context which inevitably situates them in terms of what *has* been, rather than of what is happening *now*, or may happen in the future. That applies broadly to the various authors who came to public attention at the same time as Arnold Wesker: they are yesterday's goods, something new has appeared in the meantime, and in any case, as is normal, one generation is naturally replaced by another, coming along with its own ambitions, its own determination to make its mark. This point is of course underlined by the recent death of John Osborne.

Whether or not such considerations apply more to Wesker than to others of his generation is open to discussion. In the specific case of the *Trilogy*, it has to be recognized that there are additional factors which are of significance. The fact is that the three plays, although written in a short space of time, between 1958 and 1960, cover a much longer period—a slice of what must now be seen as history, from 1936 to 1959. At a time when celebrations of the Allied invasion of occupied France have been closely followed by those to do with the end of the war in Europe in 1945, we are reminded that those momentous events happened half a century ago, and it is worth remembering that those who were *born* the year in which Act 1 of *Chicken Soup with Barley* is set are now over sixty years old, that those whose birth coincided with the end of *I'm Talking About Jerusalem* are now in their mid-thirties. That chronological remoteness is accentuated, even for a British audience, by the nature of the concerns which are at the center of the *Trilogy*: living, as we do, in a world where there has been a movement towards a radical, and even ideological, form of economic and social "liberalism," we are bound to find that concerns with 1930s fascism and a post-war belief that, at last, social and economic justice were about to be realized, are to do with a world which seems to have gone for good.

One of the things we shall need to do, therefore, is to resituate the *Trilogy*, to evaluate it in relation to the concerns of that fast-receding period of English history. One point is clear from the outset: we shall make little progress if we attempt to see the *Trilogy* as characterized by the labels of "kitchen sink" or "Angry Young Men." The reason is not that kitchen sinks are absent from Wesker's theatre; on the contrary, one of the characteristics of his work for the theatre is that he frequently includes very specific sequences of everyday activity in his plays and, given his interest in food, both as gastronomy and as an essential part of the structure of the relationships between people, there is always a good chance that the kitchen sink will be close at hand. The stage directions with which *Chicken Soup with Barley* opens include the sentence "*To the right is another door which leads to a kitchen, which is seen.*" Immediately afterwards comes the first indication of action: "SARAH KAHN *is in the kitchen washing up, humming to herself.*" One may go so far as to say that without her kitchen, Sarah would be lost: her automatic reflex on the arrival of any other character is to make tea for them; if she can also encourage them to eat, so much the better. But the important point is that Sarah's kitchen, sink and all, is part of *living* rather than an indication that some sort of theatrical revolution is taking place. It is interesting, and evidence of misunderstanding of Wesker's aim in including so much "mundane" activity in his plays, that he felt it necessary, in 1978, to write a "note to Actors and Directors of the *Trilogy*," in the course of which he says:

> Sarah should, for example, be cutting bread on a line like "You can have brotherhood without love." The family inquest at the end of *Jerusalem* should be conducted while crates are being packed, floors swept, curtains pulled; thoughts should be thrown over shoulders, down the stairs, over the washing-line, from outside while emptying garbage. If the physical business of living does not continue then the dialogue will emerge pompously and fall with dull thuds from characters who will appear no more than cardboard cut-outs. (1:7)[1]

Whether or not Wesker was an "Angry Young Man" at the time of the *Trilogy* is perhaps a more important question still, given that the phrase carries with it implications about being victims of society and its injustices in a way which justifies protest, often of a purely negative kind. Each of the authors to whom the label has been applied might well be examined with a view to deciding whether their anger (just supposing it existed) was of a passive, complaining nature, involving no action on their part aimed at putting right a situation which they found unsatisfactory. In the case of Wesker, the answer is clear, and it is interesting to see that *Roots* is prefaced with a "Note to Actors and Producers" in which he writes: "The picture I have drawn is a harsh one, yet my tone is not one of disgust—nor should it be in the presentation of the plays. I am at one with these people: it is only that I am annoyed, *with them and myself*" (1:80, my emphasis). It does not follow that Wesker is uncritical of the society in which he lives—far from it, as the plays make obvious. The world may be imperfect, society may have failings, but Wesker is concerned with *people*, and what interests him is that they, too, have their failings, that they— whether, for example, through lack of conviction, disillusion, insufficient will power—are unable to bring about the better world to which they aspire. How far that is a matter of human weakness on their part, how far a consequence of the sheer weight of existing social and economic structures, how far a direct or indirect result of the brutal- izing effect of menial work (be it industrial or agricultural) is one of the interesting questions raised by the plays.

In any event, the link between what is described in the plays and Wesker's own experience is certain. More than one critic has pointed out that the name Ronald is an anagram of Arnold, and, although it would be a serious error to see too strict a parallel between the author and his creation, we are justified in seeing the substance of what he writes as closely related to his own experience. And what is true of himself is true of others, too. If evidence were needed, it could be found here: *How do your parents compare with Harry and Sarah Kahn in the* Trilogy?

> Almost totally. They are—in so far as it is possible—total re-creations. So are most of the characters, with the only exception of me. The character of me I take liberties with. I put myself in the weak role in order that alongside Ronnie, Sarah Kahn can emerge and alongside Ronnie in

> *Jerusalem*, Dave and Ada can emerge. *Roots* was written
> after Dusty and I were married, so the fabrication of them
> not marrying could be seen as an attack on me but it
> doesn't bear with the truth. I was just using myself.
> (Hayman 1979,2)[2]

Sarah as a characteristic mother figure is easy to imagine as a representation of Wesker's own mother. The same goes for Beatie Bryant, in *Roots*, whose similarity with Wesker's wife, for those who know her, is obvious. But even those who do not can find textual evidence at the point where Beatie produces the paintings she has brought home for her mother. A stage direction tells us: "*She appears from the front room with two framed paintings. She sets them up and admires them. They are primitive designs in bold masses, rather well-balanced shapes and bright poster colours—red, black, and yellow—see Dusty Bicker's work*" (1:112). The relationship certainly exists, therefore, but we should be wrong to suppose that Beatie *is* Dusty, just as we should certainly be mistaken, as Wesker himself makes clear, to take Ronnie for Arnold: whereas Ronnie never gets beyond the succession of jobs which closely parallel those done by Wesker, for example, the character finds himself more and more threatened by the fate which might arise from his close resemblance to his father, Harry, whilst his creator moves on through a dynamic and creative life as a major figure in the theatre.[3]

When it comes to evaluating an author's work, it is of course true that any coincidence between that work and the author's biography is of little consequence. What matters, in the case of the Wesker *Trilogy*, is the reality of the events described as a factor in the author's own perception of the world. The first act of *Chicken Soup with Barley* is set in 1936, when Wesker was only four years old. We may therefore safely assume that his direct experience of the events of that year was strictly limited. It may be true that, like all of us, he was more aware of what was happening in the world outside than parents are inclined to believe; but we can be sure that the stirring happenings of the immediate pre-War years were much discussed by those around him both at the time, and in subsequent months and years. His direct memories will have been supplemented by the indirect knowledge of events which came from the conversations of his family and their friends. In a real sense, then, it is not unreasonable to assume that, for the whole of the period 1936–1959, from the beginning of *Chicken*

Soup with Barley to the end of *Roots* and *I'm Talking About Jerusalem*, we are reliving, with Wesker, that particular slice of history.

At this distance in time, it is difficult to imagine life in the East End of London in the 1930s. During the war itself, much was destroyed by German bombs. Since then, there has been reconstruction; there has also been a movement of the earlier population in the direction of the suburbs, whilst some of the territory vacated by that population has been taken over by the middle classes. London docks, so vital a component in the social and economic life of the area, have been abandoned—at any rate by the shipping trade on which they depended. There may still be a large amount of poverty and deprivation, but not of the same kind as that which Wesker knew as a small boy. His was not the only family of poor Jewish immigrants which had gravitated to that part of London. The sense of community which undoubtedly existed was based on many factors, but to be poor and Jewish and an immigrant, at a time when the threat presented by Nazi Germany was for many a matter of very recent experience, is an essential part of the background which forms the reality of *Chicken Soup*, just as it will be the source of the response to the world developed in both *Roots* and *I'm Talking About Jerusalem*.

It is easy to see Mosley's fascists as a curious, temporary phenomenon, their provocative marches and demonstrations in the East End of London as a combination of intimidation and an appeal to the xenophobic fears of an indigenous population—together with a demagogic manipulation of the general poverty and deprivation of the society of the area. Such a view might appear to gain substance from happenings like the racist attacks on Turkish minorities by neo-Nazis in present-day Germany, or indeed by the activities of the present-day British National Party in the very East End which seemed such promising territory to Mosley. What is missing, at any rate for the present, is the particular strength and virulence of the Hitler phenomenon which, as events proved too painfully, was all that many already knew it to be. A practical, concrete manifestation of that was the Spanish Civil War, an event with few parallels in the history of the twentieth century. The Dave of *Roots* was not alone in believing that he had a duty to go and fight in Spain: the particular cause was one which drew on many sections of society. Dave, as a poor East-End Jew, might be expected to see it as important to join the struggle against Franco's fascists and their German supporters, but there were plenty of others—intellectuals, artists, representatives of the favored classes in a more general sense—who, unlike those who were tempted by what they saw as the attractions of Hitler's particular type of "reforms," saw it as important to take a stand against totalitarianism, racism, and militarism.

It goes without saying that they were not all Communists, and it is that particular element which gives much of its interest both to *Chicken Soup* and to its sequels in *Roots* and *I'm Talking About Jerusalem*. Already in *Chicken Soup*, there is something touching, and even a little pathetic, in the belief some of the characters have in the ability of Communism to provide the solutions to the problems which face them. In that respect, the contrast between Monty and Sarah is interesting. Psychologically, it is easy to understand that, after the exhilaration of a day which has shown the workers successfully opposing the Fascist marchers, there should be some excess of enthusiasm amongst those who have taken part in the day's events. Even so, the reaction of a Monty must surely be the self-delusion of a political innocent:

> I bet we have a revolution soon. Hitler won't stop at Spain, you know. You watch him go and you watch the British Government lick his arse until he spits in their eye. Then *we'll* move in. (1:27)

There can be little better evidence than the events followed through in the course of the *Trilogy*.

Monty is speaking in 1936; the story of the *Trilogy* is the story of the loss of that innocence, if not the story of total disillusionment. It is worth remembering, in this context, that the three plays were written in 1958, 1959 and 1960, when Wesker himself was between twenty-six and twenty-eight years of age—a young man. *Chicken Soup* is set in London, *Roots* and *Jerusalem* in Norfolk, but the movement is a circular one, given that, at the end of *Jerusalem*, we witness a return to London, which is where—if anywhere—the characters have their roots. It would be far from true to suggest that Wesker himself comes full circle and that he rediscovers the optimism of the first act of *Chicken Soup* at the end of *Jerusalem*: he is too close to Ronnie for that to be the case. Without wishing to suggest that Ronnie is Wesker's self-portrait, we may nevertheless see in both of them *observers* of the action which is set before us. One of the main differences between

the author and his character is that Ronnie does little more than observe and, of course, like all the Kahns, talk.

But what is observed? Essentially, the events associated with specific blocks of time, important for Wesker, as for others, in the period
1936–1959. The first is the brief, but highly significant, period associated with the struggle against fascism in the East End of London in
1936. Hitler's regime was already firmly established in Germany, and
the threat of the spread of fascism seemed real—especially in the light
of the Spanish Civil War. The Kahns of *Chicken Soup*, like their friends,
are largely communist, immigrant, and Jewish: three good reasons
for being particularly sensitive to a political movement which was,
amongst other things, highly nationalist in nature. The first act of
Chicken Soup thus provides the background against which the whole
of the subsequent action of the three plays will take place, and it is in
that respect striking, and surely significant, that none of the plays
contains anything about the period 1936–1946.

In 1946, Wesker is a boy of fourteen, embarked upon adolescence and, we may suppose, political awareness at a time in England
when the future seemed to hold out much promise for the rising
generation. That is not to say that those immediate post-War years
were easy. The United Kingdom was exhausted by war and had somehow or another to rebuild its economy and, in many ways, its society.
It is one of the ironies of the situation at that time that the United
Kingdom, having done all that could be asked of it in the war, and,
having emerged victorious, was actually worse off than countries where
that was not the case. For reasons to do with what was perceived as
the Soviet threat, Germany received massive aid to put it back on its
feet. France, which had suffered defeat, had not been subject to the
same destruction as Great Britain and, thanks to its strong agricultural base, was quickly able to restore the standard of living of its
population. In contrast—an astonishing fact, looked at from this distance in time—food rationing came finally to an end in the United
Kingdom only in 1954.

Even so, there was cause for optimism for the likes of the Kahns.
The general election of 1945 had given a landslide victory to the
Labour party, which came to power with a strong program of social
and industrial reform. Nationalization was intended to take the potential riches of the country out of the hands of the few in order to
improve the lot of the many. The creation of the "Welfare State,"

with universal health care and proper concern for the old, the infirm,
and all others unable to fend for themselves, was intended to remove
some of the blights of pre-war society. In that, it was undoubtedly
successful, a success underlined by the reappearance, in recent years,
of beggars, homeless, individuals released into the community whilst
still in need of professional care. And yet the image provided by
Wesker's plays is not a particularly rosy one. The period 1946–1947,
which is the subject of both the second act of *Chicken Soup* and of Act
1 of *Jerusalem*, is not presented in terms of total optimism.

The second act of *Chicken Soup* shows us the Kahns "uprooted"
from their East End slum and rehoused in an *"L.C.C.* [London County
Council] *block of flats in Hackney"* (1:36). The sense of community of
the slum has been exchanged for the anonymous impersonality of
apartments as depressing as they are isolated. That, as far as we can
tell, is the extent of the advantage derived by the Kahns from this
particular promised land: Sarah, still maintaining her faith in Communism, though faced with the problems she has always known; Harry,
continuing on his ne'er-do-well way until he takes refuge in his first
stroke; Ronnie, now a fifteen-year-old, *"enthusiastic, lively, well-spo-
ken like his sister"* (1:37), talks and bubbles but does little—too much
like his father for his own good. But the truly significant character is
Ada:

> I'm tired, Mother. I spent eighteen months waiting for
> Dave to return from Spain and now I've waited six years
> for him to come home from a war against Fascism and
> I'm tired. Six years in and out of offices, auditing books
> and working with young girls who are morons—
> lipsticked, giggling morons. Dave's experience is the
> same—fighting with men who he says did not know what
> the war was about. [...] Oh yes! the service killed any
> illusions Dave may have once had about the splendid and
> heroic working class. (1:42)

This, of course, is the Dave who, in 1936, had left for Spain with
such high hopes and ideals. What he has discovered is that men and
women are just that, for the most part low-grade individuals incapable or unwilling to aspire to anything beyond their next orgasm or
their next pay-packet.

Ronnie will stay in London, will go on talking, will continue to
delude himself about his own possibilities without ever actually *doing*

anything worth doing. The Act 2 curtain comes down on an exchange
which clearly reveals the identity between father and son:

> RONNIE: [...] Your weakness frightens me, Harry—did
> you ever think about that? I watch you and
> I see myself and I'm terrified.
>
> HARRY: [*wandering away from him; he does not know what
> to say*]: What I am—I am. I will never alter.
> Neither you nor your mother will change
> me. [...] You can't alter people, Ronnie. You
> can only give them some love and hope
> they'll take it. I'm sorry. It's too late now. I
> can't help you. (1:55–56)

Ronnie will indeed not change; apart from some moments of depression, he will retain his surface enthusiasm and, above all, his need to
speak, but that, after all, is itself evidence of lack of change.

The period 1946–1947 is paralleled in Act 1 of *I'm Talking About
Jerusalem*. Dave Simmonds has finally been released from the army,
and has married Ada. The loss of their illusions has produced in them
also a sense of defeat. Before he left for Spain, Dave believed that the
inevitable killing was a necessary condition for attaining the ideal of
democracy, but the killing had to be done without hate: "You can't
have brotherhood when you hate. The only difference between them
[the Fascists] and us—we know what we're fighting for. It's almost an
unfair battle" (1:22). Given his realization that he was wrong to believe that everyone shared his ideals, he will not spend his time fighting for something he has no chance of achieving. Instead, along with
Ada, he will quit the urban mass and attempt to bring about a limited, romantic type of socialism through a return to a simpler, artisan's
life in which, thanks to his own labor, he will be able to set up his own
"socialist" community, based on self-sufficiency and the creation of
objects with his own hands. They will build their Jerusalem in the
isolated wastes of rural Norfolk. But even here, he will not be safe
from the corroding influence of contemporary society. This is made
clear through two events which occur in Act 1, Scene 2. The first is
the visit of Libby Dobson: that Libby whom Dave had met during
his military service, a man who shared his ideals but who shares them
no longer. His attempt to put socialism into practice by sharing out
an inheritance with a number of friends failed because those friends
either did not share his ideal or found it impossible to remain faithful

to it once they glimpsed the possibility of gratifying their self-interest. In addition, he has been disappointed by the two women in his life: his description of his successive wives reminds us inevitably of the "lipsticked, giggling morons" whom Ada so despised. The first, once married, "became so gross, so undelicate, so unfeeling about everything" (1:183); the second, possessive to what Libby considered an intolerable degree: "She marries a man in order to have something to attach to herself, a possession!... She grows and she grows and she grows and she takes from a man all the things she once loved him for—so that no one else can have them" (1:184). As a result, he has become what he calls a "cynic", not so much disillusioned as deprived of illusions to a destructive degree. That is certainly how Dave and Ada see him. We can understand Ada's response when she says "I suddenly feel unclean" (1:185). The fact of the matter is that he states a certain number of home truths: Dave and Ada have copped out, and Libby is to some extent right to "call the idealist soft and flabby" (1:183) as Dave puts it.

The second event is also a visit, that of Dave's employer, Colonel Dewhurst: he sacks Dave for having taken some unwanted linoleum without asking permission and then lying about it. Why exactly Dave should have done so foolish a thing is not satisfactorily explained in the play, but his action is certainly one which reveals him as falling short of his own ideals. It also has practical consequences in that it forces him to embark, earlier than he had intended, upon his own furniture-making enterprise. We may suppose that, in its early days, the project worked well: Wesker skips over six years, and opens Act 2 at a moment when things are again about to start going wrong: the scene is noteworthy in that it is set in 1953, and unrelated to any specific outside events, provided at any rate that we do not consider the deterioration of Ada's father, Harry, as such an event. The specific fact at the focus of this moment is that Dave's problems are of a kind which are part of the history of industrialization: the fragility of the artisan when faced with mass production. The coming to power of a Labour government has done nothing to change that. Not only does his apprentice, Sammy, decide to leave him to earn more money carrying out repetitive work in a factory, but his customers either fail to take up their orders or simply fail to place orders because they can buy factory-made goods more cheaply. He has no choice but to follow the movement, an implicit admission that his ideals are not possible in the real world he has to live in.

It is here that *Chicken Soup* and *Jerusalem* come together once more, first of all in time, in the period 1955–1956, and, second, in terms of the characters' experience of life. Strikingly, Act 3 of *Chicken Soup* opens with a scene very closely related to the Libby episode in *Jerusalem*—the visit to Sarah of Monty and his wife, Bessie. Monty is the lively militant lad, described at the start of the play as "*about 19, Jewish, working-class, and cockney*" (1:16). He is also the one who, in the excitement of the clash with the fascists, predicted that England would soon have its revolution. Things have changed radically, as Bessie explains: "Monty's got a nice little greengrocer's shop in Manchester, no one knows he was ever a member of the Party and we're all happy. It's better he forgets it" (2:61). Such talk is scandalous to Sarah's ears, depicting, as it does, the abandonment of what gave Monty's pre-war life meaning, but the scene is a necessary preparation for what is to follow, and which shows how Ronnie and Dave, though moving in different directions, have come up against what is for them a brick wall of reality.

For Ronnie, that reality is political. Wesker-like, he has been working in a restaurant in Paris, and now, in December 1956, in the final scene of the play, he is expected home. Little does Sarah suspect that, far from bringing a little light into her life, now clouded with increasing years and isolation, in addition to the burden of a Harry, reduced to an incontinent ruin, her son is returning for a crucial confrontation. Sarah, come hell or high water, has retained her faith, a faith, of course, in communism. Faith in a political creed is no different than religious faith in that it can accommodate itself to what, for the outsider, is unacceptable. Sarah is as unconditional in her belief in communism as those present-day followers of extravagant religious movements. To be fair, she has kept her faith, less in an abstract theory of communism, than in her fellow humans: "There will always be human beings and as long as there are there will always be the idea of brotherhood." We need look no further than her experience of life to understand why she should think in such a way; that same experience explains her plea to Ronnie when she says: "Please, Ronnie, don't let me finish this life thinking I lived for nothing. We got through, didn't we? We got scars but we got through" (2:75). Socialism may be her "light," as she calls it, but it is not a light which shines brightly enough to blind Ronnie to the brutality with which the Soviet Union put down the Hungarian uprising of 1956, any more than it can make him overlook the "murder of the Jewish Anti-Fascist Committee in the Soviet Union." Any social or political achievements in post-War England seem insignificant in the light of the broader political scene. "What has happened to all the comrades, Sarah? I even blush when I use that word. Comrade! Why do I blush? Why do I feel ashamed to use words like democracy and freedom and brotherhood? They don't have meaning any more" (1:71). Now he can understand his father's indifference, even though he knows that such an understanding may lead him along the same path as that followed by Harry. The reality of the post-war world, the failure of the aspirations which, in 1945, seemed to promise a better world for all, even if not the "strawberries and cream for everyone" that Ronnie accuses Sarah of expecting— that reality has caused his ideal to crumble.

At the same time, post-war reality is actively bringing Dave's and Sarah's attempt to live their ideal to an end: even Dave's concessions to an industrial society have not been enough to save him. Act 2, Scene 2 of *Jerusalem* takes place in the "*warm autumn*" of 1956—just a couple of months before the end of *Chicken Soup.* Hungary apparently leaves no impression on Dave: his ideal is attacked not by the Soviet form of socialism but by the harsh reality of capitalism. Having been forced to abandon his own artisan workshop and to compete with a factory culture on its terms, he finds himself, inevitably, at the mercy of the bankers to whom he must turn for capital. People may pay lip-service to quality as represented by his carefully designed and hand-crafted furniture; they are not prepared to pay the price for that quality. The choice he faces is that of producing window-frames as cheaply as possible or allowing himself and his family to starve. But not without protest: "I wanted to do something. Hands I've got— you see them? I wanted to do something" (1:205). The drama is that the something he wanted to do is not something people wanted to buy. Even so, he still believes that he was in the right: "No one's ever heard of me and no one wants to buy my furniture but I'm a bleedin' prophet and don't anyone forget that. As little as you see me so big I am. Now you look at me. I picked up my spear and I've stuck it deep. Prophet Dave Simmonds, me. With a chisel. Dave Simmonds and Jesus Christ. Two yiddisha boys—" (1:206). And, he might have added, two prophets who are not honored in their own country.

Dave holds out, at least for a time, and always, it has to be said, with the support and active help of Ada. But the last straw comes in 1959. If we may consider the pre-war opening act of *Chicken Soup* as a prologue to the main action of the *Trilogy*, this is the point at which the story comes full circle. After the surge of hope and optimism of the years immediately following the reestablishment of peace in 1945, the return of Dave and Ada to London in the last scene of *Jerusalem* finally marks the end of that stage of euphoria. It is significant that, just as the young Ronnie was a passive witness of the events of 1936, so he now makes a return to observe the final crumbling of Dave's dream. Significant, too, that this should coincide with a victory of the Conservatives in the 1959 general election. Not only has England not had the revolution predicted so confidently by Monty, it has also seen the people of the country turn its back on the democratic social-ist adventure ushered in by Labour's landslide victory of 1945. Dave must accept that he is not a prophet, just as Ronnie, unlike his mother, Sarah, has lost faith in any possible rosy future: "Nothing surprises you does it Sarah?" he asks his mother. "You still think it'll come, the great millennium?"

SARAH:	And you don't?
RONNIE:	Well, I haven't brought it about—and they [*of Ada and Dave*] haven't brought it about, and the Monty Blatts and Cissie and Esther Kahns haven't brought it about. But then Dad said it would never happen in our life-time—"It'll purify itself" he used to say. The difference between capitalism and socialism he used to say was that capitalism contained the seeds of its own destruction but social-ism contained the seeds of its own purifica-tion. Maybe that's the victory—maybe by coming here you've purified yourselves, like Jesus in the wilderness. (1:211)

But we know that what he says is not true. Jesus was a carpenter, too, but, whereas he left his craft to become a leader of men, the carpenter Dave will sell out to industrialization without providing any message. As for Ronnie, he is just talking, as he has always talked.

And it is here that we see how *Roots* fits into the general theme. That play is set totally in the same year, 1959. The whole action takes place over a period of two weeks or so, in a Norfolk different from that of Dave and Ada, in that it is inhabited by authentic Norfolk people: the family of Ronnie's girlfriend, Beatie. In *Roots*, Ronnie himself is like God in his universe: everywhere present, nowhere visible. If Dave is no prophet, we might say that *Roots* reveals Ronnie as a false prophet, the individual who promises much and delivers nothing. Beatie is under his spell—or, more precisely, under the spell of his words, which, as always, are little but empty air. Throughout the play, she has promoted him as the great revealer, the man bursting with ideas, capable of putting the world to rights, of bringing her to self-realization, of showing the plodding feet-in-the-mud Norfolk workers how to seize life and to live it. As in other plays by Wesker (especially one like *Love Letters on Blue Paper*) we see a woman growing in stature by learning to free herself from the man she believed to be her better. For the greater part of the play, Beatie is little more than a ventriloquist's dummy, speaking the words which come from Ronnie, presenting him as someone who deserves special consideration and who will lead the Bryants and the Beales to some sort of intellectual promised land.

She has not seen the emptiness of Ronnie's grand talk because, most of the time, she has not understood it. She believes that to be her fault, the result of her inability to follow him on the highroad to some sort of superior truth. It is only when he breaks with her, in the most brutal way imaginable, that, far from destroying her, he at last reveals her to herself. He does it at the price of destroying himself in her eyes, and he does that by his lucidity with respect to himself:

> My dear Beatie. It wouldn't really work would it? My ideas
> about handing on a new kind of life are quite useless and
> romantic if I'm really honest. If I were a healthy human
> being it might have been all right but most of us intellec-
> tuals are pretty sick and neurotic—as you have often ob-
> served—and we couldn't build a world even if we were
> given the reins of government—not yet any-rate. (1:142)

His lucidity is not total, or not quite, if only because his particular kind of romanticism shows him as not having an intellectual approach to life or even to the analysis of the problems life presents us with. At the end of *Roots*, in other words, he still has illusions about himself. They will have been dissipated by the time he comes to help Dave and Ada to pack up and return to London at the end of *Jerusalem*: "No one listens to me now. Funny that, everybody loo-ves me but nobody listens to me. I can't keep a job and I can't keep a girl so everyone thinks what I say doesn't count. Like they used to say of Dad. Poor old Harry—poor old Ronnie." And a little later, he adds: "*That's* all I ever get away with—gestures" (1:208). That is all he is in fact left with: gestures, as well, perhaps, as impossible dreams. When Dave tells him that visions do not work—and he is well placed to know—Ronnie protests. "They *do* work. And even if they don't then for God's sake try and behave as though they do—or else nothing will work" (1:216). This is the cry of a desperate man, one who has been eroded by time and events and disappointment, above all disappointment with himself.

In the end, Sarah is the one who has survived with the least damage. That is partly because, despite everything, she has maintained her political faith. But, as she shows in the closing moments of *Jerusalem*, her faith is based also on a clear view of human reality. She is not a utopian who deludes herself that the Good is there for the taking:

> Who says evil ever finishes? Nothing finishes! A Rasputin comes, you oppose him; a Bismarck comes, you oppose him; a Hitler comes, you oppose him! They won't stop coming and you don't stop opposing. Stop opposing and more will come and the garden'll get covered with weeds and that's life you mad things, you. (1:214)

She is still the Sarah who, right at the beginning of *Chicken Soup*, made her position clear: "Love comes now. You have to start with love. How can you talk about socialism otherwise?" (1:30).

How indeed? This might be the point at which the *Trilogy* should be analyzed in terms of its strictly dramatic structure. What is perhaps more interesting, given the preceding analysis, is to look at the evolution of the plays in terms of some constant characteristics to be observed in Wesker himself. Once again, it is not a matter of attempting a biographical reading of what is, after all, the work of a creative artist. But there is enough of Wesker in Sarah, as well as, more obviously, in Ronnie, for some parallels to be drawn. Looked at in political terms, for example, the *Trilogy* shows us responses which are emotional rather than theoretical or intellectual, as we might expect when we consider the circumstances of the characters involved. Whatever may have been their attitudes or their circumstances in their countries of origin, the East End Jews of *Chicken Soup*, living in a threatening world of spreading fascism, could hardly be expected not to have political views of the left, and even of the extreme left—although they could never be defined in terms of doctrinaire communism. The Wesker who writes the plays, born into that atmosphere but growing to political awareness during and immediately after the Second World War, reached adulthood in a significantly different world. He nevertheless shares the idealism and the dreams as well as some of the illusions of his characters. It is the illusions which mean that they are in practice incapable of bringing their dreams into the world of reality. That is one of the reasons for his writing in the note preceding *Roots*: "I am at one with these people: it is only that I am annoyed, with them and myself" (1:80). That he is not, however, the Ronnie of the end of *Chicken Soup* or of the final scene of *Jerusalem* but on the contrary very much the "son" of Sarah is made evident by two facts: the first is that Wesker actually went to prison in 1961 as a result of his anti-nuclear stance; the second is his involvement from 1961 to 1970 with Centre 42, an attempt to set up an organization intended to promote the arts with the backing of working-class institutions (especially the trades unions). Both are evidence that he did not give up the fight at the time his *Trilogy* came to an end; both are evidence that, like Sarah, his primary interest was in the well-being of his fellow men.

His dream of a popular culture is related to another thread running through the *Trilogy* as it does through other works of his: that thread is a love of music and a respect for learning. The music tends to be turned off by those who do not appreciate it. Act 2, Scene 2 of *Chicken Soup* has Ronnie "conducting" the *Egmont* overture. When Cissie turns the volume down, he protests: "Aunty! Please! Beethoven"—it is almost as though Beethoven should for some reason be untouchable. In *Roots*, it is Beatie's turn, trying, at the end of Act 2, to persuade her mother that Bizet's *L'Arlésienne* suite is not "squit." At the beginning of *Jerusalem*, we find Ronnie conducting Beethoven's Ninth symphony. In each case, the music in question runs up against a lack of appreciation. This is no doubt partly because the love of music is that of the neophyte (it is certainly true in the case of Beatie, whose appreciation is in any case shown to be only skin-deep), involving the dream of access to great art.

Similarly, in the case of learning. some of the most striking examples of this are to be found elsewhere than in the *Trilogy*. Wesker's Shylock, for example, in the play of the same name, is keen to share his love of books and of scholarship with his friend, Antonio. It might even be said that one of the weaknesses of that play is Shylock's excessive zeal to communicate what he has learnt to others. In *Caritas*, the research carried out by the author in preparation for the writing of his play is laid out for all to see, with the result that the mechanisms involved become more intrusive than they should. (It is interesting, incidentally, to note that *Caritas* was inspired by a suggestion made by an academic friend—an intellectual, rather than an artist.) Victor, the self-taught trade union leader of *Love Letters on Blue Paper*, would not only like to write a theoretical work on the history of art; but at the same time educate his fellow trade unionists in the appreciation of painting. In the *Trilogy* itself, Harry's first independent statement is of a related kind: "Hey, Sarah" he says in the opening scene, "you should read Upton Sinclair's book about the meat-canning industry—it's an eye-opener" (1:13). In other words, if Harry does anything, he reads. Would it therefore be wrong to see as significant Beatie's response to her mother's asking whether Sarah is educated: "Educated? No. She's a foreigner. Nor ent Ronnie educated neither. He's an intellectual, failed all his exams. They read and things" (1:124). What saves Ronnie is that he is enough Sarah's son and Wesker's creation never to see art and the intellect as a substitute for life. Beatie says: "Ole Stan Mann would've understood everything Ronnie talk about. Blust! That man liked living'." And she adds, again on the subject of Ronnie: "He's *not* trying to change me Mother. You can't change people, he say, you can only give them some love and hope they'll take it. And he's tryin' to teach me and I'm tryin' to understand—do you see that Mother?" (1:128). Here, Beatie is quoting Ronnie, who was himself quoting his father, as he recognizes in *Jerusalem* (1:210).

It is at that particular point that Sarah says: "I'm always telling you you can't change the world on your own—only no one listens to me." Logically, that should mean that the world can never be changed: Sarah's conclusion should be that only a superhuman degree of collaboration could actually succeed in bringing about change. That does not, of course, exclude the possibility of self-improvement. The failure of his characters to achieve that may be one of the reasons for

Wesker's annoyance with them. Whether that would also apply to him personally may be another matter. Self-improvement is no easy task; doing what we do to the best of our ability may be the closest we can come. In that respect, it is perhaps significant that Wesker never tires of revising his own work. The script of one of his later plays ends with: "6th typed draft." When he directs his own plays, the experience often leads him to producing a revised version. That may not lead to the building of a new Jerusalem, but, apart from any technical theatrical reason which may motivate him, it is certain evidence of a continued questioning of his response to people, both in the form of those with whom he works and in terms of the characters he creates. One of the constants in the *Trilogy*, and one of the principal reasons for its continuing appeal, is that the focus is always on the human, on characters who certainly have their weaknesses and their failings but who are all endowed with that degree of universality which makes it possible for them to speak to us across time as well as beyond the particular time or place in which the author has situated them.

ಌ

ENDNOTES

1. References in square brackets are to Volume 1 of the Wesker *Trilogy*, Penguin Books, 1964, including the revisions to *I'm Talking About Jerusalem* in the 1979 reprint.

2. Ronald Hayman, *Arnold Wesker* (Contemporary Playwrights), 3rd edition. London: Heinemann, 1979, p. 2.

3. On the relationship between Wesker's life and his work, his recently published autobiography, *As Much As I Dare, An Autobiography (1932–1959)*, is of the highest interest.

The Failure and Promise of "Socialism as Personal Contact" in Arnold Wesker's *Roots*

Kevin G. Asman

In his collection of published lectures, *Fears of Fragmentation*, Arnold Wesker says that "those of us who dare to speak before people must choose our words with care and honesty, and that is not easy and I want you to know that I know it is not easy" (105). That Wesker sees honesty as a moral imperative is not surprising. He is a playwright, after all, who has been nothing less than completely candid with people about why he writes. He has never been afraid to proclaim that his writing reflects his political agenda. For Wesker, writing is a form of political activism, and he has spent much of his career experimenting to find ways in which art could help to bring about meaningful change. In a 1960 lecture at Oxford, for instance, Wesker castigated the "Labour movement for neglecting the role of art and the artist in society" and made suggestions for how the Left could use art effectively to convey its message of socialism to the working-class (Hayman 8). His most significant recommendation was for the establishment of a center for the arts which he envisioned would provide a forum for the production of works by working-class and socialist artists and would also reach out to working-class people whose lives had never been touched by the beauty and power of live performance. In part because of Wesker's plea, which was reiterated in pamphlets sent to every trade union general secretary in Britain, in September 1960, the British Trade Union Congress passed Resolution 42, a petition which called for a "greater participation in the cultural life" of the working class and which helped spawned the establishment of "Centre 42," a production company housed at the Round House Theatre in London (Dornan 6; Hayman 8). Throughout the 1960s, Centre 42 sponsored art festivals which were intended to make art more accessible and politically relevant to the working class (Dornan 6, 44). After a short stay in prison for taking part in an illegal protest against nuclear proliferation, Wesker made a full-time commitment to Centre 42 as its managing director in 1961, a position which he held until he formally dissolved the project in 1970 (Leeming, *Arnold Wesker* 9).

From its inception, Centre 42 was plagued with difficulties. There was, for example, rarely enough money to pay the lease on the Round House Theatre in the early days of the project.[1] Most significantly, from the beginning, the artists involved often could not agree on what the purposes of Centre 42 were. In particular, others working with the project criticized Wesker for not being aggressive enough in pursuing the propagation of socialist ideas. The playwright John McGrath, for example, who had been one of Centre 42's founders and a member of its Council of Management, discontinued his involvement because he felt that Wesker's particular socialistic principles did not reflect enough of a commitment to the Marxist ideal of revolutionary change (Dornan 7). Indeed, in response to charges such as McGrath's, Wesker has always made it clear that his conception of socialism has very little to do with the programmatic formula for social change that McGrath was espousing when he abandoned Centre 42. Wesker contends that, while economic change is certainly desirable, "...there is such a problem to being a human that to complicate it even more with economic problems is to confront people with the wrong battle.... It follows that once the economic battle is over there is still the battle of being alive, of being a human being..." (Gordon 140). As this statement suggests, Wesker's intellectual and political relationship with orthodox forms of socialism is, at best, problematic. I contend that Wesker, like Betty Lemon from his play *Whatever Happened to Betty Lemon?* (1980), only ever identified himself with socialism in the early of stages of his career "because in those days there was no other name for what [he] believed" (5:30). Arnold Wesker has always favored the concerns of the individual over abstract conceptions of collective political action. In these terms, he has always been an individualist, though for most of his career, his individualism has been qualified by a preoccupation with the necessity and value of human relations. Perhaps the most striking aspect of Wesker's later writing, however, is the growing vehemence with which he espouses an "unqualified" individualism. In "A Miniautobiography in Three Acts and a Prologue," Wesker's preoccupation with relationships has been supplanted by an "exposed nerve" for people "whose minds are so crippled by stupidity that they need the crutches of

bureaucracy to support them" (238). He is more interested in asserting that "all writers are free and ambivalent spirits" and that "the free
spirit implies the supremacy of the human being over…that which
aims to frustrate initiative, cripple imagination, induce conformity"
(234).[2] He adds with conviction, "A sense of 'the free spirit' is what
I'd like to think pervades all my work" (234).

Nonetheless, in the early stages of his career, Wesker did readily
identify himself with socialism, and this identification has had a lasting impact on the reception of his work. Specifically, many critics
have been quick to accept his association with socialism uncritically
and, as a result, have labeled Wesker didactic, assuming that he is
merely reiterating the often-repeated slogans of Marxist politics in his
drama (Hayman 41; Findlater 237). In his plays, Wesker does not
present a prescriptive formula for how society should be changed to
benefit those who suffer from social structures of domination and
oppression. Wesker has an ideological agenda, but he does not pros-
elytize. He problematizes. As Glenda Leeming argues very cogently,
"…the image of Wesker as a strident moralist, whose plays therefore
must have a strident moral, should be modified because it simply gets
in the way of what is actually there in the plays" (*Arnold Wesker* 3).
Wesker, in other words, is not interested in dogma, and to suggest
that his plays are dogmatic, as too many critics have done, is to ignore
their complexities.

Arnold Wesker has repeatedly demonstrated an interest in the
development of individuals and, especially in his early works, in the
dilemmas that they face as they attempt to interact in meaningful
ways with other individuals. His "socialism" has always been more
about exploring how individuals can work through those dilemmas
to form meaningful relationships than it has about shifts in economic
paradigms. In response to the charge that his three plays, *Chicken
Soup with Barley*, *Roots*, and *I'm Talking About Jerusalem* (collectively
known as the Wesker *Trilogy*) are "primarily political," Wesker says,
"Not merely. The plays continue human relationships as well as arguments—relationships that have gone wrong—and the pause that art
gives you is the opportunity to rectify those relationships or explain
them" (Trussler 192). In particular, Wesker says of the most successful play of the *Trilogy*, *Roots*, that it "deals with socialism as personal
contact" (Rothberg, "Waiting" 497). *Roots* is the story of one person's,
and specifically Beatie Bryant's, ineffectual attempts to work through

the problems of being human to develop "socialistic personal contact" and thus intellectually rich and emotionally supportive relationships, with the members of her working-class family. The purposes of
this essay will be to analyze how and why Beatie attempts to bring
about these relationships, to understand why they do not form, and
most significantly, to demonstrate how Beatie's moment of transcendent self-realization at the end of *Roots* makes plausible the possibility
that these relationships might still develop.

Too often, critics of *Roots* have accepted Beatie Bryant's self-dep-
recations as legitimate assessments of her intellectual capabilities. In
particular, they have been all too ready to accept as incontestably true
Beatie's declarations in Acts 1 and 2 that she has never really compre-
hended the complexities of Ronnie Kahn's socialistic ideals in a way
that would allow her to engage him in a meaningful exchange of views
(1:95,143).[3] To argue that Beatie does not understand at least something of Ronnie's ideas from the very beginning of the play is to over-
simplify her character and, more importantly, her dilemma. While
Beatie does merely regurgitate much of what Ronnie has said (at least
what she indicates he has said), her imitations of the speeches and
mannerisms which she attributes to Ronnie signify that she has, on
some level, internalized the maxims which he has conveyed to her
over the years of their engagement. Ronnie's views and conceptions
are meaningful enough to Beatie that she commits them to her very
formidable memory, something which critics in their rush to malign
her intellect have been unwilling to acknowledge. Her struggle is not
merely to understand what Ronnie has taught her but to comprehend how what he has taught her can be applied in a world where his
ideas are foreign, and it is, in part, to bridge the gap between Ronnie's
theories and the world of human experience that Beatie returns to the
Norfolk community where she grew up. She is, from the very beginning of the play, working toward the realization of Ronnie's understanding of socialism. In one of her imitative moments, Beatie con-
veys Ronnie's definition of socialism to her mother: "Socialism isn't
talking all the time, it's living, it's singing, it's dancing, it's being interested in what go on around you, it's being concerned about people
and the world" (1:129). It is precisely because she has never seen the
members of her family express a concern "about people and the world"
that Beatie feels they need Ronnie's socialism. As Wesker notes in an
Act 1 stage direction, "Throughout the play there is no sign of

intense living from any of the characters—Beatie's bursts are the exception" (1:92). Beatie recognizes this lack intensity in her family, and she wants desperately for them to feel passion for their "roots," the connections which develop between individuals and which give people the emotional nourishment for life (1:145–46). She wants her family, in others words, to live intensely by caring about who "[they] are [and] where they come from" and by taking an interest in the world around them (1:146). Beatie wants them to do nothing less than become aware of their humanity and of their human capacity to express deeply felt emotions for other people and, in particular, their feelings for her. She understands enough of what Ronnie has said about the value of human interaction that she works toward developing more meaningful relationships with her family members from the moment that she arrives at her sister Jenny's house in Act 1.

I am responding, in part, to Abraham Rothberg's assessment of the play which he sees as flawed because "almost nothing happens in the first two acts, which are filled with Wesker's talkiness and set speeches" ("East End" 375). On the contrary, the first two acts of *Roots* are filled with instances where Beatie is trying to reach out to the members of her family on emotional and intellectual levels to which they are unaccustomed. Beatie attempts, for instance, to discuss the merits of reading with Jenny and Jimmy shortly after she arrives at their house. While imitating Ronnie, she contends that reading comics is an acceptable activity—after all, even Ronnie reads them at times—but that one should not confine oneself simply to the reading of comics as is commonly the case among her relatives, as suggested by the large stack which Jimmy and Jenny possess (1:89). Beatie suggests that she has moved beyond what she thinks of as the cultural limitations of her working-class background when she says that "sometimes I read books as well" (1:89). On the one hand, Beatie is trying to encourage Jimmy and Jenny to open themselves up to new forms of artistic stimulation. She is trying to enrich their lives by introducing the world of books into their discourse. On the other hand, she is presenting them with her new identity of increased cultural awareness and asking them to assess and understand what she has become as an individual. She seeks their approbation because she wants some indication that she has become a better person as result of her interaction with Ronnie. On another level, Beatie also seeks their compassion for her dilemma. She opens herself up emotionally to Jimmy and

Jenny when she tells them she would often get a "copy of the *Manchester Guardian* and sit with that wide open—and a comic behind" (1:88). Far from being a simple admission that she does not understand the newspaper, Beatie is pointing out to Jimmy and Jenny how much difficulty she is having negotiating who she is as a result of her life in Norfolk with whom she wants to be so that she can appease Ronnie and live up the values which are expressed in his maxims. However, Beatie receives neither their approbation nor their compassion. Instead of embracing the cultural values Beatie is trying to convey and, thus, showing their approval, they respond defensively and dismissively, telling her, "…don't come pushin' your ideas across at us—we're all right as we are" (1:94). In a very moving appeal for Jenny's understanding, Beatie explicitly tells her sister of how hurt she is by the difficulties she is having living up to Ronnie's expectations. She says, "I pretended I was interested—but I didn't understand much. All the time he's trying to teach me but I can't take it" (1:95). Rather than trying to understand her sister's trouble so that she can help her work through it, Jenny responds dismissively by telling Beatie that she is "not right in the head" for staying with someone like Ronnie (1:95). Jenny does not respond to Beatie with a careful and honest expression of deeply felt emotions. Despite Beatie's effort to reach out to Jimmy and Jenny, the culturally rich and mutually nurturing relationships which she desires do not develop. Beatie is unable to bridge the gap between Ronnie's socialistic theories of human interaction and the Norfolk world of human experience.

Undeterred by her failure with the Beales, in Act 2 Beatie reaches out to her mother in an effort to increase the cultural richness and emotional intensity of their relationship. She begins by showing her mother that she has developed artistic sensibilities as a result of Ronnie's tutelage. She says, "Mother! Did I write to tell you I've took up painting? I started five months ago. Working in gouache. Ronnie says I'm good" (1:113). Beatie is trying, first of all, to expose her mother to a new artistic form which could increase the complexity and intensity of their interaction by introducing into their world the richness and beauty of visual art. She is also asking her mother to acknowledge and celebrate the fact that she is not the same person who left Norfolk three years earlier. Whatever else she is, she is now a painter, and Beatie wants some indication that her mother approves of and values her individuality. She explicitly asks for this confirmation when she says to her mother, "Like 'em?" (1:113). Mrs. Bryant's response does not, however, provide the affirmation which Beatie desires. She "is unmoved," to quote the stage direction, and only says to Beatie, "Good colors ent they" (1:113). Mrs. Bryant shows no appreciation for what Beatie has done with those colors, and, thus, demonstrates neither an approbation of Beatie's new identity nor a willingness to open herself up to the unaccustomed forms of art which Beatie has brought back with her.

That Beatie feels intensely about bringing about a meaningful change in her familial relations is evident in her persistence. Beatie refuses to give up on her mother despite Mrs. Bryant's initial indifference to what she is trying to accomplish. She reaches out to her mother a second time by sharing a poem. However, Mrs. Bryant neither acknowledges Beatie's accomplishment in having memorized the poem, nor does she demonstrate a willingness to open herself up to the enriching possibilities of poetry (1:114). If anything, her assessment of the poem is even more dismissive than her appraisal of Beatie's painting. Mrs. Bryant refuses to acknowledge that there is any aesthetic value in the poem, and her only response is "them's as good words as any" (1:115). Beatie's mother only demonstrates a reserved willingness to accept what her daughter is offering when Beatie plays Bizet's "L'Arlésienne Suite" at the end of Act 2, but Mrs. Bryant's defensive response to the suite of "I ain't sayin' it's all squit" qualifies her willingness to accept the cultural and aesthetic possibilities of the music (1:129). She may not be dismissive, but neither does she admit that there is beauty in Bizet's art, although Beatie explains its aesthetic virtues *in her own words* with a sensitivity and perceptiveness that critics have not acknowledged (1:129). In a 1960 interview with Jill Pomerance, Wesker asked rhetorically, "In *Roots*, when Beatie dances isn't this poetry?" (6). He was challenging Pomerance, in other words, to understand that Beatie's response to the suite is a complex and meaningful expression of her individual humanity and, most especially, her human capacity to feel passion for beauty. Mrs. Bryant, however, does not share Beatie's passion. There is, for instance, no indication in the stage direction at the end of Act 2 that she joins in the dance which Beatie performs when she is caught up in the emotion of the music: "Beatie claps her hands and dances on and her Mother smiles and claps her hands and—The Curtain Falls" (1:129). The conjunction does denote that something else happens, but the act ends before the audience sees what that action is. We never see Mrs. Bryant participate in the dancing (if she even does), a significant omission because dancing, as noted above, is very much a part of Ronnie's understanding of socialism. It is a communal activity, something which people share and which reinforces their connectedness as human beings, a point which Beatie makes just before she begins dancing (1:129). Mrs. Bryant's taking part in the dance would signify her unconditional acceptance of both Beatie's new identity and the idea that these unfamiliar forms of artistic expression could help increase the emotional intensity of her relationship with her daughter. Despite the qualified optimism of the Bizet episode, Beatie's attempt to build a mutually nurturing and culturally rich social relation goes unfilled. By the end of Act 2, though she is intense and persistent, Beatie is unable to bring Ronnie's conception of socialism into realization. Wesker leaves his audience anticipating whether that realization will be explicitly dramatized in Act 3, whether, in other words, Beatie will succeed in getting through to her family.

That Mrs. Bryant does not open herself up in Act 3 to the emotional depth and cultural richness which Beatie is trying to bring into their relationship becomes apparent in her response to Beatie's heartfelt admission that she has been having difficulty negotiating what Ronnie is asking of her. After Ronnie has sent his letter breaking off their engagement and indicating he is not coming to Norfolk, Beatie says, "I *never* discussed things. He used to beg me to discuss but I never saw the point on it" (1:143). Much as she was doing in Act 1, Beatie is trying to indicate to her family that she has been having difficulty reconciling who she is with whom Ronnie wants her to be; she is reaching out to them, asking for their compassion in a moment of intense self-doubt. Instead of trying to understand Beatie's dilemma and offering emotional support, Mrs. Bryant seizes upon this moment of despair to attack both Beatie's new identity and her efforts to enrich the lives of her family members by bringing to them unfamiliar forms of art. Mrs. Bryant's most vehement condemnation of Beatie occurs when she says, "The apple don't fall far from the tree—that it don't" (1:144). She argues, in essence, that Beatie has not really changed and, therefore, has no right to set herself up as an authority on artistic forms of expression such as painting, poetry, and music. Mrs. Bryant contends that all Beatie has offered is "high-class squit and then it turn out that she don't understand any on it herself" (1:145). Mrs.

Bryant is so determined to undermine all that her daughter has been trying to do that she cannot see that Beatie has already demonstrated the intellectuality and sensitivity necessary to appreciate art, and nothing better illustrates Beatie's capacity for appreciation than her deeply emotional response to the Bizet suite at the end of Act 2 (1:129). Instead of helping Beatie overcome her self-doubt by pointing out what she has already demonstrated, Mrs. Bryant seizes on this moment of insecurity to both humiliate her daughter and drive a wedge between them. Thus, despite her persistence, Beatie's attempts to reach out to her family have the reverse effect of what she intended. The familial relations at the end of the play are neither culturally rich nor, as Mrs. Bryant's slap in Act 3 indicates, mutually nurturing (1:144). Beatie is never able to see Ronnie's conception of socialism brought into realization by play's end. If *Roots* is about "socialism as personal contact," as Wesker argues, then is it a story of Beatie's failure to achieve the socialistic personal contact that she has been striving for since her arrival in Norfolk?

To understand why these mutually nurturing and culturally rich relationships do not develop, one must begin by looking at Beatie's family. In my analysis of her family, I am responding, in part, to Laurence Kitchin's assertion that "Wesker's people are less characters than personalities, indeed it is part of the statement that they are not characters, but...they refer to a social context bigger than themselves..." (177). Without quite using the term, Kitchin is arguing that Wesker's characters are allegorical, that they represent "subjects of mid-century life" such as "boring work" and "misused leisure" (177). Kitchin's assessment is, however, an oversimplification of the people in Wesker's plays. There is no better refutation of his contention than the "Note to Actors and Producers" where Wesker says, "My people are not caricatures. They are real (though fictitious), and if they are portrayed as caricatures the point of all these plays will be lost" (80).[4] If one reduces characters such as the Bryants to exaggerated personalities, then one fails to acknowledge they are people (though fictitious) with emotional dimensionality. In particular, it is essential that Beatie's family not be reduced to characters who simply reject deep emotional involvement with other people because they are too simplistic to want emotional depth in their lives. As Michael Anderson argues, "One of the achievements of *Roots* is that Wesker manages to condemn the dull existence of the Bryants without condemning the Bryants" (15).

There are episodes in the text which suggest that these people, like Beatie, also feel the need to reach out to those around them in a way which offers some emotional fulfillment. When Beatie first arrives at Jenny's house, for instance, Jenny's first action is to say, "Sit you down then an' I'll get your supper on the table" (1:86). Far from being an insignificant activity of daily life, Jenny's attempt to feed Beatie is a meaningful gesture of nurturance and caring. As Wesker himself says, "When you invite people into your home you touch them through food" (Itzin and Leeming 21). How much it means to Jenny that she "touch" Beatie in some fashion becomes apparent in her offer of strawberry ice cream, something which Beatie particularly enjoys and which could not have been easy to keep in a rural Norfolk home without modern conveniences (1:88). This pattern of offering food as a gesture of communal benevolence is one that recurs throughout the play. When the Bryants are anticipating Ronnie's arrival, for instance, Mrs. Bryant prepares "an enormous bowl of trifle," a dish which Beatie says Ronnie enjoys (1:131–32). The trifle becomes Mrs. Bryant's way of "touching" Ronnie, of doing nothing less than welcoming him into the family.

What becomes apparent through these repeated offers of food is that the Bryants and Beales mediate their human interrelationships through material objects which, in turn, become inadequate substitutes for meaningful expressions of emotion. When Mr. Bryant, for instance, wishes to express a rejection of Jenny Beales (perhaps because of the illegitimate child she bore before she married Jimmy), he does so by refusing to allow Beatie to bake to a sponge cake for Jenny using his electricity (1:120–21). He does not, however, verbalize his condemnation of his daughter, and there is certainly no indication of what his emotional rationale for rejecting her might be. When it comes to expressions of emotion, Mr. Bryant's motto is "let's hev grub [or not] and not so much of the lip ..." (1:121). Mr. Bryant does not have the capacity to express his feelings in language, but he is not alone. When Jenny and Beatie are discussing the concept of love, Jenny says, "Love? I don't believe in any of that squit" (1:97). Jenny, nonetheless, does feel something for Jimmy; she expresses some compassion for him when she agrees with Beatie's contention that "he's a good man" (1:96). There is an emotional bond between Jimmy and Jenny. She is, however, incapable of verbalizing her emotions and so dismisses their existence, much as Mrs. Bryant does when she says,

"The world don't want no feelings" (1:116). Jenny cannot bring herself to call what she feels for Jimmy love because she does not know what the word means. Jenny exists, to use Beatie's expression, "wi' no tools for livin'" (1:145). She does not have the words to convey her feelings, and words are, in Wesker's view, the basic components of human relationships because, as he contends, "[humans] understand experience through them" (Stoll 425). It is with words that human beings work through the problems of being human. Words are what individuals need to reach out to other people, to develop what Beatie calls, in one of her imitative moments, "bridges," the things "that help you get from one place to another" and, I would add, from one person to another (1:90). As Beatie herself says, when people do not have the bridges to reach each other, they "hev a row" instead (1:90). That *Roots* ends with "a row" between Mrs. Bryant and Beatie suggests that the "bridges" are not yet there which will allow them to interact with emotional depth. After she reads Ronnie's letter, Beatie screams, "Well! help me then! Give me words of comfort! Talk to me—for God's sake, someone talk to me" (1:144). Mrs. Bryant's response is one of bewilderment. She asks her family, "Well, what do we do now?" (1:144). Beatie's relatives do not know how to communicate the approbation and compassion that Beatie is asking of them throughout the play. It is, in part, because they do not have the tools that the mutually nurturing and culturally rich familial relations which Beatie wants do not develop.

   Beatie's relatives are not, however, solely responsible for inhibiting the development of these relations. A. M. Aylwin argues "that the failure of communication is caused by Beatie's shortcomings as well as those of her family" (2). In particular, Beatie's major shortcoming is her inability to accept her family because they represent what she has so desperately been trying to leave behind, the outward markings and limitations of her working-class identity. Beatie is, in short, ashamed of her family because she sees in them too much of what she does not value in herself anymore. In her recent book on working-class writing, Pamela Fox argues, that "shame can serve as an actuating force in [working-class] revolt" because it signifies "an active refusal to wear the badge of [class] Otherness" (127). In part, Fox is correct. Beatie's shame, for instance, is born out of a desire to actuate change in her life and the lives of her family members. Through Ronnie's influence, she comes to resist the notion that she must live

an intellectually stifled existence because she was born into a working-class community and grew up to acquire working-class views and
conceptions. *Roots* is the story of her attempt to free herself and her
family from the limitations of their working-class lives. However, as
she begins to open herself up to forms of artistic expression which are
not predominant in the working-class Norfolk community, she also
begins to distance herself from the people and customs of that community in a way that ultimately leads to the alienation of the very
people to whom she is reaching out. Therefore, her shame also has
the effect of limiting her ability to achieve the relationships that she
desires. Beatie's shame inhibits change; it does not "actuate revolt."
She says to her mother, "I don't want Ronnie to think that I come
from a small-minded family" (1:111). Beatie's recurring emphasis on
the shortcomings of her family makes them intractable and defensive. They feel besieged by her attacks on their way of life, and so
cling to and defend that way of life, including its limitations. As Mrs.
Bryant says, "All right so I am a bloody fool—all right! So I know it!
A whole two weeks I've bin told it. Well, so then I can't help you my
gal, no that I can't, and you get used to that once and for all" (1:145).
Ultimately, because Beatie cannot accept who they are as individuals,
they resist what she has to offer, both culturally and emotionally.

Wesker says in his "Note to Actors and Producers" that "the picture I have drawn is a harsh one, yet my tone is not one of disgust..."
(80). One should not, therefore, translate Wesker's harshness into fatalism. *Roots* ends without a positive resolution between Beatie and
her family. The socialistic personal contact which Beatie has been
striving for never occurs, but *Roots* does not end by positing that
mutually nurturing and culturally rich social relations can never occur. Beatie's moment of transcendent self-realization indicates, optimistically, that she is better equipped to bring those relationships into
existence at the end of the play than she was when it started. Beatie
resolves her dilemma of reconciling who she is with whom Ronnie
wants her to be. She discovers, specifically, that she does not have to
imitate Ronnie if she wants to share her feelings and perceptions with
those she loves, something which the audience should have been aware
of since the end of Act 2 when they saw Beatie's reaction to the Bizet
suite. Beatie realizes that she has the ability to use words. As she says,
"I'm talking. Jenny, Frankie, Mother—I'm not quoting no more,"
and she adds, "It does work, It's happening to me, I can feel it's

happened, I'm beginning, on my own two feet—I'm beginning…"
(1:148). As John Russell Taylor argues, Beatie not only begins to speak
for herself but she also beings to doubt whether Ronnie's truisms are
all that true. Taylor notes that Beatie "sees the falsity of Ronnie's idea
about country workers, living in mystic communion with nature"
(149). Beatie finally realizes that she has the capacity to analyze and
appreciate things in her own terms, that she is, in other words, an
individual.

The play is a celebration of Beatie's individual accomplishments,
and, therefore, an endorsement of individualism in that it suggests
that her personal development must necessarily precede the development of the relationships which she is seeking, but it is an endorsement of individualism which is qualified by a preoccupation with
those relationships. Even at play's end, although she has suffered much
rejection from everyone to whom she has opened herself emotionally,
Beatie still feels compelled to share her new identity with those around
her. They are not listening to her, but her concluding speech begins
with the very significant imperative "Listen to me someone" (1:148).
She is still reaching out, still trying to share something of herself with
her family. The difference is that she is now beginning to understand
what she has to offer. As Beatie begins to understand and accept who
she is, it opens up the possibility that she also will be able to accept
who her family members are and that they will, therefore, be more
likely to find some common ground for growth and understanding
or, if you prefer, building bridges.

In the end, Wesker does not, however, present a prescriptive formula for how those relationships can be achieved. The play ends before Beatie can employ the tools that she has discovered as a result of
her self-realization. As Thomas P. Adler contends, Beatie's self-discov-
ery is "but a prelude to action and not a substitute for it" (429). The
audience members never see the bridges being built because Wesker
is asking them to consider how those bridges can be built. Rather
than make a declaration of how to work through the problem of being human, he describes the problem as he understands it with great
"care and honesty" and asks the audience to figure out how the "tools
for livin'" can help solve the problem of bringing individuals together
in a way that allows them to realize their full human potential. This is
what his "socialism as personal contact" is all about. That Wesker
does not have the solution for the problem becomes evident when he

says in the "Note to Actors and Producers," "I am at one with these people" (80). With *Roots*, he is trying to work through the same dilemmas that they are; he, like Beatie Bryant, is trying to understand how to bring individuals together in meaningful relationships. Ultimately, what I find compelling and what has kept me coming back to *Roots* is my sense that, unlike much of his later work where he expresses a sense of resignation about human relations, this play is a carefully and honestly constructed attempt to build bridges with his audience so that we all can work toward the same goal of solving the problem of being human.

૨૭

ENDNOTES

1. The lease on the Round House Theatre was donated to Centre 42 in 1965 (Dornan 47).

2. In "A Miniautobiography in Three Acts and a Prologue," Wesker attributes these lines to an article called "Hebrew and Jewish Legacies—A Symposium" which appeared in the *Times Literary Supplement* of May 3, 1985. The lines are not, however, included in the article as *TLS* printed it.

3. All references are to the 1979 Penguin edition of the Wesker *Trilogy* (Volume 1). *Roots* was originally staged at the Belgrade Theatre in Conventry where it opened May 29, 1959, under the direction of John Dexter and featured Joan Plowright as Beatie Bryant (Leeming, *Wesker on File* 16).

4. In the 1964 Penguin edition of the Wesker *Trilogy*, the "Note to Actors and Producers" is entitled "Author's Note to Actors and Producers" and is on page 7 before *Chicken Soup with Barley*.

WORKS CITED

Adler, Thomas P. "The Wesker *Trilogy* Revisited: Games to Compensate for the Inadequacy of Words." *Quarterly Journal of Speech* 65 (1979): 429–38.

Anderson, Michael. "Arnold Wesker: The Last Humanist?" *New Theatre Magazine* 8.3 (1968): 10–27.

Aylwin, A. M. *Notes on Arnold Wesker's Roots*. London: Methuen, 1975.

Dornan, Reade. *Arnold Wesker Revisited*. New York: Twayne, 1994.

Findlater, R. "Plays and Politics." *Twentieth Century* 168 (1960): 235–42.

Fox, Pamela. *Class Fictions*. Durham, NC: Duke UP, 1995.

Gordon, Giles. "Arnold Wesker." *Behind the Scenes: Theater and Film Interviews from the Transatlantic Review*. Ed. Joseph F. McCrindle. New York: Holt, Rinehart and Winston, 1971. 137–48.

Hayman, Ronald. *Arnold Wesker*. London: Heinemann, 1970.

Itzin, Catherine, and Glenda Leeming. "Wesker: A Sense of What Should Follow." *Theatre Quarterly* 28 (1977–78): 5–24.

Kitchin, Laurence. "Drama with a Message: Arnold Wesker." *Experimental Drama*. Ed. William A. Armstrong. London: G. Bell, 1963. 169–185.

Leeming, Glenda. *Arnold Wesker*. Harlow, Essex: Longman, 1972.

——. *Wesker on File*. Ed. Simon Trussler. London: Methuen, 1985.

Pomerance, Jill. "Question and Answer, Arnold Wesker." *New Theatre Magazine* 1.3 (1960): 5–9.

Rothberg, Abraham. "East End, West End: Arnold Wesker." *Southwest Review* 52 (1967): 368–78.

——. "Waiting for Wesker." *The Antioch Review* 24 (1964–65): 492–505.

Stoll, Karl-Heinz. "Interviews with Edward Bond and Arnold Wesker." *Twentieth Century Literature* 22 (1976): 411–32.

Taylor, John Russell. *Anger and After: A Guide to the New British Drama*. Rev. ed. New York: Hill and Wang, 1969.

Trussler, Simon. "His Very Own and Golden City: An Interview with Arnold Wesker." *The Drama Review* 11.2 (1966): 192–202.

Wesker, Arnold. "Note to Actors and Producers." *The Wesker Trilogy*. 1964. Harmondsworth: Penguin, 1979. 80.

——. *Fears of Fragmentation*. London: Jonathan Cape, 1970.

——. "A Miniautobiography in Three Acts and a Prologue." *Contemporary Author's Autobiography Series*. Vol. 7. Ed. Mark Zadrozny. Detroit: Gale Research, 1988. 24 vols. to date. 227–63.

——. *Roots. The Wesker Trilogy*. 1964. Harmondsworth: Penguin, 1979. 79–149.

——. *Whatever Happened to Betty Lemon? One Woman Plays*. Harmondsworth: Penguin, 1989. 23–36.

——, et al. "Hebrew and Jewish Legacies—A Symposium." *Times Literary Supplement* May 3, 1985: 499–500.

Arnold Wesker and the Desire for Utopia
Utopia's Enemies and Wesker

Heiner O. Zimmermann

Utopia has always been severely criticized by conservative thinkers. After the Second World War, the liberal philosopher, Karl Popper, denounced utopian societies as authoritarian and "closed" and their designers as enemies of the pluralist "open" society which admits the equality of different ideologies and ways to happiness.[1] He accused utopia of having furnished the model for both fascist and communist totalitarian states such as Hitler's Third Reich and Stalin's Soviet empire. The dream of utopia will survive, however. Ernst Bloch showed both its historical importance and the need for it in his study, *The Principle of Hope*.[2] It will persist because it liberates the forces of imagination and hope to produce a necessary counter-image to an ever imperfect reality. It represents the desire of its time. This is also the reason why the tenacious and at times desperate interrogation of the idea of utopia which forms the center of Arnold Wesker's plays still attracts our attention—in spite of all the corrosive criticism of utopian thinking which would denigrate this desire as naive. The endeavor to achieve utopia in Wesker's plays reflects an emotional reality of their time.

At the birth of the new political drama after the Second World War, John Osborne's *Look Back in Anger* identified the loss of meaning and political perspective in the late fifties as the loss of belief in the socialist utopia which had turned from an ideal into Aldous Huxley's horror vision: "If the big bang does come, and we all get killed off, it won't be in aid of the old-fashioned, grand design. It'll just be for the Brave New-nothing-very-much-thank-you."[3] Parallel to the anti-utopian novels of the time by Anthony Burgess or William Golding, Harold Pinter presented the sufferings of the individual crushed by a society which enforces conformity and a state which smothers him with care in *The Birthday Party*.

Literary utopias between More and Bellamy, it is true, nourished the hope that universal happiness could be achieved by perfect planning and order. But it is nevertheless a fallacy to take the possible decay into totalitarianism as the very essence of utopia.[4] Its dangerous potential has been denounced even from the utopian point of view itself, since writers like George Orwell in *1984* drew horror visions of a society whose members are incapacitated by an order which manipulates them like objects. These negative images, however, do not necessarily intend to refute utopia altogether. They can even—as in the case of Orwell's works—dialectically allude to another utopia.[5] The vision is thus preserved in the negative.

In this situation, where positive utopian designs seemed no longer possible, where even socialists joined in the general criticism of the vision, calling it a chimera,[6] Wesker advocated a revival of the utopian ideal.[7] He was convinced that it could be a means of retrieving hope, and show a way out of a general dilemma. At a time when Beckett's metaphysical despair left no hope for any action in the sense of fundamental change, Wesker announced that the belief in the utopian ideal could provide a meaning and order for life.

What gave him the confidence to revive this conception? First, he took advantage of the chameleon-like nature of the term "utopia" itself. According to Plato and More, to Cabet and Saint-Simon, rules, bureaucracy, and obedience triumph in the ideal state in which equality comes before freedom. But from the time of its first descriptions, this idea of utopia has provoked an opposed Arcadian vision.[8] The latter is propagated by authors such as Aristophanes, Rabelais, Swift, Owen, and Fourier, who prefer the individual to the state, nature to technology, organic to artificial organization, and spontaneity to precepts. In contrast to the other utopian ideal, these counter-images are not discredited by analogies with totalitarian states. The pastoral dream has even had a come-back during the last few decades with the ecological movement's opposition to industrial society.

Wesker faced up to the dual nature of the utopian concept in his writing and in the foundation of Centre 42. As early as the 50s he anticipated a movement which for the rest of society commenced only around the mid-60s with a wave of new utopian communities trying out alternative ways of living.[9] They extolled the exodus from an alienated, competitive capitalist society whose industry destroys the natural environment and advocated the return to a natural lifestyle based on the introduction of alternative technologies. They saw themselves as catalysts for radical general change. May 1968 brought a temporary climax to this new belief in utopia. Wesker's vision, however, was firmly rooted in the British Labour Movement, and fully conscious of its history. He had hardly anything in common with the spontaneous outbursts of the young rebels of 1968, who hoped to triumph over history by ignoring it, and believed rather in imagination, spontaneity, and anarchy than in reason. The few ideas he shared with them derived from the utopian socialists of the nineteenth century, such as Robert Owen and in particular William Morris. His obstinate belief in the middle-class tradition of humanist culture, however, fundamentally separated him from them.

The Fear of Fragmentation and Utopia

Wesker is no philosopher. Attempts to distill a coherent conception of socialism from his lectures and plays will only lead to the feeling that his ideas are diffuse and contradictory.[10] Yet it would be wrong to dismiss his theories, for they offer essential insights into the patterns of thought from which his plays arose.[11]

At the centre of Wesker's reflections on the fundamentals of his writing in the 50s and 60s stood the opposition between the negative principle of fragmentation and the wholeness of an integrated utopian perspective[12]:

> Somewhere in the total history of man, in his thoughts and his actions and his hopes, there is a delicately woven vision of a just and beautiful society; and if most religions, philosophies and political ideologies could be analysed in incredible detail then this vision would be found to hold them more in common than in conflict. (*Fears* 110)

As Morris had, Wesker blamed the fragmentation he saw all around him on capitalist methods of production and the resulting social order. Without their abolition, all other efforts could only remain "patchwork." Capitalist society takes away the workers' freedom of self-determination and so shatters their identities. The competitive system estranges one worker from another, and the class system, with its hatred, alienates whole parts of the society from one another.

Wesker's fear of losing the wholeness of vision is also related to the fragmentation of all knowledge into more and more specialized compartments. This fragmentation in turn leads to a narrow-minded concentration on detail, and the mistaking of partial insights for the whole truth. Not only superficial and trivialized information from the mass media is pernicious, but the sheer quantity of information imposes arbitrary self-restraint on the recipient. The eclecticism of contemporary artists makes Wesker uneasy. According to him, they cannot cope with the mass of information offered by science, art, and literature, and consequently they make some arbitrarily chosen detail the centre of their work. He is equally depressed by the satisfaction of the masses with a shallow art of fragments and their rejection of a more demanding kind of art. "Chaos," "disintegration," "confusion," "waste," are the terms which he uses to characterize the central idea of fragmentation. Wesker thus expresses his own sense of a disorientation which pervades modernist literature. This disorientation is felt to be a consequence of the individualistic concept of reality, of the alienation of subject and object, and of the loss of any metaphysical hope that could provide meaning.

The "Total Work of Art" and Utopia[13]

Wesker never draws a detailed picture of a utopian vision which promises order, wholeness and solidarity. Only some outlines can be discerned. As he believes that enlightenment leads to emancipation and social progress, his ideal is the humanistically educated *uomo universale*. In an all-embracing synthesis, the New Man endeavors to assimilate the cultural heritage, the accumulated knowledge of history, in order to achieve autonomy. He is a perfectly rational being in command of his passions, fully comprehending his social and economic situation and consequently self-determined (*Fears* 122f.). Wesker's ideal of a wholly integrated way of life, an active and a creative life which is lived consciously, which ignores the separation between work and play, is inspired by Morris.[14] Yet in contrast to his model, Wesker begs the question of how, exactly, this utopian life is to be economically and socially organized.

Utopia needs the visionary artist who is totally imbued with its idea and who is conscious of his obligation: "...to trace sections of this fragile vision and leave clues about its existence" (*Fears* 110). Only a utopian perspective restores unity and general validity to artistic work. An awareness of the ideal allows art to fulfill the task of conveying a real understanding of the human condition (*Fears* 69). It must both explain the causalities underlying reality and suggest a possible order and unity: ...the truth about ourselves as we are and the vision of what we could be" (*Fears* 30). Thanks to its obligation to utopia, art preserves the hope of healing the division between subject and object. Like utopia itself, art should be "a sort of hymn in praise of man" (*Fears* 18).

Since Plato's *Politeia*, skepticism towards art has frequently accompanied utopianism in literature. Wesker, however, attributes to art a key function in society, for it can release the working classes from their cultural inferiority to the educated middle class; art will enlighten them and so bring about their social emancipation. Thus social antagonisms will disappear. In this endeavor Wesker wages war on two fronts: against the capitalist system as the origin of alienation and fragmentation, and against the Labour Movement, which takes care of the physical, but not the spiritual, well-being of the workers and so neglects part of the wholeness of human nature. While the unions struggle to transform the worker economically into a member of the middle class, Wesker battles for his intellectual metamorphosis. He conceives of the emancipation of the working man mainly as a result of a change of consciousness. Once this transformation of consciousness is achieved, economic change and the promotion of the working classes to social equality will follow. This vision of revolution means that Wesker can ignore the problems of political violence.[15]

In an experiment, a model community would search for the ideal image of a socialist society through the common study of historical utopias, utopian art, literature, and architecture; through the analysis of religions, philosophies, and political ideologies. This would be a kind of permanent university (*Fears* 124ff.). Wesker thus makes education the "categorical imperative" with the defining of utopia as its aim. This exploration of the idea of utopia simultaneously creates the condition of its achievement: a critical, enlightened and humane "community that knows," united to make the analysis of art and literature the center of its life and so to draw nearer to the ideal of the New Man.

The concept of utopia is transformed into a principle of evolution, an ideal which shows the way. In its essential parts it remains, however, indeterminate. This indeterminacy produces its own dynamic. It stays forever ahead of all historical situations, thus generating the energy for all development and guiding evolution like a lodestar. It creates a meaning for this world and suggests an ethical system. The transformation of the ideal into practice, however, remains a never-ending process which constantly demands new efforts.

The utopian idea is for Wesker not only the business of literature but above all an eminently practical political matter. He made this evident by his project, "Centre 42," which was to change the conditions of the reception of art and in particular of the theatre.[16] True to his ideal of wholeness, all arts were to find a home in this temple of the muses for the people. By living in a community, workers and artists were to enjoy access to one another entirely unhampered by the laws of the market. This would strike the spark that was to kindle the fire of a general cultural revolution. The failure of this project at the end of the decade also marked a turn in Wesker's confrontation with utopia.

The Biographical Bias and the Inherited Dream

Wesker's desire for the enlightenment of the working class betrays the inferiority complex of the working-class author, who was barred from the middle-class privilege of a university education as well as from bourgeois culture. His emancipatory zeal is ultimately motivated by his need to compensate for his repressed contempt for the state of mind of one part of the working class: "...we do inherit from our parents that slight distaste for the *Lumpenproletariat*."[17] Without a critical examination of the values inherent in this tradition, he adopts it as the absolute norm. He reduces both the question of the genesis of art forms and aesthetic concerns to a simple value judgment: "We are not looking for a working-class art—we do not know what this is. There is only good and bad art and there should never be any other criterion" (61). This is the only way for him to remain faithful to his principle of the unity of art, which is eventually to lead to the unity of society. His subsequent argument, however, makes it evident that by good art he means the art of middle-class high culture above all else. He is unaware of the problems that lurk in the use of bourgeois aesthetics for the emancipation of the working class or in the authoritarian tendencies of an educational theatre. He ignores the dilemma caused by the fact that his drama asks for an audience which, in order to be able to appreciate it, ought to be already blessed with the knowledge and taste which the plays are intended to convey.[18] Overestimating the possibilities and means of enlightenment, his pragmatic optimism seems like an attempt to purge his own secret fears as a Jew subjected to the racism of the working class.[19]

Wesker's reactions to the controversies over his utopian vision, and even his attempt to rationally distance himself from it, reveal his deep psychic entanglement with it. Not without reason does he speak of "the dream I've inherited."[20] Although not a practicing Jew, elements of the Messianic dream of the millennium, which brings salvation on earth, appear everywhere in his plays accompanied by humanistic and socialist conceptions. The essential field of reference for the author's dream is formed by the exodus and the return to the Promised Land, and also by the expectation of the Messiah, who will bring peace and happiness, abolish injustice, and establish a kingdom of God for the Chosen People with Jerusalem as its center. The distinct worldly orientation of Messianism,[21] in spite of all its eschatological implications, favors a broad Jewish commitment to secular concepts of the ideal community. This can be observed equally well in Theodor Herzl's Zionist movement, in the concept of the kibbutzim or in the socialist vision of utopia. Wesker, a comparatively feeble voice in this choir, does not deny his commitment first to the Young Communist League and later far more intensely to the Zionist Youth Movement.[22] In a daring "biblical genealogy" of the utopian tradition in "The London Diary," the syncretist character of his concept of utopia appears quite distinctly: "From Isaiah to hand a piece to Jesus, Jesus to Wat Tyler and he to Winstanley and he to William Morris and Marx to Lenin and Lenin to Castro and the students of Paris and the workers of Prague."[23] This sweeping overview ignores Marx's critique of the authors of social utopias as "prescientific." Intuitively, Wesker seems to assimilate Marx's belief in progress in history into other eschatologies.

Wesker's writings blend inherited Messianism with socialist utopia, in effect, Robert Owen's New Harmony with the Heavenly Jerusalem. This fusion reveals the mystical sources of energy from which his hope springs and also reveals the function of a utopian society for the author: utopia replaces religion and creates meaning. The sacral connotations of Wesker's concept of art accordingly assume their specific significance, and the poet often appears with the missionary halo of a

Jewish prophet. His ideal artist fulfills a priest-like function in society. He is the born guardian of utopia, for "only the poet is capable of a view of man as he could be, rather than as he is."[24] Art possesses a redeeming force in so far as it transmits the message of utopia.[25] For Wesker the paradox is that art is the medium of the utopia which it may not itself become without betraying it.[26] The holistic utopian vision thus is that which cannot be represented, the sublime, whose loss rouses the modernist Wesker's melancholy.

A Vision of Enlightenment

Roots (pf.1959, pb. 1959), the centerpiece of the *Trilogy*, propounds a complementary vision to the hope of achieving happiness and justice by reinventing the whole system of social relations: it is the dream of the working class's emancipation through enlightenment. It is founded on the hope that the workers' tutelage, their moral and intellectual immaturity, which is due to the capitalist system of production, will be remedied by their instruction. In order to achieve the free use of their own reason they must, however, overcome the moral and intellectual limits imposed upon them by their social status. Better insight into themselves and their condition as well as an improved command of language would lead the working class to a self-determined and active life of self-realization.

A family of Norfolk farm laborers serves for a dramatic case study. Their deficient understanding of themselves and of their situation alienates them from themselves, their work and their surroundings. Their lack of articulateness and their passiveness predestine them to become victims suffering from ailments of which they neither perceive the origin nor understand the cause. The imperative of enlightenment is thrust upon them by their daughter and sister, Beatie, on visit from London. The origin of this discourse, which she only quotes, is her absent boyfriend Ronnie, a failed student committed to socialism whose visit is prepared for as the play's climax. But he never turns up. Beatie, his mouthpiece, is not so much moved by the force of conviction of what she rehearses as by her love for him and by the desire that her family should please him. Ronnie and the principle of enlightenment thus appear like Beatie's superego, whose claims she projects on her family, having largely failed to meet them herself. This marks the distance between the working-class way of thinking and feeling and the discourse which promises them a fuller humanity, justice and happiness.

"Roots" thus refers to the patterns of thought, the values and habits which determine and mutilate the farm laborers' life as Beatie perceives it thanks to Ronnie's influence and her years of separation from them. But it also evokes the knowledge accumulated by humanity in the course of history, the cultural heritage which the individual must appropriate in order to achieve full humanity. This entails a demand for permanent learning which is considered a moral duty. A historical, critical understanding of themselves and their situation will be the way to the workers' self-determination and independent democratic practice in spite of the capitalist system. The belief in the basic socialist values of "human dignity and tolerance and co-operation and equality"(1:141)[27] relies on enlightenment to create the new wo/man capable of implementing them. The hoped-for experience of enjoying life through autonomous, meaningful and creative activity providing the feeling of being fully "alive" also always implies an aesthetic satisfaction. It presupposes intellectual curiosity, openness to communication, willingness to teach and to learn. Contrary to the stultifying smoke screen of popular forms of entertainment preferred by the working class, which are disqualified by Beatie as third rate, creative intellectual activity and critical insights are furthered by bourgeois literature and painting or by classical music.

The authoritarian character of this way to emancipation is evident. It not only establishes a hierarchy of forms of culture but also demands the workers who are to be liberated subject themselves to the authority of those who know. The family's critical rejection of the new ideas demonstrates this as does Beatie's own development from dependence through a painful disillusionment to maturity. Ronnie tries to shun the issue when he denies that he attempts to change people and insists that by teaching them he only proposes his ideas to them, leaving them free to choose (1:128).

Articulateness and free communication are the indispensable prerequisites and vehicles of this process of transformation. The play features Beatie's transgressing of the taboos which impede communication in her family as well as her development from quoting to autonomous speech. The catastrophe in the final scene when Ronnie abandons her and her mother slaps her face shocks her into articulateness. This is a *mise en scène* of her emancipation from the authority of her mother and from that of her spiritual "father," as both refuse to take further responsibility for her. It portrays an improbable revolution which completes the process of enlightenment and breaks the fetters of heredity and socialization. The end of the play attempts to inspire the audience with the enthusiasm of Beatie's vision: "That it does work" (1:148). Her liberation, however, alienates her both from her former self and from her family.

An Alternative Way of Life

The last play in the *Trilogy*, *I'm Talking About Jerusalem* (pf.1960, pb. 1960), bears in its title the allusion to Zionist and chiliastic concepts. Jerusalem, the capital of the promised realm of God, the heavenly, the Golden City, shall also be the centre of the prophesied Third Kingdom of the Holy Ghost on earth.

Since the play's protagonists are weary of endless and fruitless political discussion, they take direct action. Straightaway they want to jump into a private "paradise now," in order to live according to their ideals.

Ada and Dave Simmonds turn their backs on the organized Labour Movement and on capitalist industrial society. They follow the ecological principles already established by William Morris and dedicate themselves to a way of life close to nature. Their return to craftsmanship and creative unalienated work rescues them from the blessings of modern technology. A place of work near home and nature, the quality and the aesthetic design of the goods produced are more important for them than profit. A mere glance into history, however, could have taught them that their individual journey to Arcadia is foredoomed to failure, because they, like their predecessors, ignore the fact that indispensable preconditions for the practical execution of the project are not fulfilled. In the long run, no increase in individual effort can remove their economic inferiority to the capitalist industrial production around them or their dependence on the latter. This, as well as society's immutable hostility, at last exhausts the outsider's resistance. When he returns to London at the end, the vision has lost its glamour.

The insuperable problems and enormous misunderstandings which weigh down Ada and Dave's attempt to build themselves a utopian island become evident in their isolation even within their family. The objections to their enterprise range from non-understanding of their renunciation of electricity, water on tap, and asphalt roads, to their mother's more fundamental criticism of their escapism into an "ivory tower" (1:164) outside the Labour Movement. Workers in particular cannot understand their behavior. The objections that their ideas are outdated and that their project is irresponsibly egotistical—since a universal rejection of industry and technology would lead to a catastrophe—expose the fundamental shortcomings of their behavior. It is a debate which anticipates the ongoing discussion about an ecological reorganization of industrial society.

"Mad" is the epithet most frequently used by other people for those who are "possessed" by the utopian idea. The allegation of a distorted relationship with reality is not wholly unjustified but can also be understood as a self-protective reaction to the Simmonds couple's provocative rejection of the ordinary way of life.

The protagonists' failure is not simply caused by the fact that it is senseless, in the twentieth century, to try to put the utopian models of the nineteenth century into practice. Like the rest of society, the central characters lack the altered consciousness which is the prerequisite for the new mode of life. Moreover, a disturbing plurality of opinion shows no sign of disappearing in favor of a uniform New Man. The dilemma cannot be solved by sacrificing freedom for equality, as Libby Dobson proposes (183). His demand for a benevolent dictatorship reveals the danger which lurks in the gap between human reality and the utopian ideal.

Since the characters in *I'm Talking* are imbued with their Jewish background, their utopian project includes chiliastic concepts originating in the Old Testament. Ronnie quotes the episode concerning Moses and Zipporah at the well (*Exodus*, 2:16–22), and thus identifies the Simmonds' exodus from London and their arrival at their new home with the central vision of the *Pentateuch*: the Exodus from Egypt and the conquest of the Holy Land. He speaks of the advent of the millennium and, at the beginning as well as at the end of the play, he compares the quest of the "wandering Jew" for the New Jerusalem with the protagonists' quest for utopia. Dave declares himself inspired by the spirit of the Old Testament prophets, who inveighed against riches and luxury and preached a return to the original ideals. Like these disturbing mentors, he sees himself isolated with his model of a utopian counter-society. Conscious of his mission, he even feels like a companion to Jesus in his struggle (1:207). The socialist ideal is given roots in Jewish traditions, in the myths and the faith of the Simmondses' ancestors. The connections with the transcendental realm explain both its eschatological features and its strong emotional implications. The Jewish belief in belonging to the Chosen People who will be redeemed is married to the optimism of the Marxist view of the future. The meaning which used to be derived from religion is now furnished by the utopian vision. Ronnie's desperate mourning in the end therefore transcends the failure of the experiment and demonstrates the fundamental need for the ideal.

The Architecture of Utopia

Their Very Own and Golden City (pf.1965, pb. 1966) resumes the dramatic confrontation with the dialectics of the utopian ideal versus reality. The city, like the island, is the traditional location for utopia. The idea of a New Jerusalem, the Golden City of Messianism, is evoked in this play with the well-worn quotation from Blake's Preface to his "Milton."[28] Like Jerusalem in Blake, this Golden City represents for Andy Cobham the epitome of a liberated, enlightened secular society. He hopes that this enclave in capitalist territory will spawn the transformation of the whole of England into a "Promised Land," Cobham therefore not only designs a town, but considers himself to be the architect of an ideal community, as did his predecessors from Fra Giocondo, Ledoux or Fourier to Le Corbusier. He expounds this conviction in his motto: "In the way you shape a city you shape the habit of a way of life" (2:173ff.). Cobham's city no longer has the town hall as its center, but cultural institutions such as theatres, concert halls, art galleries and libraries. In its economic organization, this project resembles Robert Owen's Villages of Unity and Co-operation or his New Harmony in Indiana. The communities are founded on an associative basis (2:130); the houses belong to those who live in them and the factories to those who work in them; the exchange of goods is taken over by co-operatives. Cobham's architecture is designed to overcome the geometrical uniformity of the historical utopian towns of the age of positivism. Variety is the principle of their design. It creates the space for the contrary needs of a pluralist society. The new utopia avoids uniformity and allows for differences between individuals. The Golden City is distinguished by the same kind of transfiguration which is to be found in the prophets' vision of the millennium in the Old Testament.[29]

The overwhelming enthusiasm which the idea of the Golden City is supposed to inspire and which animates its founders, excludes the possibility of its concrete visualization. Wesker appeals to the audience's imagination to flesh out emphatically enunciated but vague suggestions.[30] The allusions, however, communicate so little that is extraordinary and exciting in this bold, revolutionary project that the effusions of joy of its originators and their patrons can hardly be plausibly sustained by it.

The scene of the young friends' enthusiastic commitment to the utopian dream is the cathedral of Durham. The daring Promethean proportions of this Norman building, its negation of the dimensions belonging to the everyday world, make it a *Gesamtkunstwerk* and an ideal symbol of utopia. At the sight of the cathedral, Andy Cobham is moved to ecstasy. He goes mad, stands on his head and wants to fly. This is an epiphany to him and inspires him with the idea of the totally different life of the Golden City. "Soar," "audacious," and "mad" are the keywords, evoked by the impact of the visits to the cathedral, which characterize the spirit of utopia.

The paradox of utopia's perfection as a pure idea and its inevitable perversion in practice determines the form of *Their Very Own*, with its point-and-counterpoint confrontation of two levels of action. In alternating scenes, the utopian vision, which anticipates the future, is contrasted with a series of pragmatic objections to it in "flash-forwards." On one level, immutability prevails and time stands still; on the other, a development of sixty-five years is condensed into a rapid movement from progress to decline. On one plane, the protagonists are eternally young, inexperienced, and inspired by the utopian vision; on the other, the process of experience and age leads them from enthusiasm to disappointment and resignation. Andy Cobham pays no less a price for the implementation of his vision than its betrayal in pragmatic compromise.

The incorruptible and unpopular trade union official Jake Latham imperturbably claims that revolution is the precondition for the practical realization of utopia. He distinguishes between the true revolutionary and the short-sighted rebel who is not inspired by any vision but only obsessed by rage against the establishment. His main concern in preparing this revolution of the mind is the intellectual emancipation of the workers. But the trade unions and the working class do not understand him and reject his efforts.

Andy Cobham's success, held up as an alternative to Jake Latham's failure, is achieved only by self-deception. He suppresses the historical knowledge which teaches him that his effort to attain utopia by forming islands is hopeless. Through their dissociation from the utopian ideal—which is after all a part of their constitution—and through their contempt for "Robert bloody Owen" (2:184), the trade unions show the extent to which they have internalized the dominant system. In order to continue his project, Cobham abandons his principles and thus sacrifices the spirit of utopia. He even appeals to capitalists and to the Conservative Party for the financing of the industry in his City. This obliges him to relinquish the principle of common ownership of the means of production and forces him to go back on the decision that the City's future inhabitants should participate in its planning. His utopian idea shrinks to the mere aesthetics of his architecture. Andy comes to realize eventually that by compromising with the Conservative establishment he has become its collaborator, "to stave off the real revolution for yet another century"(2:165).

Cobham's relationship with Kate Ramsey, the daughter of an aristocrat, illustrates the danger which arises for utopia from compromise with the middle and upper classes. It is her influence on him which alters the utopian project so decisively that its essence is spoilt. His commitment to the working class becomes a burden for him as does his relationship with his wife. That he does not help her to achieve her own emancipation gives the lie to his ambition to lead the working class to autonomy. No doubt Cobham unconsciously hopes to solve his identity problem by realizing his ardently defended utopian project. Working on the ideal design compensates for feelings of guilt caused by his critical distance from his working-class origins.

As at the end of *I'm Talking*, the question of meaning in the struggle for the utopian idea comes down to the question of the sense of inevitable failure in its service. The play ends with an enthusiastic declaration of faith, by young Cobham and his friends, in the goodness of man and in their ideal. Jessie is carried by them in triumph out of the cathedral which for a moment threatened to become their prison. Through direct juxtaposition with the negative experience which has shown the day-dream to be impracticable, the unabated enthusiasm for the vision takes on an auto-suggestive character and becomes an act of faith. Andy preaches the gospel according to Blake, the archprophet of the Golden Jerusalem. Thus the protagonists, and possibly their creator, protect themselves from loss of purpose. Because only utopia can show the way and mobilize the forces necessary for social change, Wesker insists on its validity in spite of the impossibility of ever attaining it.

Utopia's Necessity in Spite of Disillusion

Whereas Wesker's preceding plays managed in the end to strike sparks of hope even from the failure to realize the utopian ideal, in *The Friends* (pf.1970, pb. 1970)[31] a disenchantment with a decade and a half of fervent commitment to the dream of the social emancipation of the working class through improving their aesthetic sense prevails. Utopia has faded into the distance and with it the Jewish friends' belief that they are God's elect. In a tired joke God is asked to "choose someone else" (3:89).

Esther, who is dying, is the group's main authority. She never loses her faith in revolution, which she conceives as a radical change of consciousness resulting from the knowledge of history. She repeats Jake Latham's charge from *Their Very Own* that the destructive revolution of power is an action of blind rebels, disregarding their cultural heritage. Their bloody violence terrifies her no less than it does Wesker (3:106). Manfred fails to master the cultural heritage transmitted by history and to weld the discoveries of modern natural sciences into an all-embracing synthesis. He believes that his failure is due to a lack of a university education. His personal failure thus makes him realize the implausibility of his hoped-for enlightenment of the workers. Simone's rudimentary definition of utopia emphasizes, in addition to traditional values such as "justice" and "the pursuit of happiness," the necessity for "order" in order to attenuate human weaknesses. She repudiates the anarchist utopia of the generation of '68. In the play's final tableau she demonstrates to the friends as well as to the audience that commitment to life in the jaws of death demands a renewed devotion to the ideal. Without a confession of faith in utopia, life is meaningless and aimless. Reality needs to be transcended by the dream, in order to protect people from despair and degradation, as much as the dream needs to be corrected by the attempt to transform it into reality, if it is not to degenerate into escapism.

In this play, the author manifestly tries to come to terms with the personal problems caused by his fight: the failure of Centre 42, the controversy surrounding the bourgeois character of his ideal of emancipation[32] and his plays' lack of success on stage.

Utopia's Deceptiveness

The plays following *The Friends* focus on the dangers of utopia rather than on the indispensability of the ideal. Wesker's critique in his play *Shylock* (pf.1976, pb. 1983) of the antisemitism in Shakespeare's *The Merchant of Venice*[33] is dominated by the protagonist's humanist vision of an enlightened society which education and knowledge protect from racist prejudice, injustice and intolerance.

Antonio and Shylock's friendship embodies the ideal and therefore must end tragically. It is based on their shared love of books, their high esteem of knowledge and the arts and their rejection of material values as merely functional. Their mutual affection is rooted in the idea of equality and respect for each other's otherness. They address each other as "brother." Shylock metaphorically conceives the historical interdependence of Jewish and Christian cultures as a parent-child relationship.

All this stands in opposition to the racial discrimination against Jews by the Venetian laws which order the official relations between both communities. They relegate Jews to the ghetto, refuse them landed property, inflict exorbitant taxes on them and confine them to morally despised but necessary professions such as money-lending. They are complemented by everyday antisemitic prejudice and repression, which in Wesker's play come from the merchants of the young generation who disdain learning and lack historical insight. They disclose the instrumentalization of racism by desires and passions which are impervious to reason.

By cultivating his friendship with Antonio as well as by inviting scholars and artists to his house, Shylock deceives himself about this reality. Unlike ideology, which conceals the real condition of society in order to stabilize existing power-structures, Shylock's utopian thinking makes him misconstrue social reality by his wishful anticipation of change.[34] His vision makes a hostile reality bearable for him. In a monologue he extols the importance of the book as a medium for the transmission of knowledge in history. This confession of faith in historical progress through enlightenment culminates in an outburst of visionary enthusiasm reminiscent of Beatie Bryant or Andy Cobham (4:229). The bell summoning the Jews back into the ghetto interrupts his ecstasy and he has to don the yellow hat which stigmatizes him as an outcast. In spite of his confrontation with a reality contradicting his hope, he defiantly resumes his vision of humanism through enlightenment, which, although sometimes disappearing like a subterraneous stream, will always well up again. Only when he finally has to face the consequences of his bond does he realize that his books witness not only the progress of learning but also the history of man's unchanging cruelty and violence.

His self-deception inevitably leads to catastrophe. When reality finally catches up with him, he loses child, friend and possessions. His disregard for the prevailing order and public exposure of the injustice inherent in it must lead to his annihilation. In tragic self-punishment he offers his books to the justice, admitting the failure of his vision.

Portia, the "new woman," inherits Shylock's dream of emancipation through enlightenment. Her philosopher father favored her with an education surpassing that of most men. She is aware of the injustice of antisemitic prejudice and also stands up against the racism of patriarchal privilege. Like Andy Cobham, she could found cities with her strength. After the Jew, another victim of social inequality takes up the torch, restating the hope of liberation through knowledge.

Utopia as a Prison

Caritas (pf.1981, pb. 1981)[35] relates two narratives of mediaeval attempts to achieve liberty and happiness. The play focuses on a young woman's pursuit of spiritual fulfillment by mystical union with God in the life of an anchoress. The individual religious attempt to anticipate heavenly bliss on earth is inscribed in the social context of the peasants' rising of 1381 led by Wat Tyler and its religious equivalent, the Lollards' movement inspired by John Ball and John Wycliffe. Striving for liberation from the mediaeval bondage system as well as from the tutelage of the church, this rebellion dreams for the first time the dream of liberty, equality and the abolition of private property. The change the young anchoress hopes for, however, is to take place exclusively in her soul. It is to be achieved by complete abdication of the world and negation of her body and self (6:105).

The anchoress's sequestration from the world, her solitary life in search of union with God and her mysticism of obedience "should bring freedom" (6:87) of the spirit. Like the utopian who hopes to create a "new man," Christine strives "to put off the old woman with all her works and become a new woman"(6:71). In aspiring to represent the ideal, free from the deficiencies and irreconcilable contradictions of everyday reality, mystic and utopian imagination resort to the same language, evoking imaginary perception beyond reason and the senses. Both use concepts such as ecstasy, dream, vision or revelation in order "to reconcile the knowledge that we inhabit an irretrievably fallen and divided world in which the ideal state is unattainable, with the irresistible and mysteriously present idea of unified perfection."[36] Immurement, solitude, darkness and sensory deprivation are to create a void preparing Christine for the reception of God's word, His image. She is to become His medium. A vision will transform her into a sign of eschatological deliverance. Her existence as an anchoress is thus accompanied from the beginning by a chorus of children who tauntingly repeat the aim of her endeavor and the measure of its success or failure: "Christine, had a revelation yet?" (6:75).

Both the individual endeavor to transcend the world by retreat into spirituality and the attempt to change society fail. The peasants are blinded by hatred, try to achieve justice by committing injustice and become involved in a vicious circle of violence which destroys them. Christine's hope for transformation through mystical union comes to naught as it completely negates her physical existence. Mortification of her body makes her lose the feeling of the oneness of body and soul and thus her oneness with God (6:83). When she is finally transported into ecstasy, her vision confronts her with what she has rejected. She suddenly apprehends the teleology, harmony, and beauty of the world. This makes her realize the misery and torture of life in her squalid cell. Her growing desire to return to the light and life of the world and the Church's refusal to allow her to do so drive her mad. In her final delirium her subconscious haunts her with the hallucination of the negative side of her ideal of pure spirituality. She rediscovers natural sensual pleasure (6:114). Orgasmic bliss overcomes her as she imagines the feeling of her naked body exposed to the sun and the sensual experience of the beauty of nature in spring. The world and the flesh, which she rejected, have finally become the inaccessible objects of her utopian desire.

The peasants' aims and the object of Christine's struggle differ fundamentally. Both worldly and otherworldly ideals, however, determine the evaluation of reality and shape life in their image. The play stages the danger of the worldly and otherworldly visions which distort the view of reality and lead to inhumanity, violence and a crippled life in anticipation of their future implementation. Whereas the closed cathedral in *Their Very Own* pictured the greatness of the utopian vision as well as the friends' confinement in it, Christine's immurement in a cell attached to a church becomes the image of her spiritual imprisonment in her mystical belief.

The story of the joyless life of self-denial and the suicide of a young Chinese hardliner which precedes the medieval play like a motto relates the meaning of this parable to mysticism as well as to social utopia in the past and the present. The author moreover insists in his preface: "All dogma is anti-human because it presumes the way life *must* be lived, which kills spontaneous creativity" (6:61). The danger of being seduced into adopting a false consciousness inevitably comes into existence with the ideal. The reminder that the ideal is never attainable is thus necessary to prevent intolerance, constraint and disproportionate individual sacrifice.

A recent play, *Lady Othello* (pb. 1990)[37], is a counter-piece to *Caritas*, which explores the ideal of sexual love. Emerson's idea of love serves as the model. His poem "Give all to love" precedes the text and is quoted in a central scene (6:220). With utopian absoluteness, it decrees love and therewith passion the centre of life, the "Hope beyond hope,/High and more high" for which everything must be renounced: family, friends, reputation, even artistic achievement. It has to be granted absolute freedom and its temporary nature must be respected. The individual self is the centre of this ethic which refuses the tyranny of social norms.

An aging professor dreams the dream of a second youth, of renewing his sexuality by changing his partner and his mode of life. He desires to be reborn as a different person in a different life (6:242). The circumstances of the episode are reminiscent of the central motifs in utopian fiction. The encounter implies a long-distance flight from the old world to the new. It means leaving behind wife and children, friends and colleagues, work and habits of life. The trial of the power of the passion, as well as of the new life governed by it, is a moment of time clearly detached from the continuity of the everyday life which precedes and follows it. The limitation to a short period safeguards the experience from routine and heightens its intensity. The object of the professor's desire is a thirty-year-old black student from New York. Her youth, love and uninhibited sexuality promise the retrieval of a youthfully passionate life and therewith a new self. He hopes "to be overwhelmed" (6:253) by ecstasy, to forget his past and abandon the principle of reason.

The couple's feelings evoke images which in earlier plays denoted the enthusiasm inspired by utopian visions. The professor calls the sublime irrationality of the enterprise "madness." Like Andy Cobham in Durham cathedral, he feels as if he were "soaring" when he rediscovers his body in the movements of dance at a disco. Both lovers excitedly repeat that they feel "alive," meaning by this an intense, non-alienated existence which brings to mind the aim of the utopian experiment in *I'm Talking About Jerusalem,* a *carpe diem* of self-determined, spontaneous enjoyment of life ignoring conventions.

But the utopia of love is as elusive as that of the ideal society. The momentary harmony of their bodies is a deception. Cultural, racial, social and economic differences from the very start provoke clashes, resentment and frustration in both. They are finally forced to realize that it is man's irrationality, passion, egotism and ignorance which pervert social systems (6:223).

Like Ada and Dave in *I'm Talking,* the professor returns in the end to his former life. Whilst the Simondses abandon their utopian project because of insurmountable obstacles and exhaustion, the lovers' ideal proves to be a mirage, shortsighted and too exclusive. Whilst the socialist utopian models sacrificed the individual's idea of happiness to the well-being of all, the utopia of self-realization in love, which finds its ethical norms in the individual, rejects all social conformity and responsibility.

Wesker's Changing Attitude towards Utopia

The form of Wesker's early plays is determined by the dialectics of utopia and reality. The tension between social criticism and utopia as well as the contradiction between imperturbable belief in the ideal and the failure to realize it is the mainspring of their dynamics. They dialectically relate the critique of historical social developments to the attempt to escape from historical constraints into a timeless vision. Wesker's theatre is part of his dream of the emancipation of the working class through enlightenment which also engendered Centre 42. He wants to educate his audience according to his humanist ideal of wholeness. His plays are thus repeated efforts to reveal the entire chain of causes which lie behind social and political situations.[38] Many of his earlier dramas thus cover long periods of time. None of them, however, dares to sketch even the outlines of a total world model. Even the attempts to establish small-scale prototypes of an ideal society, which are based either on historical blueprints of utopia or on messianic and chiliastic ideas, are doomed to fail. Most of Wesker's plays reveal the impossibility of realizing an ideal which by definition cannot survive the exigencies of reality. Initial enthusiasm for a utopian project is gradually stifled in the abortive effort to implement it.

In *tours de force*, the conclusions of the plays try to resolve the contradiction between failure and belief in an endeavor which acknowledges that the ideal is impossible to attain and yet, in spite of all, must not be abandoned. The meaning and solidarity which faith in utopia creates, as it overcomes the loss of orientation and the fragmentation of society into egotistical interests, is more important than the disappointment at the inevitable failure to realize it.[39] The insight won from disillusionment moreover unmasks the enemies of utopia. These are both the conservative, external opposition to it and its own congenital risk of decline into possessive individualism, reformism and compromise, or totalitarianism and repression. These dangers, however, cannot cancel out its necessity as a guideline.

After *Their Very Own* (pf. 1965, pb. 1966) Wesker abandons the idea of utopia as a grand design of the life of society from its economic order to its leisure pursuits. He overcomes his fears of fragmentation and faces the totalitarian threat in the modernist desire of unity, planning and control. The designs of the utopian city in this play abandon the idea of unity and allow for the difference between people by anticipating their contrary needs. This is a first step towards a utopia of plurality which is to succeed the totalizing vision imposing a single form of salvation. In the motto of *Distinctions* (pb. 1985) he quotes Isaiah Berlin's avowal "that pluralism and untidiness are, to those who value freedom, better than the rigorous imposition of all-embracing systems." Utopia has assumed a new meaning for Wesker.

With *The Friends* (1970) the plays' structure changes. Whilst the earlier dramas start with enthusiastic strife for utopia and end in disillusion, the protagonists' loss of faith in the project of emancipation through enlightenment already dominates the beginning of this play. Unlike his earlier plays, Wesker's drama now exposes the dangers of believing in utopia, revealing the distorted vision of reality which results from the protagonists' dream. They transfigure reality in the light of the ideal, anticipating the desired future in the present. This inevitably leads to a clash with reality and thus to catastrophe. The belief in the ideal is shattered, the foundations of a meaningful life break down. Shylock's and Christine's tragic delusion destroys their lives. The process of disillusion in the later plays threatens to include even the dream of enlightenment. Like his Shylock the author seems to have lost faith in the "expectation that the arts and sciences would promote not only the control of natural forces but also understanding of the world and of the self, moral progress, the injustice of institutions and even the happiness of human beings."[40] And yet like Habermas, Wesker wants to hold on to the intentions of the enlightenment in spite of postmodernist scepticism.[41] Shylock's loss of hope through experience is balanced by the resuscitation of utopian belief in Portia, who starts a new cycle. The faith in the ideal remains a matter of youth, ingenuity or innocence. It provides a concept for a meaningful life which has to be constantly revised and restated.

Wesker makes no attempt to sketch the utopia which "would respect both the desire for justice and the desire for the unknown."[42] He barely hints at the new ecological vision or the battle for the equality of the sexes. His most recent plays warn, however, against the vision which becomes ideological doctrine and thus turns into a prison for the mind as well as for the body. He equally denounces the individualist dream of love and happiness which rejects rationality and social responsibility.

వ

ENDNOTES

1. Karl Raimund Popper, *The Open Society and Its Enemies* (London: G.Routledge, 1945), and "Utopia and Violence," *The Hibbert Journal*, 46 (1947/1948): 109–16. In the chapter "Paths of the Denunciation of Utopia," Arnhelm Neusüss in *Utopie: Begriff und Phänomen des Utopischen* (Neuwied: Luchterhand, 1968), 33–81, distinguishes between the conservative and the eschatological criticisms of utopia as well as the reproach of totalitarianism.

2. Ernst Bloch, *The Principle of Hope*, 3 vols (Oxford: Basil Blackwell, 1986). The original German version was finished in 1947.

3. John Osborne, *Look Back in Anger* (London: Faber, repr. 1957), 84ff.

4. Hans Ulrich Seeber, "Bemerkungen zum Begriff 'Gegenutopie,'" in Klaus Berghahn and Hans Ulrich Seeber, eds., *Literarische Utopien von Morus bis zur Gegenwart* (Königstein: Athenäum, 1983), 164.

5. Ibid., 165ff.

6. The socialists' scepticism concerning utopia is as old as Friedrich Engels, *Die Entwicklung des Sozialismus von der Utopie zur Wissenschaft*, Karl Marx, Friedrich Engels, *Werke* (Berlin Ost: Dietz Verlag, 1956–1968), vol. 19. The disappointment of the failure of socialist utopia in the states of eastern Europe was already influentially articulated in the fifties by André Gide, Arthur Koestler and Stephen Spender in Richard, Howard, Stafford Crossman, ed., *The God that Failed* (London: Hamish Hamilton, 1950). In the sixties, criticism was particularly aimed at the Welfare State, by e.g., Anthony Hartley, *A State of England* (London: Hutchinson, 1963), or Richard Hoggart, *The Uses of Literacy* (Harmondsworth: Penguin, 1966).

7. Valeska Lindemann, *Arnold Wesker als Gesellschaftskritiker* (Diss. Marburg, 1972), refers to the significance of utopia for Wesker's writings in her chapter "Traum, Utopie, Parabel als Mittel zur Loslösung von der Gegenwart und zu ihrer Bewältigung," 227–36.

8. Gilles Lapouze, "Le lieu glissant de l'improbable," *Magazine Littéraire*, 139 (1978), 16. This pastoral version of utopia advocates the liberty of the individual and closeness to an unspoilt nature in anarchist forms of society with as little technology as possible.

9. Philip Abrams, Andrew McCulloch, *Communes, Sociology and Society* (Cambridge: University Press, 1976); Dennis Hardy, "Communities and Twentieth-Century Decentralism," in *Alternative Communities in 19th Century England* (London: Longman, 1979), 219–24; and Rodney Barker, *Political Ideas in Modern Britain* (London: Methuen, 1978): "1968, the year which provided visions and memories for radicals and the left in western Europe, saw the publication of *Communes*, the journal of the commune movement" (206).

10. Rüdiger Hillgärtner, "Arnold Wesker: *The Chicken Soup Trilogy*," in Heinrich Plett, ed., *Englisches Drama von Beckett bis Bond* (München: Fink, 1982), 119; and Valeska Lindemann, "Weskers offener Sozialismusbegriff," in *Arnold Wesker als Gesellschaftskritiker*, 170ff.

11. Hillgärtner, "Arnold Wesker: *The Chicken Soup Trilogy*," is one of the first critics to evaluate the significance of Wesker's theoretical statements for the appreciation of his theatrical practice.

12. Wesker, *Fears of Fragmentation* (London: Jonathan Cape, 1970). All following quotations of this text are taken from this edition and are

indicated by page numbers in parentheses and abbreviated to *Fears*.

13. By "total work of art" is meant a Gesamtkunstwerk less in the Wagnerian sense of a fusion of music, poetry, dance and painting, than in the sense of a work of art which is intended to express a total worldview.

14. William Morris, *Signs of Change*, Lectures on Socialism, in *The Collected Works*, 23 (London: Longmans, 1915): e.g., "Useful Work versus Useless Toil" (1884), and "Art, Wealth and Riches" (1883).

15. Being himself an opponent of nuclear weapons, he warns in *Their Very Own* and in *The Friends* of the foolhardy rebels engaged in the student revolution or in the revolutionary movements of the Third World.

16. Frank Coppieters, "Arnold Wesker's Centre Fortytwo: A Cultural Revolution Betrayed," *Theatre Quarterly*, 18 (1975): 37–54.

17. *The New Theatre Magazine*, II, 2 (1971); see also Wesker, "East End Roots," *Times Educational Supplement*, 7 March 1975, 25.

18. The dangerous entanglement of enlightenment with power and capitalist production remains a central topic of the contemporary philosophical debate. Max Horkheimer, Theodor W. Adorno, *Dialektik der Aufklärung* finished in 1944 in USA. Jürgen Habermas in "Modernity—an Incomplete Project"; Michel Foucault, "Qu'est-ce que les Lumières?", *Magazine littéraire*, 309, April 1993, 71.

19. Interview with Rainer Taeni, *Die Neueren Sprachen*, 20 (1971), 417 and *Shylock*.

20. Wesker, "The London Diary for Stockholm," in *Six Sundays in January* (London: Jonathan Cape, 1971), 186.

21. *Encyclopaedia Britannica*, Macropaedia (London, 1974), vol. 11, s.v., "Messiah and Messianic Movements," 1017ff.

22. Interview with Simon Trussler, in Charles Marowitz and Simon Trussler, eds., *Theatre at Work* (London, 1967), 80.

23. "The London Diary for Stockholm," 186.

24. Wesker, *Fears of Fragmentation*, 76; see also *Fears* 121.

25. Theodor W. Adorno, *Ästhetische Theorie* in *gesammelte Schriften*, 7 (Frankfurt: Suhrkamp, 1970), 200.

26. Adorno, 55.

27. Wesker, *Roots* (Harmondsworth: Penguin,1960). All following quotations of this play are taken from this edition, Volume 1.

28. Wesker, *Their Very Own and Golden City* (Harmondsworth: Penguin, 1981), 2:147. All following quotations of this play are taken from this edition, Volume 2.

29. The importance of light (2:161) recalls the radiance emanating from God in Isaiah (60.19). Parallel to the millenary reconciliation of contradictions in Isaiah (II.6–9), Cobham's cities offer architectural diversity (2:48).

30. The playwright asks for an "abstract set of a building site" (192).

31. *The Friends* (Harmondsworth: Penguin, 1980) 3:89. All the following quotations of this play are taken from this edition, Volume 3.

32. Simone's settling of accounts with the group of friends in the second act aims at Wesker's critics in his own camp who condemn his unreserved appreciation of the bourgeois artistic tradition. John McGrath answers this in his review in *Black Dwarf*, 15.

33. The play's original title was *The Merchant*. The text is quoted from Wesker, *Shylock* (Harmondsworth: Penguin, 1990), vol. 4.

34. Karl Mannheim, *Ideology and Utopia* (London: Routledge & Kegan Paul, 1954), 36; "In the utopian mentality, the collective unconscious, guided by wishful representation and the will to action, hides certain aspects of reality. It turns its back on everything which would shake its belief or paralyse its desire to change things."

35. Quotations are taken from Wesker, *Lady Othello and Other Plays* (Harmondsworth: Penguin, 1990), Volume 6.

36. Jan Relf, "Utopia the Good Breast" in Krishan Kumar, Stephen Bann eds., *Utopias and the Millennium* (London: Reaktion Books, 1993), 110.

37. Quotations are taken from Wesker, *Lady Othello and Other Plays* (Harmondsworth: Penguin, 1990) Volume 6.

38.   Wesker, *Fears of Fragmentation*, 112ff.

39.   The author insists on this: "But with the question of ideals it is a case of convincing the audience that to be concerned about disillusionment is to be concerned about anything worthwhile anyway" "Let Battle Commence," in Charles Marowitz et al., eds., *The Encore Reader* (London, 1965), 100.

40.   Jürgen Habermas, "Modernity—an Incomplete Project" in Patricia Waugh ed., *Postmodernism, a Reader* (London: Edward Arnold, 1992), 165.

41.   Jürgen Habermas, "Modernity—an Incomplete Project."

42.   Jean-Francois Lyotard, *The Postmodern Condition: A Report on Knowledge* (Minneapolis: University of Minnesota Press, 1984), 67.

II. Biographical Notes

Arnold Wesker
Margaret Drabble

"Those who dismiss me" is a characteristic Wesker phrase, these days: though perhaps it always was. He is sensitive to attack, and admits that one adverse criticism hurts him more than many praises can cheer him. There is nothing odd about this: probably most writers (and most people) are the same. But there is something odd, or at least unusual, in the way that Wesker responds to hurt and dismissal. Unlike most, he fights back. "I have," he says, "this—perhaps paranoid—sense that I must fight to maintain acknowledgement of my continued existence as a writer." And fighting is something that comes easily to him. He wonders if he is paranoid, brooding over remarks like those of the critic in *The Guardian* who reviewed his collection of short stories in 1971 with a piece beginning "There is this plot afoot to rehabilitate Arnold Wesker," and puzzling, still, over an anonymous and incomprehensibly cryptic letter of abuse which reached him in 1961. But unlike most people who feel hurt, he doesn't care who knows it: most of us are restrained by a kind of pride from answering back to our attackers, but not Wesker. He conducts long battles in newspapers: he is even prepared (and considers he ought) to take more serious offenders to court. Perhaps times are harder than usual at the moment, for he has two completed full-length plays (*The Journalists* and the *Wedding Feast*) as yet unperformed here, perhaps he is displaying the irritable symptoms of a once highly fashionable writer, struggling with an uncongenial theatrical climate, and trying to survive the effects of his own early success?

But there is more to it than that. Wesker's character, like his plays, is more complex than it seems at first sight. For one thing, his desire to fight back now is not a new thing, and has little to do with present fortunes, for Wesker has been fighting back all his life. It is a habit of mind with him. He does not merely brood, he takes action, which is what he was brought up to do. He says:

> Did I tell you, I'm getting out this book called Battles—
> it suddenly occurred to me that right from the days when
> I lived in an LCC flat and was writing letters to the LCC
> urging them to get a new flat for us—because we lived on
> the third floor, and my father had this stroke which left
> him paralyzed and incontinent—I've just got back these
> letters from the GLC, dating back to 1952, a correspon-
> dence that goes on and on, past the time of my first play,
> past the time my father died—and I suddenly realized
> that right from the time when I'm writing letters to se-
> cure a flat, through letters to the Ambassador of Brazil
> protesting against torture, or to the Soviet Ambassador
> about the Jews, or writing attacks on the critics—I real-
> ized how all my life has been engaged in battles.

Fights about his own rights, the rights of his family, and the rights of
others, are clearly less separated in his mind than they are for most:
his mother brought him up to fight back against the machinery, to
get up petitions and write letters, and he is still doing it. Many of the
public causes he has taken on have been nothing to do with his own
career: CND, for example, or more recently, Northern Ireland. This
autumn, he published a long open letter in the *Sunday Times*, sparked
off by the report of the shooting of two friends, one Catholic and one
Protestant, assassinated simply because they were friends. "This really
offended me to the depths—then I said to myself, what really pushed
me into action was this—I said to myself—But you're really too fright-
ened to write that letter, aren't you? And once I'd said *that* to myself...."

This is very much a part of his attitude to life: an accepting of
challenges, a defiant leaving of his name in the telephone directory,
despite the swastikas on the anonymous cut-out of a model in a night-
gown, and the fear of Irish bombs through the letter box. Some find
it maddening, masochistic, pointless, as he knows.

His feelings about his own success are as deeply rooted as his
habit of public protest. It would be very easy to see Wesker as a writer
who would inevitably have suffered crises of identity about his own
power and recognition. How could he keep a sense of perspective, the
son of a Jewish tailor from the East End, whose plays have been (and
are constantly) produced and translated in 45 different countries? He
still shows anxiety about some of the shortcomings of his origins—he
regrets that he didn't have a formal education, is afraid of mispro-

nouncing words, and considers himself ill-read, despite the fact that he comes from a family of readers, and was given his first reading list by his brother-in-law at the age of twelve. But he feels at a loss with professional literary people, who reel off lists of authors whom he has never embarked on, and says that Doris Lessing (an old friend) thinks he is ill-read, as though that clinched it. A classic case, one might think, of someone likely to be bowled over by early and unexpected success—he was only twenty-six when his first plays were produced in the West End. But, he says, this isn't quite how it is. He has always considered himself lucky, even when there was no evidence. When he was working in the Bell Hotel on three pounds ten a week, he clearly remembers saying to himself: "It's all going too well: nobody can be as fortunate as I have been. I've got good looks, happy disposition, good parents. Something's bound to go wrong." And he is still waiting for things to go wrong, never quite sure if they are doing so.

He certainly has plenty to feel pleased with himself about. If parochial British critics sneer and say that Wesker needs rehabilitating (or if they fail to review his short stories), he can reflect on the enormous success he has had abroad. His plays have been performed all over the world, and he has himself directed them in Cuba, Sweden, Germany and Denmark, and visited productions of them as far afield as Japan, where a whole Wesker Project in 1968 was devoted to him and his work and the idea of Centre 42. The English have always thought there is something suspect about an English author with a large foreign following: Kingsley Amis, in his splendidly xenophobic novel *I Like It Here*, sums it up when he writes of the high regard the French have for Charles Morgan, Grim-Grin, Ifllen-Voff, Zumzit-Mum and Edge-Crown. And the fact that nine tenths of Wesker's income now comes from abroad would appear, to such xenophobes, not as a tribute to his international stature, but as some kind of black mark. Wesker would probably not see the point of this, and rightly. The great success of, for instance, *The Kitchen* in Poland must be a real comment on the play's power, both as a drama and a message. Wesker is perhaps right to feel (as he does feel, a feeling manifested by his withdrawal of the ban on production of his plays in South Africa) that drama is important, and can effect change. One would like to have seen *The Kitchen* in Poland; the Poles' appreciation of it was no doubt rather different in kind from the admiration of the French (whose views on the novel are rather odd these days anyway) for Charles Morgan.

Wesker would agree that he lacks one of the qualities almost essential for success in the English literary scene, self-mockery. He is not at all in touch with the kind of cliqueish in-jokes of which, for instance, *The New Review* has been accused. He knows and talks to plenty of writers, but he doesn't do it with self-mockery. Perhaps it is partly the absence of this untranslatable (and at times, in my view, highly valuable) ingredient that make his plays communicate so directly in other languages and to other cultures. I asked him why he thought he lacked this edge of self-mockery, and he said that he thought it was probably because of the Jewish seriousness in his nature. This is doubtless true, though it may also have something to do with his lack of early acquaintance with the literary and academic world. Those who have struggled through university churning out essays on D. H. Lawrence, or progressed to writing theses on minor Victorian novelists, tend to be a little more skeptical about the writer's role, and the whole business of scholarship. Arnold Wesker comes from a background where the artist was regarded, genuinely, as remote and special, if odd: the world of the literary hack or the thesis writer which was unknown to him, and he has never looked on himself as mere thesis-fodder. When people come to him to ask his views and to interview him, he actually thinks they are really interested in his answers. He is remarkably hospitable to those who want to talk to him, particularly to foreigners, and says that it is the sheer impossibility of talking to everyone, rather than cynicism about other people's motives, that has led him to cut down, and to delegate certain information-dispensing jobs to a secretary. Wasn't he aware, these days, I asked him, of thesis-writers and interviewers on the scrounge for a free meal and a free quote? But he denied that this was so; when pushed, the most that he would admit was that he does get fed up with those who come and ask him silly questions about when he was born, which they could easily have got out of a book.

So Wesker communicates to foreigners, is well known in other countries and knows them well, is interested in public and international affairs, and is hospitable to visitors, even to those with language problems. All of which is very un-English. But he also reaches audiences in this country which few writers hope for. A few years ago, I went on an Arts Council Writers' tour of the Northeast with him, and was much intrigued by his fame, and by his contact with audiences. He was then in his Japanese days, and appeared as an exotic figure, with long hair and Japanese shirt: when we visited schools, he would read intimate passages to impressionable school girls from his Stockholm Diary, which was written on a strange long unfolding piece of Japanese paper. (A good attention-grabbing gimmick, I enviously noted.) It was very noticeable that everybody, but everybody, knew who he was. The children knew who he was because *Roots* was on the O-Level syllabus: one school put on a scene for us, from *I'm Talking About Jerusalem*, which I thought sounded good in the accents of Tees-side, though I seem to remember that Wesker himself was rather critical of the production. (Characteristically, one could construe that as Wesker taking his own play seriously, or as Wesker taking the school children seriously, whilst I was patronizing them—I don't know which it was.) The adults, in the adult audiences in the evenings, also knew who Wesker was, because they'd seen or read his plays, or knew about Centre 42, a very live issue in the provinces: and even those who didn't know his plays, knew their titles, for I remember one angry old man in Darlington yelling crossly that Wesker had chips on his shoulder with everything, and that was what was wrong with him. This is fame, I said to myself. One evening, we got round to discussing why it was that Wesker was so popular on the Literature syllabus, and I came up with the theory that his plays appeared so often because they had no sex and violence in them. I don't think he thought that was very funny. The little girls at the schools used to try to stroke his hair.

So Wesker does all right, except with the reviewers of *The Guardian* and the secret powers behind the RSC. Nevertheless, I asked him, didn't he perhaps feel, these days, that his protests were having less and less effect and that his plays were becoming more depressing? He conceded that he does protest less, these days, and that he hadn't yet persuaded the UK and Russia to abandon their nuclear programs: but in the same breath, he went on to say that perhaps CND had "sharpened a consciousness, a world consciousness of the need for nuclear disarmament," though we would never know whether this was in fact so or not. He claimed a small victory over a housing problem in the East End ("so it sometimes works"), and told me at length about a letter he had received from a woman bringing to his attention the recommendation from the Pugwash conference that there should be an international monitoring of world supplies of uranium, to prevent the build-up of nuclear power. "This seemed to me," he said,

a perfectly sensible simple thing to do. And what's more,
it's very interesting, because in *Their Very Own and Golden
City*, which a part of Andy's character is based on Ernest
Bevin, there is a speech which Andy gives which comes
from Bevin, that very famous speech in the big debate
over whether the British should go to war, in the Second
World War, in which he knocks the old socialist—what's-
his-name-Lansbury—on the head, and in which he says
in passing "There was a time when we could have stopped
this war, there was a time when we could have had international control of the seas and the world raw materials...." So even as far back as that, there was this suggestion, and it was Bevin, the arch Labour reactionary, who
was making it.

He went on to discuss proposals for monitoring world food supplies,
and said "Now this seems to me a *necessary* step to be taken in terms
of food, and yet it's only in the last week or two that the necessity has
been brought to our attention...." These are not the reflections of a
man who is too depressed to go on thinking, despite the lack of response to his own letters. "Much more depressing," he says, "than
wondering about whether one's letters have any impact, is trying to
get one's mind round the enormous problems we read of every day."
He went on to talk of Northern Ireland. He has no solution for Northern Ireland: he wants to understand it, to get his mind round it.

So, politically, he has become less optimistic, but has by no means
retired from the effort. What of the depression in the plays, I asked
him. A few weeks ago, over Sunday lunch, I heard a friend say to him,
"Ah, Arnold, what we miss in your plays these days is the old uplift,"
to which Wesker replied, as usual, that his plays have never been uplifting, or only one of them, *Roots* (financially the most successful).
He expanded this to me; in fact, he said, all his plays had been about
failures of attempts, not about successes. The family in *Chicken Soup
with Barley* disintegrates; Dave and Ada's rural dream in *I'm Talking
About Jerusalem* ends in defeat as does the architect's dream of a Golden
City. The rebellion in *Chips with Everything* fails, the love affair in *The
Four Seasons* comes to an end, the Friends, once successful, split up in
disillusion and death, and the Old Ones are, simply, old. So how did
Wesker ever get a reputation for being a playwright who provided
uplift? This is his own explanation, which has taken some time to
work out: "There's just this one play *Roots*, in which the girl survives

the traumatic experience of having been ditched by her boyfriend, and in a strange way I think that all the other plays have been incorrectly seen through the rose glasses of this one play." *Roots*, his most successful play, has colored our reception of all the others, and our interpretation of them. I find this explanation satisfying, because it charts my own experience of Wesker's work: *Roots* was the first play of his that I saw (and one of the first plays that I ever saw), and I saw it at the Arts Theatre, Cambridge, in 1959, with Joan Plowright giving her unforgettable performance as Beatie Bryant, and I must say that it *was* an uplifting experience, such as one rarely hopes for—a unique, accomplished complex but affirmative piece of theatre, and one through which (Wesker is quite right) I have seen the whole of the rest of his work.

His other plays, though, his plays about failure, although they are not uplifting, are not depressing either. They are, as he says, "about defiance, about a refusal to accept defeat quietly." "If you don't care, you'll die," shouts Sarah Kahn to Ronnie, in the last line of *Chicken Soup*, a line which the whole play works towards, through the slow defeats of two decades. "My characters are defeated and the reasons for their defeat measure up to a political, a social, an emotional psychological truth—but they are defiant, that's what it is. I think that what people have difficulty coping with are the two things together—a chart of defeat, and yet the people remain defiant." A chart of defeat ought to end with people "being completely broken," but his don't. They shout back, even when beaten. And so, although not optimistic in tone or message, the plays do have a certain exhilaration or most of them do, at least.

Wesker, like his characters, remains defiant, though some of his projects have taken hard knocks: impossible not to see the ghost of Centre 42 hovering behind some of his plot structures. A project which aimed so high and achieved so little might have been enough to depress anyone. But Wesker is not embittered. He does tend, as some of his friends complain, to go on a bit these days about middle age and death, both in his plays and in conversation, but he isn't depressing company. Occasionally humorless in print, he is rarely so in life, though his brand of humor does lack "that malicious edge which often thrills people"—as he describes it. He tells good stories against himself, he finds it hard to understand ill-nature in others ("I'd rather be a victim than a con man"), he is sociable, he likes to be host, and, on the whole, he still likes people. "I do have this capacity," he says, "for retaining, for squeezing out some pleasures, some joys. I won't let Them get me." He also has a capacity for making himself and those around him comfortable. Does he feel guilty, as a socialist, for having a large and comfortable house in London, and a beautiful cottage, for work and holidays, in Wales? Yes, he says, he does, and describes how it crept upon him—when the third baby was on the way they had to move out of their small flat, and he wanted to have room to entertain, to receive foreign visitors, and then he wanted somewhere to escape from the visitors and work in peace, and before he knew where he was he was the owner of two houses and mortgaged for the next 20 years. But he's never been the kind of socialist who believes in austerity as though it were in itself a virtue: he enjoys the pleasures of life, and even when he lived in a small bed-sit in the Bell Hotel he managed to make himself comfortable. He had the talent and the impulse before he had the money. His mother's house in the East End was constantly full of a stream of visitors speaking all languages, and his own home is the same. He likes to keep open house and encourages his children to bring their friends home and tries not to complain when the apples and cakes and kipper paté disappear.

One of the dominant images of his plays is the image of community—a family, a group of friends, even a group of National Servicemen. They make community, often against the odds. One would say that this was one of Wesker's more noticeably Jewish characteristics, this feeling for and ability to make a sense of community out of sometimes conflicting elements. In his plays, as has often been noted, the acts of cooking and eating are central to much of the stage activity. One of my own favorite Wesker memories is of a visit I made one half-term with the children to the cottage in Wales: when we arrived, Wesker was making two enormous puddings, one of creamed rice, one of raspberries. He showed the kids how to make a forcing-bag out of a paper bag and how to decorate the pudding with cream. How could one be depressed in the company of a man making a raspberry pudding? "I have a happy disposition," he says. "It's like having black hair, or blue eyes. I can't help it. You know that game, where you guess if people are happy pessimists, or gloomy optimists? Well, I'm a happy pessimist."

Even so, despite the raspberry puddings, the *Old Ones* (1972) struck me as a singularly depressing play: so, in its more complex way, had *The Friends* (1970). And his two most successful short stories, "Six Sundays in January" (1969) and "The Man Who Became Afraid" (recently published by Cape in a collection called *Love Letters on Blue Paper*), are very bleak. I asked him about the *Old Ones*, a play which deals with a group of elderly Jewish people against a background of illness, thuggery, family conflict, and violence and suggested that it might have been the play's subject as well as Harold Hobson's eccentric and personal attack in the *Sunday Times* that had limited its success at the Royal Court. Wesker directed it himself in Munich not long after the massacre of the Israeli hostages at the Olympic Games—another act of defiance. He replied: "Again, it seems to me that the *Old Ones* is about people who are defiant...and I so warm to those two brothers. Just the fact that they exist, I find uplifting.... It raises the question of what is uplifting, and I think I have that old-fashioned view of the artist bearing witness. And the act of him bearing witness is enough. Someone is there to record. That is enough."

I put it to him that he has often been accused of doing far more than bearing witness: that to many, he appears as a moralist, a didactic paternalist, who dared to say out loud that the music of Beethoven is better than the music of the Beatles. (He rang me up the next night to say he hadn't meant "better": he had meant "musically more interesting.") The accusation of being paternalistic always annoys Wesker: "Far from *me* being didactic in *my* views, insistent on imposing my views, I am confronted with a world which imposes on people the lowest common denominator of taste—and *I* am fighting back." Does the fact that his plays contain several denunciations of working-class ignorance and apathy make his attitude paternalistic?

He quotes, twice, William Morris on this subject, once as a preface to *Their Very Own and Golden City* (first performed 1966), and once as part of a lecture called "Tarnished Virtues and Confused Manners," which he delivered in Sweden in 1966, and which was printed in *Fears of Fragmentation* in 1970: the Morris passage, from a lecture on socialism given in Norwich in 1886, urges the Trades Unions not to be driven into the blind alley of respectability, as negotiating cogs in the capitalist machine and says

> I say again that if they are determined to have masters to manage their affairs, they must expect in turn to pay for that luxury...remembering that the price they pay for their so-called captains of industry is no mere money payment,

> no mere tribute which once paid leaves them free to do as
> they please, but an authoritative ordering of the whole
> tenor of their lives, what they shall eat, drink, wear, what
> houses they shall have, books, newspapers rather, they shall
> read, down to the very days on which they shall take their
> holidays like a drove of cattle driven from the stable to grass.

Fine stuff, which goes to the very heart of the conflict dramatized in *Roots*, in *Golden City*, in *Friends*—but in all these plays Wesker poses very forcefully the arguably paternalist view that high art *is* better than low art, that Mendelssohn is better than pop music, that a handcrafted chair or handpainted wallpaper is better than mass-produced rubbish, and that the ignorant, by refusing to draw distinctions, are wallowing in their own ignorance. Bourgeois art, houses, books and chairs are better than chocolate box art, council architecture, strip comics, utility chairs. Which is the authoritarian arbiter of taste, Wesker or Woolworth's?

Wesker is in good company with his problems: the company of Ruskin and Morris. The authorities he quotes reveal much about his affinities with an old-fashioned English socialism, an idealism little suited, some think, for the second half of the twentieth century—though those who think so have to come to terms with the fact that Wesker made more real effort to contact, and succeeded more in contacting, the Union Movement than any individual had bothered or tried to do for many years. Because his protagonists are craftsmen and thinkers, architects, chefs, talkers, makers, are they therefore less revolutionary, more paternalistic, than, say, the criminal, in submitting proletarian heroes of Silitoe? It is, as Wesker himself says, a complex problem, and one that he dramatizes in all its complexity: his answers are indeed far from simple.

He admits that many people do think of him as a moralist and pedagogue, and are surprised to find he isn't, in real life. Again, he thinks much of the confusion springs from *Roots*: audiences identify him with Ronnie, who ditches Beatie Bryant. ("I didn't ditch Beatie," says Wesker indignantly, "I *married* her, that's what people forget"— thereby simultaneously accepting and rejecting the identification.) Ronnie comes across, through Beatie, as a priggish young man, uttering slogans—but, says Wesker, if we examine what Ronnie is actually said to have said, he emerges as a searching, worried, confused, anything-but-self-satisfied young man. And Wesker himself is certainly not a didactic bore, though he is not afraid of a straight point or two—while we were talking about Ruskin (whose name came up in response to the statutory question: "Which critic do you respect most?"), I expressed the view that Ruskin, as a man, worried me slightly, and went on to chat idly about Effie in Venice and Ruskin's alleged fear of and aversion to female pubic hair. Whereupon Wesker looked at me firmly but kindly and said: "Your objections to Ruskin are trivial." Quite so.

On the subject of paternalism, it is interesting to watch Wesker with his own (or indeed other people's) children: he tends to take the ability to get on with young children as some kind of touchstone of character, and unlike some who take that view, he certainly has a gift for getting on with them himself. (One sometimes wonders how the word "paternalism" acquired quite such derogatory overtones—there is nothing wrong, surely, about being fatherly, though there may be good or bad fathers?) Family games, so often an embarrassment, blossom at the Wesker touch, making one appreciate why it is that the game played by Ada and her son in *I'm Talking About Jerusalem* is not the uncomfortable dramatic moment that it could be. Games feature largely in the plays—like eating, they are a symbol of community, and even the most fragmented of his characters can sit down together to a game of cards. There is nothing much of the heavy father about Wesker, and unlike many socialists with houses in Highgate [the Weskers' address until 1986] and country cottages elsewhere, he actually sends his children to the local Comprehensive, to pick up there what they like: I asked him why.

> What I felt was—and it's not working out or rather, it's working out as I thought it would—is that they needed something to balance what they have at home—and sure enough, they're having it. My children talk in a semi-Cockney voice, they have all the limited values of—well—of minority ethnic groups and repressed working-class groups. They don't read. They're not interested in classical music. So my attempt to balance things, the atmosphere of the house, has been more than successful.

So much for another Wesker project. Though, while one can't review people's children as one would review their books (it would be quite amusing if one could), I ought to add that the Wesker children seem to do all right to me and are very good company.

What does Wesker think that the future holds, for him? He is writing a play, he says, about the Merchant of Venice. He has an idea, an idea he has had for a long time, for a novel about Beatie Bryant, a sequel in the life of Beatie Bryant, though it would start not from the Beatie of *Roots*, but from a Beatie just leaving the gates of Oxford. (Would it be about Dusty Wesker? Well, not exactly, he said. But Dusty, a remarkable woman, would make an interesting subject for a novel.) And he is also writing more short stories, which he finds "fantastically exciting." To change from plays to prose fiction is a drastic change of medium, and Wesker has been offended by the lack of response to the two volumes he has published so far. In vain does one point out, in a cynical and worldly literary way, that short stories just don't *get* reviewed like plays at the Royal Court, and that short stories are even less marketable than novels. Only writers like Doris Lessing get their short stories reviewed, one tells him. He does not seem to think much of this kind of excuse, and, talking about the matter to him, one becomes aware that the world of the dramatist is very different indeed from the world of other writers: it is a specialized, self-enclosed yet public world, where reputations tend to be larger (and briefer and more fashion-tied) than in the rest of literature.

(For all this, Wesker says he doesn't have theatre friends or a theatre crowd—"acquaintances, yes, but I feel very very cut off from the theatre." And it's worth noting that just as he lacks self-mockery, he lacks also the almost inevitable theatrical quality of camp. An actor told me a story the other day about a moment in *The Golden City* when something went wrong with the Royal Court's machinery, and one of the leading players was left with a very difficult scene in front of a table which had failed to arise, as it should have done, from under the stage: the actor extricated himself from this embarrassing position by what seemed to me a very funny ad lib. But Wesker didn't like it at all. Whether this story is true or not, it illustrates the gap that the theatre believes to exist between Wesker and itself: a gap which got him into considerable difficulties, which have been recorded elsewhere, over his production of *The Friends* at the Round House.)

To return to the short stories. Two of them at least seem to me to be remarkably good, and good in quite a different way from the ways in which his plays succeed. In his plays there is little place for malice, or even for irony: they show people exposed to life, vulnerable, aspiring, naked to themselves and the audience. Some of his stories are

like this too—his first, "Pools," and his last two, "A Time of Dying"
and "Love Letters on Blue Paper," are also vulnerable, even painful
with emotion, one might say with sentiment. But two of the stories,
"Six Sundays in January" and "The Man Who Became Afraid," struck
me at least as something new. The first of them deals with six days in
the life of a middle-class woman in her thirties, who has three children whom she takes for walks on Hampstead Heath; a scenario which
I know fairly well, and which Wesker describes with complete conviction. The woman is a Jewess from the East End, with a mother
who reminds one clearly enough of Sarah Kahn in the *Trilogy* and
Sarah in the *Old Ones*, for she, like Mrs. Leah Wesker, is a communist
in a council flat. But this time, this is not what the story is about at
all. It is not that the woman's background is irrelevant—on the contrary, two of the focal episodes in the story are the woman's return,
one Sunday, to the street where she was born, and the suicide of a
friend from the same neighborhood. But the center of the story is the
woman's realization that

> she could not bear her husband. Not the sound of his
> voice nor the shape of his body; not the conversation he
> made nor the feebleness of his gaiety…. And more than
> that: she knew that for her children's sake she would not
> leave him because it was not in her to do so, and this
> knowledge reduced and rendered her spirit incapable of
> growing beyond where it now stood. So, she would re-
> treat, retire, she knew this. She would care for nothing,
> for without love nothing could be cared for.

We have here, as we do not and cannot have in the plays, a moment of silent and completely inner realization, that can never be
expressed in words, in action, but only inwardly. In the plays, Wesker's
characters communicate: they manage, as Beatie puts it, to build
bridges, to reach one another across the most unlikely gaps, they talk
themselves into existence and into contact. In the short stories, the
characters are alone. There is a whole new area here, which Wesker is
exploring. In "The Man who Became Afraid" Wesker also deals with
an experience of private disillusion, with a failing marriage, with a
person coming to terms not with the outward, visible failure of an
enterprise, but with an inner knowledge of failure of faith: and the
story has a hard, sardonic edge to it. The moment of truth, in this
case, is the moment at which the protagonist, Sheridan, realizes that

he is no longer a socialist: "The depressing conclusion faced him: if men could never be equals wasn't it unfair to create equal opportunities in which their inequalities would be seen? It was an awful moment. A skin dropped from him. Not only did he see men as unequal, he felt relief that it was so, and the sense of relief disgusted him. His soul turned grey with fear."

This is a powerful ending, to a powerful tale, and the way in which Wesker leads up to it is impressive: we see Sheridan, the mocker, who tells people he is afraid of everything in order that he need not be tricked by fear: we see him suffering fear on airplanes, fear abroad, we see him try to defend himself from fear by hoarding, by insurance, by Vitamin C tablets, by investing in vintage wines, first editions, art. The chart of middle-class, middle-aged defense mechanisms is scathingly accurate, and one wonders, do we have here, perhaps, the satire, the self-mocking voice that has not needed to speak so far?

I have to ask myself whether perhaps I like these two stories through a kind of Schadenfreude, for the wrong reasons: because they take the reader into the familiar territory of doubt, the homely land of self-doubt and disillusion. If that were so, it would be an interesting comment on oneself, and on Wesker's earlier successes. His defiance, his largely unrewarded faith and perseverance, have made us uneasy: perhaps something in us would like to see him forced to accept the grim, dull realities of life more quietly. But I don't think that is all the stories mean. They do lead in a new direction, but with any luck it will not prove a dead end. And Wesker has always been lucky. At the very least, it will be interesting to follow the progress of a writer who has committed himself, and continues to commit himself, to the most important issues of our time. His response has become less general, more personal, but it is no less valuable for that. If anyone is going to rehabilitate Wesker, it will be Wesker himself, by refusing to sit back in the comfortable slot of Angry Young Dramatist, or to grow into the role of Betrayed Middle Aged Man. He does not fit as easily into slots as people would like.

ન્જ

Reprinted with permission from *The New Review,* Vol. 1 #11, Feb. 1975.

Vision and Reality
Their Very Own and Golden City *and Centre 42*

Clive Barker

In my album I have some photographs taken early in 1963. The photographs give an odd feeling when I look at them since I do not appear in any of them. I took the photographs, and that fact makes it appear as I was not part of the activity that was captured on film. The settings for the photographs are the cloisters of Durham Cathedral and the North Yorkshire Moors. There is a heavy fall of snow visible in all of them. What the photographs show is a group of young people in their twenties and early thirties fooling around. They strike poses in the windows of the cloisters and throw snowballs as they roll around on the moor. The four people are Arnold Wesker, Beba Lavrin, Mike Kustow, and Geoffrey Reeves. The timing of the photographs was propitious and accounts for the presence of all four and myself as photographer. All of the people were connected with the project Centre 42, which underlies but is not directly depicted in Wesker's play, *Their Very Own and Golden City*. Wesker was Administrator, Beba Lavrin his assistant. I was Festivals Organiser, Mike Kustow my assistant, and Geoffrey Reeves was its Technical Director.

The time at which the photographs were taken represents the high point of Centre 42, riding on a wave of optimism, six major Trades Union Arts Festivals organized in 1962, 13 envisaged for 1963 and 20 for 1964. The 1963 and 1964 Festivals never took place, and the tone of *Their Very Own and Golden City* carries the frustration, bitterness, and pain of the failure to carry the project forward.

Centre 42 bore its curious name because of Resolution 42 of the Trades Union Congress of 1960, which called upon the Trades Union movement to support artistic activities, particularly those which were in keeping with the aims and objectives of the movement. The lead-up to the framing of this resolution had been a lecture tour by Arnold Wesker in which he presented a view of Trades Unionism moving beyond simply battling for better pay and working conditions for its members but taking into its sphere a concern with the whole range of living conditions, the total culture in which they lived. This view of Trades Unionism presents positively what William Morris issues as a warning of what will happen if the Trades Union movement does not adopt a radical political role in the long quotation with which Wesker prefaces the play in the published text.

These ideas arose in the late 1950s and early 60s out of a network of social processes. Wesker was born in 1932, which makes him a member of a generation with a specific history. He belongs to the last generation who would experience consciously the deprivation of working-class life in the Great Depression before the Second World War, who were the first generation, in the main, to be offered a much wider range of educational opportunities than previous generations of their class, who grew to awareness during the war-time period, in which a new society was being planned and the dream of socialism was presented as a social necessity and inevitability, who experienced in adolescence and early manhood the failure of the working-class movement, Labour Party and Trades Unions to establish the socialist utopia and who found themselves, after yet another war to end all wars, fighting in a range of colonial wars or in Korea.

It was this generation, fired by a belief in social progress and haunted by a sense of disillusionment, which was responsible for the breakthrough in the British theatre from 1956 onwards. Among others, John Arden, John Osborne, Harold Pinter, Dennis Potter, Trevor Griffiths, and John McGrath were responsible for breaking through the hermetical sealing off of the theatre from society, which Arthur Miller found so distressingly apparent in the mid-1950s British theatre, only to find yet more disillusionment, as Wesker records in his essay "Oh, Mother, Is It Worth It?" He accepts that his plays are well and frequently performed, no-one is censoring his works, but he complains that the audience he is writing for, the working class, are notably absent from the audience.

It was this frustration which moved Wesker into contact with the Trades Union movement, led to Resolution 42 being passed, against the advice and wishes of the ruling General Council, and was the inspiration behind a group of artists meeting at the end of 1960 to discuss their feelings of discontent about the commercial valuation of their work, and the absence from the audience of the formative communities for whom their work was conceived. This group discussed a range of other discontents, principal among them the ways in which the socialist dream had been sold out for material consumer benefits and the ways in which the rebuilding of Britain after the war had taken no account of the existence and continuation of the sense of shared community which characterized the old working-class neighborhoods. In *Their Very Own and Golden City*, Wesker projects backwards in time to look at the ways in which the dream of a new postwar world was lost through the sheer enormity of the task of reconstruction, a lack of vision and capital resources and the resulting necessity to compromise. All of which resulted in the patching up of the old and the preserving within the new much of the inequality, shoddiness, and spiritual poverty of the old.

The group meeting at the end of 1960 included writers, actors, and directors, principally, and their discussion focused on the above discontents and on how the artist could combat both the cultural poverty left over from the past and the materialist consumerism which had come in with the short, post-war economic boom. To this group Wesker introduced the idea of making a parallel gesture, comparative to the passing of Resolution 42, by means of which artists and Trades Unionists would join and work together to create new cultural structures. The first plans were to build a literal Centre, which would serve as a laboratory within which ideas could be discussed and tried out and which would serve as a display place for exhibitions and performances of all kinds. It was envisaged that participating artists would give their services for as little as they could afford and that wealthier writers and artists would contribute some portion of their royalties to help finance the running of the Centre. By projecting a possible multi-activity centre, drawing in a public directly through Trades Union memberships, Centre 42 drew on the experiences of some continental models but introduced to Britain the idea of the Arts Centre, which has become a standard feature of British cultural life.

However, the physical Centre 42 remained a dream and was never built. Early in 1961, a group of Trades Unionists from Wellingborough, a small town in the Midlands, approached the members of Centre 42, asking for a festival. Since this was the first positive demand made upon the proposed alliance, it was impossible to turn the request down and a Trades Union Festival was organized in November 1961. This admittedly small festival aroused such interest that invitations were received to mount six large-scale festivals in 1962, in Wellingborough again, the major cities of Leicester, Nottingham, Birmingham, Bristol, and the industrial conurbation of Hayes and Harlington on the western edge of Greater London.

The festivals were mounted during the autumn of 1962 in alternate weeks—one week of festival, one week of preparation. The content of the festivals was constant, the first compromise, since resources did not allow making each festival specific to the host town. The program included theatre, music theatre, poetry, jazz, and exhibitions of local artists and children's art. The first major concerts of the folksong revival movement were given in the program and a sixteen-piece band was formed, including most of the leading modern jazz soloists in Britain at a time when big band jazz desperately needed some encouragement. The production of *Hamlet*, by the National Youth Theatre, in which the title role was played by Simon Ward, included many young actors who in the 1990s are leading members of their profession. The festivals also included a documentary production *The Maker and the Tool* which was the first example of multi-media theatre in Britain and was certainly the most advanced experimental work seen in the two decades after 1945. The events were mounted in a variety of environments. In Leicester, a theatre was built in an ice rink. Folk singers and poets performed in public houses, schools, and factory canteens. In Birmingham the exhibition of children's art was estimated to have been seen by over a million people as it was sited in a wide corridor which linked two halves of a giant department store.

The organization of the festivals was split between committees of artists, responsible for the artistic content, and committees of Trades Unionists who were responsible for the local arrangements. The financial agreement was that the Trades Unionists would raise as much money as they were able and Centre 42 would raise the rest. In the event, the Trades Unions were unable to raise any money, although in Leicester they persuaded the local authority to contribute £1,000. Centre 42 enjoyed strong support at grass-roots level, where there was no money to spare, and failed to gain the support of the union leaders, who were passively sitting on massive sums of money as a precaution against having to support possible future strike action.

Money was slow to come in, and the organization was stretched simply by having to mount the festivals and had no time to spare for fund-raising. The Arts Council of Great Britain, whose function it is to subsidize the arts, gave a derisory £250 and that was paid directly to Wesker as a commission to write a music theatre piece, *The Nottingham Captain*. In a desperate attempt to raise money at a moment of crisis, Wesker offered to sell the television rights to the *Trilogy* of plays with which he first established his reputation, *Chicken Soup with Barley, Roots*, and *I'm Talking About Jerusalem*. One of the major independent television companies, which boasted a socialist as its chairman and major shareholder, made an offer of a derisory £250 for the full screening rights.

The six festivals, accordingly, had a loss of somewhere in the order of £38,000, which was below the cost of a small Bach Festival in Oxford. Of the many hundreds of artists taking part, only one, who had special skills, demanded the market price for his appearance. All accommodation was in the homes of Trades Unionists. This financial deficit was ultimately to dog the rest of Centre 42's career and to lead to its demise. A hope, which was understood to be a promise, was held out by Harold Wilson, who expected to be, and was, returned as leader of a Labour Party Government in 1964, that this deficit would be wiped out and future activities subsidized after the election. In the meantime, as part of a package deal, Wilson insisted on the appointment of an advisory board of financial experts and businessmen, to oversee the running of the project. Not only did this board fail to raise any capital; it effectively put a stop to any interim Centre 42 activities and, towards the end, succeeded in taking over the large premises in London, which had been donated to the project free of charge, for commercial exploitation. The support of Wilson's government failed to materialize, largely through Wilson's failure to establish direct subsidy, outside the control of the Arts Council of Great Britain, as a principle. Centre 42 was left without a home; its activities largely prohibited. The great optimism reflected in the games played in the photographs taken at Durham Cathedral led through a slow decline to the abandonment of the project and an end to the dreams. A challenge put down to tear the arts loose of commercial domination and bureaucratic control, to halt the drift towards a centralized metropolitan culture and to restore to people the means to create their own cultural environment was not taken up.

This was the major loss caused by the failure to sustain Centre 42. There were many gains arising out of the life of the project. The whole nature of the debate about the relationship between the arts and the community changed. Many other projects learned from the experience in constructing their own work. Most of these projects were grass-root organizations where artists moved out to live and work in communities. One, Inter-Action, started by the American Ed Berman, was large-scale and very ambitious, earning for itself the compliment of being called the most successful community arts venture within Europe. Although nothing would permit the bureaucrats to admit it, the policy underlying arts subsidy changed over the next years and a greater emphasis was placed upon provision for the regions outside London. In the new building program which resulted from this, many of the points raised by Centre 42, about freer access and a more positive policy towards building a socially, more broadly based audience, were incorporated. But for those who were closely involved in the running of the project, the great realization was that among the workers in any community there were enough skills and energy to change the nature of that society, if they could be harnessed. What the Trades Unionists brought was a range of practical skills and organizational capacities which made the running of major arts festivals a relatively simple matter. If a temporary theatre had to be built, the carpenters and builders would do it. If there were eight box-offices, running simultaneously, the bank workers union could handle that with no trouble. Transport problems, ring the transport workers union. With no vision this would be a way of exploiting cheap labor. What made it more than this was the engagement of the Trades Unionists in creating their own cultural event and the amount of control they were able to exert over it.

However, the ultimate astonishing achievement of Centre 42 lay in proving that any community has within it the capacity and power to create its own culture, which is a revolutionary concept. In *Their Very Own*, Wesker attaches to Centre 42 an affiliation to the overall dream of building a new world and appropriates for it the same level of importance as the play ascribes to the building of the Golden Cities, the design of which will be democratically determined by the choice of the future residents. The artist/architect will be given the opportunity to be truly creative in the service of the community. By extension, the artist can only be truly creative in the service of the community. At no point does Wesker present a utopian dream as a reality. Although he presents, through the character of Bill Matheson, a rampant philistine, a picture of small-mindedness, petty jealousy, and political reaction, Wesker elsewhere is concerned to be fair minded. The Trades Union leaders and politicians in the pla may be blinkered in their vision and timid in their actions, but they are constrained by pressures arising out of the real, external world they live in and not simply by limitations inherent in themselves. They are not fools, villains, nor bloody minded, and, in the course of the play, the visionary Andy Cobham has to learn to live with the same constraints and to make similar compromises. Wesker shows us the great efforts that have to be made to achieve no more than a token gesture towards progress and the effects that the necessary, if excessive, compromise has on the human mind, body, and spirit.

The play is written in episodic form, utilizing many short scenes, covering a period of almost sixty years. It concerns the plans and deeds of an architect, Andrew Cobham, and a group of friends, to build a network of new cities, which will constitute the ideal environment in which to live. In any event, only one of these cities is ever built; Cobham grows old, loaded with honors, bitterly frustrated that his grand dreams have only resulted in contributing one more piece to the patchwork, shoring up of the old society, which characterized the death of the war-time dreams of building a new society upon its conclusion. Along the way, Cobham has to learn many lessons. Through his friendship with the aristocratic Kate Ramsay, he learns that he who wants to create must learn to be assertive and elitist, if he wishes to bring in democracy. He has to learn to be a politician, a diplomat, and ultimately to accept compromise as the price of a minimal success. Politics, as we are told, is the art of the possible, but those who accept this without testing how far the possible can be pushed must bear the responsibility for stagnation. Cobham learns that those who give their lives to pursuing high ideals and progress can never enjoy the fruits of their labors themselves. One part of the price of Cobham's limited success is the slow destruction of his marriage and the enslaving of his wife.

In constructing this episodic play, Wesker cunningly uses the technique of flash-forward. The play opens with the friends playing games amid the glorious architecture of Durham Cathedral. At various points the play returns to this setting and the time of youthful dreams. The use of this time and place as a framework places a positive emphasis on what follows. To have used flashback would have been to create a play of despair and disillusionment as the aged Cobham looked back at his failures. In using flash-forward, Wesker asserts that, in spite of all the pain and compromise to come, there is value in the attempt. In every age people have to assert positive principles and to stand by their beliefs:

> I've no time for rebels, they hate the past for what it didn't give them.... Revolutionaries is what we want—they spend less time rebelling against what's past and give their energy to the vision ahead. (2:138)

> Defeat doesn't matter; in the long run all defeat is temporary. It doesn't matter about present generations but future ones always want to look back and know that someone was around acting on principle (2:141)

This positive intention is further borne out by the instruction Wesker gives in the text:

> N.B. If the cathedral scenes in either Act are heavily played this entire play will fail. Innocence, gaiety and a touch of lunacy is their atmosphere. (2:127)

The play becomes an assertion of the human spirit in the face of all opposing forces and adversity. The motto Wesker chose to embody the spirit of Centre 42 was a statement made by D.H. Lawrence, "If you are going to make a revolution, make it for fun." Those who are true revolutionaries, in Wesker's opinion, are those who aim to change people, not those who battle to bring down governments.

In beginning his play in 1926, the year of The General Strike, the high point of working-class militancy and the low-point of Trades Union leadership, Wesker tacitly acknowledges that Centre 42 was behind its time. 1945, not 1960, was the time when it should have been founded. But it would be foolish to write the project off in those terms. The value of Centre 42, and the Golden City of the play, is difficult to assess in concrete contemporary terms. I have tried to set out some of the positive influences the project was able to assert, but ultimately, the true and lasting value lies in the hearts and minds of those who were involved and touched by it. I have the photographs to remind me of the joy we experienced. My subsequent life and career have been molded by that experience. I recently met up with someone who had been involved. She asked me, "How did we manage to do so much?" Because we had a vision and we pursued it as far as it was allowed to go.

ↀ

Well-nigh Wesker
Paul Levitt

Several years ago, Reade Dornan asked me for a letter of introduction to Arnold Wesker. I wrote to Arnold, whom I had met in the early 70s, and asked him to see her. He graciously agreed. Reade talked to him in London and came away a friend of Whizzy's, as his wife Dusty affectionately calls him. (The name comes from his school days; his family called him Whiz, owing to his speed of foot.) So when Reade asked me to contribute to this collection, I felt she was returning a favor and responded that really she ought to include only those scholars who had previously written about Wesker, a select group that I've never joined. I did not wish, moreover, to trade on my friendship with Arnold. But Reade persisted, pointing out that since Arnold had already thanked me in the printed edition of *Caritas* for suggesting the story of Christine Carpenter, I would be just the person to shed some light on his work and his sources. Here, then, are some reflections that may serve some public purpose without, I trust, violating Arnold's privacy.

My first meeting with Arnold, like Reade's, came through the agency of another. Nathaniel Tarn, Poet-in-residence at a University of Colorado summer writers' conference that I directed, had told me that he and Arnold were friends. As my own scholarly interest in modern drama had led me to read Arnold's plays, and as I had just started writing for the theatre myself, I wanted to meet the author of the Wesker *Trilogy*, a collection that made me realize the richness to be found in the Jewish family experience. Nathaniel asked Arnold to give me an audience.

I can still remember standing in the lobby of a London hotel dialing the Wesker telephone number. Dusty answered. As I subsequently learned, she vetted all Arnold's calls; I cannot remember a single instance in which Arnold ever answered the phone. Dusty knew whom to admit, whom to bar, and whom to delay. I fell into the last category. After a minute or so, I heard Arnold on the line. He invited me to their home in Highgate.

I have to smile when I think of Arnold giving me directions. He rarely used the Underground himself, preferring to travel by car. Yet there he was eagerly telling me how convenient it was to use the Northern Line and not to be dismayed if I found the long escalator from the platform to the station out of order, as was frequently the case. So off I set. Highgate, I discovered, is one of the more fashionable London communities, just the sort of place that attracts artists. According to Arnold, when I exited the escalator and reached the ticket kiosk, there would be turnings to the right and left. And so there were. By turning right, one arrives at the junction of Archway Road and Jackson's Lane. The northwest corner of this intersection houses the Jackson's Lane Community Center, a building that has frequently drawn Arnold through its doors: for meetings, for Christmas dinners to help the poor (Arnold carved the chicken), for plays and for readings.

By turning left, one comes to a steep, winding path that leads to the junction of Archway and Muswell Hill Road. Crossing Archway, a major truck artery out of London that during the day clouds the air with exhaust fumes, I walked one block north to Arnold's street. At the corner, just as he said, I found a nursery on one side and a police station on the other. Turning left (west), I walked up Bishops Road till I came to his house on the north side of the street, number 27. A low, unpainted, rough-hewn fence with a wobbly gate fronted the house, which stood virtually on the sidewalk. The grass patch between house and fence could not have measured in depth more than four or five feet. Though tall, the house itself looked pinched, hedged in on either side by its neighbors. Thinking I would find small, cramped quarters—just what one might expect of a working-class writer—I rang and waited.

Dusty Wesker answered the door and led me through a small foyer into the sitting room. Years later, I spent untold hours in this room exchanging ideas with Arnold about his work and that of others, listening to an occasional reading and attending parties fueled by Dusty's incomparable cooking. On this day, I had to wait about five minutes, ample time to admire the elongated sitting room, with its walls of original art work and its elegant fireplace at one end. Through the windows and glass doors, I could see a lovely walled garden at the back of the house. Dusty's desk, positioned so that she could see into the garden, stood covered with letters and papers. Comfortable couches and chairs abounded, nothing period, nothing pretentious. All in all, a warm, inviting, uncramped room.

A buzzer sounded. Dusty answered it and announced that Arnold was now free. I would find him up the stairs at the top of the house. Up I went and there, framed in the door of his study, stood Arnold Wesker. An immense smile, covering his broad, round face, and an outstretched hand greeted me. A short, well-built man, Arnold bristles with vitality and energy that make him seem much taller than he actually is. He ushered me into his cluttered study. There just inside the door was a bulletin board of numerous family photographs, the very pictures used in the program cover design of *The Old Ones.*

His study under the eaves had a low sloping ceiling. A single floor-length window looked out onto Bishops Road. Arnold's expansive writing table faced a wall, but by looking to his left, he could see out the window. He explained that he could never find a desk large enough to suit him, so he preferred to work at this table, with his card files at its end. Off to one side, I could see a small phonograph and a pile of records, virtually all of them, as I later discovered, recordings of classical composers. Books stacked on the floor and papers strewn everywhere—I knew the terrain.

Arnold sat down at his desk, with his back to the window, and I on a couch across from him. I remember watching the December light fading quickly. I was apprehensive as I tried to frame the question—or was it a request?—that had brought me to this room. Having just completed a historical play about ritual murder, a charge brought against the Jews of Norwich, England in 1144, I wanted to know, given the nature of the material, how to market it. At least that's what I told myself. Where should it be sent and to whom? Which theatre, which artistic director? Did I need an agent? But looking back now, I think, most of all, I wanted to know if he would read my play and give me its measure. Was it, in short, any good?

Arnold agreed to read my play but warned me that even if he liked the script, his own theatre contacts were at best tenuous. He explained that in the small theatre community of England, everyone knew everyone else and that the old boy network, which had branded him a pariah, was very much alive. I gathered that to circumvent it took some inventiveness—or just plain cash. If one had friendly relations with an "angel" or two, heretofore unavailable directors and stage designers suddenly found themselves free. Arnold, as I subsequently learned, had the respect and affection of some of these angels. But as I knew no one, I asked about an agent. He shook his head and observed that agents had a knack for writing contracts, not for selling plays. At the end, he said that if I wished to write for the London theatre then I really ought to live in the U.K. or at least try to spend long periods in the country. Given this tight little island, it was imperative that I meet people in the theatre. He could, he allowed, introduce me to several.

It was during this talk that I began to discern some of the major concerns in Arnold's work: His love of learning; his ambivalence about not having gone to university; his arguments with a critical establishment that resents his tendentiousness and tenacity; his socialist principles; his fear of received opinions, particularly when echoed by the many; his failed experiment at community theatre; and his family. From that day in the early 70s till now, I have remained convinced that to understand Arnold's plays one must grapple with these concerns.

Shortly after this meeting, my department elected me chairman. In this capacity I had the means to invite Arnold to Boulder, as visiting lecturer in the Department of English and resident playwright in our summer writers' conference, 1974. He accepted my offer and brought his family with him. Exchanging houses and cars with a neighbor of mine who lived just across the road, Arnold and Dusty immediately came under the spell of the climate. Their first day in Boulder, Dusty pulled up a chair on the back porch of the house, which has a splendid view of the mountains and called Arnold to join her. Never, she said, had she experienced such light; she felt as if she could reach out and touch the mountains. Nothing like gloomy England, she needled Arnold; no need for a slicker or Wellingtons here. Arnold took it all in good humor, though I subsequently learned from him that any second thoughts he had had about this trip were owing to his fear of leaving his aged mother behind.

I had also invited Charlotte Zolotow, the children's book author, to teach juvenile literature at the conference. She and Arnold soon struck up a friendship, which proved valuable for Arnold, as she, in her capacity as editor for Harper and Row, subsequently helped arrange for that publisher to bring out an American edition of the complete plays of Arnold Wesker.

It was during this stay that Arnold began to explore his idea for *The Merchant*. He would invite the students from his Contemporary Drama course back to his house, where they would spend hours excitedly talking about the reading list and ways of reconceiving Shakespeare's plays as well as other works. He loved those sessions, in which he used the students as a sounding board for a number of his fancies. The initial idea for *The Merchant* (later titled *Shylock*) had come to him in England, but a number of conceptual problems remained. Hoping that his students might help, he asked them to look into the legal and political customs of Venice during the sixteenth and seventeenth centuries. Were Shylock and Antonio under some legal compulsion to execute the bond that they had lightheartedly entered into, or could it have been easily dismissed? He knew that if the play were to work, the prosecution of the bond could not strain credulity. The students eagerly took up this task, and one of them, Lois Bueler, whom Arnold thanked in the printed edition of *The Merchant* was so thorough and adept in her research that she enabled him to fit the legal details of the bond to his dramatic conception. But I hasten to add that, whatever background information the students contributed, the idea of a book-loving Shylock is Arnold's own expression of his deep love of learning.

As *The Merchant* began to take shape, Arnold saw it as his vehicle to financial independence. His belief in the play's commercial possibilities soared when Zero Mostel agreed to play Shylock. Wouldn't every Jewish theatre-goer on the east coast of America want to see it, he asked me. I had to agree; he seemed to be sitting on a gold mine. So convinced was Arnold that this play would make him wealthy that, if I'm not mistaken, he established a trust fund in anticipation of the money he expected to earn. *The Merchant* was to open in Philadelphia and then proceed to New York. But as fate would have it, Zero took ill after one performance and died a week later. The person who replaced him, alas, could not on name alone fill the theatre. I had lunch in New York with Arnold shortly after the play closed. He described how everyone had gathered at Sardi's on opening night and waited for the reviews. The delight of the audience seemed a harbinger of wonderful tidings and had carried over to the restaurant. The whole Wesker party thought they had been present at the launching of a great success. But as the evening drew on, so did doubt. Could they have misread the enthusiasm of the audience, the applause? Once the newspapers arrived, and particularly the *New York Times*, Arnold's hopes were utterly dashed. Although some of the critics liked the play, and Clive Barnes subsequently praised it on radio, the damage was done. The *New York Times*, the maker and breaker of shows, had spoken. The backers backed out. A week later, the show closed. I don't think Arnold has ever completely recovered from the misadventures that befell the play: rewrites, disagreements, and death. But as he once said to me, though his luck had been rotten, Zero's was worse.

The Boulder summer of 1974 was the first time, as far as I know, that Arnold introduced *Love Letters on Blue Paper* to an audience. He had told me that he was working on the manuscript, but when he selected it for a public reading, I had grave misgivings about its reception by undergraduates. Held in the University Memorial Center, the reading attracted an overflow audience. My colleagues and I kept dragging in additional chairs and even had to leave the door open to ventilate the overcrowded room. Arnold had arranged for the reading to mirror a stage presentation: house lights off; silence; Arnold's entrance; lights up. He read in one of his stock-in-trade shirts, open down the front, exposing his shaggy chest. I have never know Arnold to read with more feeling or drama. The crowd, made up principally of students but also of faculty and other writers, sat transfixed. A woman next to me broke down in tears, and she was by no means alone. Afterwards, Arnold observed that although *Love Letters* had been written as a collection of short stories, he thought that given the audience's reaction he might reshape the work as a play. *Love Letters* rewritten for television was broadcast March 2, 1976, and the stage version performed at the National Theatre (Cottesloe) February 15, 1978.

Arnold's visit to Boulder made us good friends, and on one occasion I rented his Highgate house for a month in the summer, while he and his family went off to visit, I think, Warsaw or Budapest. Arnold's friends used to wonder why he often took trips to Poland and Hungary and other communist countries and whether his journeys had to do with his political sentiments. Not so. His plays have always been enormously popular in Eastern Europe, to say nothing of Japan, and as long as the currency in the socialist countries had little or no worth in the West, he left his royalties *in situ* to be used on some subsequent holiday.

Why Arnold's plays have been better received outside Britain has provoked endless debate. I suspect that when he made the Queen's

Honors List and turned down the CBE (Commander of the British Empire), he thumbed his nose at the very recognition that would have legitimated his non-traditional type of playwriting. (He told Harold Wilson that rather than honors, he would prefer the government's support of Centre 42.) When a society invites one of its rebels inside, a society without whose support serious stage plays and favorable newspaper reviews are virtually impossible, the rebel either accepts or invites contumely or neglect. By rejecting the honor, Arnold closed a great many doors—and put the wind up a number of influential people. Although he acted out of egalitarian principles, his motives were mocked, and he was ever after looked upon as an umbrageous socialist. But as his critics could not rail against him for being true to his principles, they shifted the grounds of the argument and began to attack the didactic intent of his work. Who was this fellow to lecture them? He hadn't even a university degree. Besides, his plays were formless and his characters often pretentiously wordy. The work that had once been found passionate and deeply moving, the critical establishment now found inchoate and muddle-headed. The English ruling class doesn't appreciate uppity behavior. Arnold had been uppity. Worse, he argued with the critics—in public. He would take reviewers to task in print for what he saw as the inadequacies of their arguments. Worst of all, he often left them looking foolish and ill informed. In short order, the word went out: Wesker was trouble.

After all, this was the bloke who had sued the Royal Shakespeare Company (RSC) for not living up to its contract to perform *The Journalists*. This was the chappy who wanted to direct his own plays, the Eastender who thought that he knew better than the actors. The one appellation that never surfaced but lay just below the dermis was "Jewish working class." The English upper classes have always had trouble with raw energy and imagination. When those qualities were found in a writer with socialist sympathies who never went to university, a writer who often bested the critics at their own critical analyses, the invitation to insinuate that his plays were simple political tracts or autobiography was too good to refuse.

I saw this behavior firsthand. At the opening nights in England of *The Old Ones*, *The Wedding Feast*, and *Caritas*, I had occasion to talk to some of the theatre critics who crowded the bar at the interval. Invariably they would praise (surely not merely for my benefit?) the emotional power of the play. And then, predictably, they would write reviews in which they complained about the play's lack of depth or its failure to translate political thought into drama. Arnold would then rise to the bait and defend himself, exacerbating his already precarious relationship with the press. I saw clearly in 1976–77, when I settled in London for about fifteen months, the dilemma of a playwright at odds with the Establishment yet dependent for a living upon its patronage. Once the Centre 42 and Roundhouse experiment had failed for want of financial support, he was at the mercy of the commercial theatres—and the popular press.

During those fifteen months, I saw Arnold frequently. He was at sea about what to write next. After all the reading and research *Merchant* had involved, he wanted to stay clear of historical plays. One evening, he stopped by my flat on Broadlands Road, a street just a few blocks away from his own. We were casually exchanging ideas about plots and story lines. He remarked that he always found it difficult to come up with the initial idea for a play. I began rifling through my notebook, sharing with him several stories that had struck my fancy. While going through my notes, I read him a brochure that I had picked up at the small church of St. James in Shere, Surrey, during a sightseeing trip. A history buff, I had been much taken with the story of Christine Carpenter, the young woman who, according to my brochure, declared herself an anchoress after a spat with her swain and asked to be immured in a cell hollowed out of a wall adjacent to the church. Her suitor came to visit her every day, stationing himself outside the wall, where they held lengthy conversations. When the bishop forbade these talks, he drowned himself. Shortly thereafter Christine requested that she be released from her vow. The church refused. A few years later, having gone mad, she died.

I saw the play as a wonderful love story, with the bishop as the heavy. But Arnold, to his credit, saw it as part of a political tapestry. It was not until at least a year later, certainly well after I had returned to the States, that Arnold got in touch with me, asking if I had any objection to his using this story in a play that he wanted to write. None at all, I said, and he went on to tell me that he had visited Shere and discovered that my original information was in error: recent research indicated that the love story owed more to fancy than fact. In that light, he fashioned his own view of Christine Carpenter, the passionate woman who utters in *Caritas* what I consider one of the most moving lines in all of Wesker's plays: "I am crucified upon the spring!"

Although in the market for new ideas, Arnold at this period was also preparing *The Wedding Feast* for its English premiere. In January 1977, he rented a bus and driver to transport dozens of family and friends north to Leeds for the opening night. The friends included Wilfred Josephs, who wrote the music for *Nottingham Captain*, performed at the Centre 42 festivals, and Bob and Nicky Gavron, people who have in one way or another significantly affected Arnold's career. Wilfred is a prominent composer who has written original music for theatre, feature films, television, and documentaries. Bob Gavron is a successful printer who frequently helped Arnold out of personal financial difficulties. Nicky, now a labor counselor for Hornsey, used to run the Jackson's Lane Community Center, the setting of the first public performance (a rehearsed reading) of *The Journalists*, with Sheila Allen and Ian McKellen.

The bus trip was particularly memorable for the goodwill and humor exhibited along the way. People walked about the bus talking to one another. Those of us new to the caravan were introduced and in no time were engaged in warm conversations. Although Arnold and Dusty were driving with their children to Leeds in their Volvo, Dusty had provided for her guests. At some point in the trip, a neatly packed basket was opened and cold turkey and salads and sweets were heartily passed around. I had hoped to see long queues of theatre goers, but the house was less than full. The play, in its dramatization of contradictions and its explorations of class differences, eloquently reveals Arnold's subtlety of mind. The critics objected, as they would subsequently object to *Caritas*, that the play lacked unity of style. They seemed unable to see the relationship of the narrative voice to the rest of *The Wedding Feast*. I found the production admirable and the play moving. After the play, we indulged ourselves in yet more of Dusty's provender. It was a Wesker family tradition for Dusty to host a party after every opening night. A word about Dusty. An immensely talented cook, photographer, and inn keeper, she was indefatigable in her support of Arnold's career. Her Sunday teas became legendary, those marvelous afternoons when out-of-town guests, including entire theatre companies like the Habima and the Piccolo, were treated to gourmet cooking and Arnold's charms. With Dusty turning out some of the best food in the U.K., Arnold had no trouble persuading his guests that the theatre world would be much the richer for taking the occasional chance.

Food figures as a major motif in Arnold's plays because food looms large in his life; and the author of these numerous meals was Dusty. Her creations, in fact, accompanied us on every trip we made together, whether to Leeds or to Wales for a holiday in the Wesker house, or the Royal Court for an opening night. Dusty's culinary genius culminated in *The Dusty Wesker Cookbook*, published by Chatto & Windus in 1985. Written in the form of a diary, the book is equally rich in recipes and names. The recipes are the different meals she prepared during the course of a year for the many who dined at the Wesker table. The guest list itself sounds like a Who's Who of British culture. Although some people have complained that the teas and parties and dinners were intended to promote Arnold's career, I never once heard him ask anyone to stage his plays. And even if he had, I fail to see the unseemliness. I think rather the point of the exercise was to bring together foreign guests and family and close friends so that people of different cultures could enjoy each other's company. The different foreign languages I have heard spoken in the Wesker house and the number of foreign guests who lodged there would qualify 27 Bishops Road as an international hostel. And the person behind the scenes who made all this activity a success, the person frantically preparing meals in a cramped kitchen with steamy windows, was Dusty.

After my 1976–77 stay in England, I spent summers in London as well as random periods when my plays were being produced on BBC radio. On one such trip, in October 1989, I arrived in time to see the opening of the rewritten *Merchant*, at the Riverside Studios, Crisp Road, Hammersmith. Arnold had rented the theatre and invited a number of critics to see the play. Although some members of the press declined his offer, his family and friends did not. They filled the theatre. Arnold was bustling about in his black velvet jacket, trying to get everyone seated. I found the performance uneven; Arnold was beside himself because of last-minute cast changes owing to illness. A day or two later, the newspapers appeared with their mostly lukewarm reviews. Arnold blamed the acting. What that venture set him back, I have no idea, but I thought it gutsy of him to produce his play at his own expense in the hope that favorable reviews might lead to its transfer to a popular theatre and a lengthy run. Alas, such good fortune never materialized.

That was the last production of a Wesker play that I saw, but not the last time that I heard from Arnold about playwriting. Not long after, he wrote me to inquire about the sources for my first play, *The Norwich Incident*, with its exploration of the motives behind the Church's invention of ritual murder. He explained that he had been commissioned to write a play for the opening of the new Norwich Playhouse and would like to use this story. I sent him not only a bibliography of works about the period, including books about medieval usury and economics, but also photocopies touching upon those aspects of the story that I thought most important. I heard nothing more of this material until Reade Dornan sent me a copy of Arnold's play, *William of Norwich*, which bore on its title page the note: "the third typed draft, Blaendigeddi, 3 September 1991," The manuscript copy that I read exhibits some of the most austere, crystalline dialogue Arnold has ever written—to great effect. His point of view, completely unlike my own, explores the tension and skepticism the clergy themselves felt about the charge of ritual murder. In this regard, Arnold has remained much closer to the sources than I. His is the play not only of a mature craftsman but also of an elegant mind—Arnold at the top of his form. The Norwich Playhouse presented *William of Norwich*, now retitled *Blood Libel*, at its opening in 1996.

The last time I saw Arnold, I had been invited to lunch at the Weskers' new house in Crouch End. Except for the addition of the solarium, which greatly pleased Arnold, this house has virtually the same floor plan as the one on Bishops Road. We sat with his granddaughter and an American woman who wished to stage some of his plays. Arnold had just returned from Wales and talked at some length about how much he liked to write in their house there. He observed that he had no telephone and that long walks on the hills were tonic. I sat there remembering the hills, spotted with ponies and horses and sheep and lambs, and the house, on the inside mostly blue and white, with its rough stucco walls, large kitchen and dining room (as one might expect), and fireplaces that heated the downstairs. The bedrooms, upstairs and unheated, required woollies. I could picture us parking the car at road's end, some distance from the house, and schlepping boxes of food down a long muddy track. The closest real town was Hay-on-Wye, which has become famous as the second-hand book capital of the world. A once-dying town, Hay owes its success to some bloke who had the bright idea of turning all the failed shops into bookshops. Now people come from all over the world to stroll this town where bookstores line the streets.

The discussion in the house turned naturally to playwriting. The American woman asked us both why we liked to write. I responded first, saying that playing with words takes me out of myself and transports me to some other imaginative place. Arnold replied that he does not like to write but that he feels driven to share his personal vision of the world, with all its sad and comic misadventures, and to leave it a better place if possible. I thought: mine was a selfish answer, and his, predictably, was an expression of his belief in sharing and community. His wish to delight and instruct, a Classical and Renaissance ideal, informs all his plays. That his critics see the didacticism and not the joyful personal vision makes the critics, not the plays, the poorer.

I think the achievements of the Renaissance frequently tease his mind. He once asked me: "Wouldn't you like to have been present when English was a fresh, new wonderful language, when all the metaphors and similes were original? How wonderful to have been there." For myself, I have my doubts if there was ever a there there, but no doubts at all that the desire for conceiving the world in new ways constantly renews Arnold's language and makes it endlessly vital.

ॐ

Writing for Radio and Radio for Writing
Yardsale *by* Arnold Wesker

Alessandra Marzola

Within the universe of the media, the radio plays a distinctive role, using techniques designed for sound only. The exclusion of the image, which has become dominant in today's culture through photography, television, and cinema, lends this old-fashioned medium an almost mythical dimension. The days of the radio's near-exclusive presence are now over, giving rise to nostalgic remembrances such as the fable of *Radio Days* presented on cinema screens by Woody Allen. In the home, radio has thus become secondary, merely a supplement to the crushing presence of the television screen. It may occasionally represent an elite, intellectual alternative, perhaps as a deliberate resistance to the invasion of the small screen. In this sense, radio programs share the same fate as theatre. Called upon to compete with the popular image, radio struggles to re-define its parameters in the light of this challenge.

During its history and due to technological developments, the radio play becomes an artistic medium in its own right.[1] In the most fortunate cases, radio even manages to empower certain features of the text, thus favoring developments hitherto unknown and encouraging the expansion of certain aspects which theatre and television inevitably suppress. From this aspect, limits imposed by the medium are not to be seen as restrictions, but rather as opportunities to expand or refine certain qualities of language.

Deprived of the concrete physicality of the stage, of the characters, and of the whole system of dynamic interactions which are part of live or televised theatre, the absolute priority of language stimulates the visualizing and contextualizing imagination of the listener who must recreate the absent setting on the basis of a code of purely sound signals. "The stage is the listener's own mind"—as Martin Esslin aptly puts it (21)—and radio drama must be articulated according to precise patterns, developing an iconic rhetoric which reinforces its nature as visual medium"(McLuhan). According to Martin Esslin the structure of a radio play can be compared to a musical piece: a careful, rhythmic orchestration measures the tempo of the performance in a calibrated way, alternating rapid movements with slower rhythms. The scanned iteration of certain key lines, the measuring of pauses and silences, the control over evocative and suggestive implications keep the re-creation of the imaginary setting in line with the directions of the text. These devices cannot be inscribed within a prescriptive rhetoric, which fortunately is fluid and variable enough to respond to commercial demands. It is the specific nature of the medium which imposes these devices, and they are the basis on which the most recent radio drama is founded.

The interesting thing to note here is that these "restrictions" imposed by radio condition the writing of authors of theatre texts, so much so that in Arnold Wesker's case we might say that the radio represents a happy alternative to the stage and becomes an ideal medium for him.

As we know, Wesker's early works (*The Kitchen, Chips with Everything* and the *Trilogy*) had great success in the 1960s. This popularity was reconfirmed by the positive reception of the recent revival of *The Kitchen*, which demonstrates the permanent effect which Wesker's theatre writing from the 1960s has had on Anglo-Saxon culture. Wesker's later work, in which he modified his writing considerably, was received much less enthusiastically. Concentrating on private and intimate themes—as in *The Friends* and *The Four Seasons* and on "public" and "social" matters, as in *The Journalists* and *Shylock*—he diluted the semantic depth of the language and at the same time made its poetic matrices more powerful. Even though Wesker has often restated the passionate need for a theatre which translates experience into message, in his later work language (the signifier) seems to be foregrounded against experience (the signified).

Yardsale, a one-woman radio play that was first broadcast by BBC Radio 3 on October 6, 1984 with Sheila Steafel and produced by Margaret Windham, provides an interesting example of Wesker's later stylistic developments.[2] Since the radiophonic strength of *Yardsale* closely depends on Wesker's stylistic developments, it could be even argued that the author's later writing is more congenial to the radio than to the stage. The specific case of Wesker's play problematizes the claustrophobia of theatrical structure, the oppression of its semiotic architecture which often flattens and deforms the creativity of theatre writing, rendering it unnatural and artificial and exhausting it of significance.

A closer reading of *Yardsale* will clarify this hypothesis.[3] *Yardsale* is the story of a marital breakdown. Stephanie, the protagonist, finds the epigraph of her marriage in a laconic letter from her husband Sheldon together with the decision to interrupt a relationship which has become too repetitive and routine. This single, external, and salient document becomes the engine for a sequence of considerations, memories, and associations which are articulated in eight scenes, carefully metronomed acoustically by the author through the ticking of a clock. After an initial "staccato" which stresses Stephanie's anxious wait while preparing her husband's meal, the eight sections ("The Homecoming," "The Discovery," "The Depression," "The Phone Call," "To the Art Gallery," "To the Bookshop," "Yardsale") cover a sequential period of time and frame the see-sawing phases of her reaction to the betrayal: from desperation, to victimization, to a liberation after a desecrating denigration of her husband. She attempts to take refuge in places which should help her to forget but which in fact serve as pitiful reminders of her loss.

Wesker does not cast the theme of abandonment into a story with a well-defined outline nor a well-rounded psychological exploration of character, but neither does he overwhelm or cancel out the theme with the rhetoric of the interior monologue. Instead, he constructs a sequence of sketches, brief profiles of emotional situations, each of which is independently a fragment in its own right (the original radio play consisted in fact only of the last section called "Yardsale"). The parts, however, make up a whole interlaced with semantic and symbolic links which both justify and reinforce it.

Each section has its own distinctive and specific nature deriving from the formal elements of rhythmic scansion. In the first section, "The Homecoming," the brief interrogative with its implicit anxious suspension—"Sheldon?"[4]—gives rhythm to Stephanie's discourse which is rapid and breathless like the anxiety caused by his delay. This discourse is interwoven with a lexis that insists on the irrelevances of daily life, without ever focusing on detail. In the indistinct torrent of banalities, this rhythmic and recurrent interrogative becomes dominant, together with the other ritual formula recalled by a scrap of family lexis:

Right, Sheldon? Right, Stephanie! (5:12)

With his strong presence in the discourse, which pivots around his strange absence hardly believable to her, Sheldon takes on the function of an eavesdropper similar to the radio listener:

> Sheldon, are you sure you're not somewhere in the house?
> I know your tricks, you let me talk to myself and that way
> imagine you're hearing what I really think but never tell
> you. (5:12)

It is a listener who waits for mysterious revelations, which contradict the transparent evidence of the words:

> I am who I am what I am that I am so you can listen to
> me talking to myself all the time and you won't find out
> more than you already know about me. (5:12)

Stephanie's waiting and her discovery of Sheldon's betrayal act as a meta-theatrical metaphor for the author's apprehensions about the audience's reactions. The anxiety is offset by Stephanie's demand to be taken at face value (an echo of Wesker's demand to be read "transparently" for what he believes he is), and it culminates in her self-ironic attempts at distancing which are supported by an erudite quotation from "Night Thoughts" by Edward Young and a refrain from the popular song "Summertime" with intermittent notes of "Jealousie" sung as "Stephanie" (5:11–12).

If the anxious and insecure Stephanie projects the profile of the author, the faithless Sheldon acts as a bored listener, worn out and deprived of independent resources, "Curiosity gone, nerve ends dead, mechanical" (5:13) and thus hungry for unusual sensations.

The Stephanie/Wesker identification is reinforced in Scene 3, in which the naturalistic aspect of the female character is further thinned out. Stephanie's language, which can no longer be traced back to a fully realized and specific subject, is dominated by repeated denials which punctuate it at regular intervals, each one typical of the renunciatory depression: "I will lie here in this bed and never get up" (5:13). These are alternated with the accusation of her rival of theft—"Husband Thief" (5:13) and a series of repeated and rhythmically intervalled interrogatives which Stephanie makes in search of her own errors:

> What did I do wrong? (5:13).... What, what, did I do
> wrong? (5:14).... Did my breath smell? Did I talk non-
> sense? Did I lack style? (5:14).... Was I too loud, too in-
> tense, too dry? Did something in me stop long ago? (5:14)

The space reserved for the hammering iteration overwhelms the argumentative fluidity. Still more repetitive motifs are worked into the rhythms of the discourse which obsessively and grotesquely go over the tortures which Stephanie imagines inflicting on the faithless couple:

> I would like to pull out her nails. No. Better. I would like to tie her up to watch while I pull out his nails. No. Better. I would like to tie them both up while I mark her and castrate him and then pull out their nails. First one from him, then one from her. Then one from him then one from her. She loves him, she loves him not, she loves him, she loves him not, she loves him. (Beat) She loves him! (Beat) O Christ, does she love him?...I would like to see her run over by a car. I would like to see her struck blind. I would like to take shit and throw it at her. (5:14)

The voice of the monologue retraces obsessively and rhythmically the ritual formulas of the betrayed wife, giving them an emphasis which the exclusion of the image further strengthens. Self-recriminations and aggressiveness alternate with each other, enabling the listener to visualize iconic masks without physiognomy or well-defined outlines. What is acted is therefore "betrayal," not a betrayal, "abandonment," not an abandonment. The overabundance of clichés worked into a lattice with comic, grotesque, self-ironic, and desecrating strips leaves spaces for a meta-theatrical listening. Thus the figure of the betrayed Stephanie is superimposed with that of the author: he, too, has been abandoned by the listener who, betraying him, unjustly robs him of the fruits of a patient labor of loving devotion. The metaphor of the theft and the economic implications which subtend the marital bond acquire increasing and threatening weight during the play and become the only important semantic connectives emphasized by the absence of other metaphors. The metaphor symptomatically reflects Wesker's private idiosyncrasy, a kind of persecution mania which recurs in the author's confessions and testimonies. The word "scavenging," which is repeated obsessively in Wesker's polemic against critics and reviewers to indicate what he experiences as a brutal sapping of the vital resources of writing re-emerges suggestively in this radio play.[5] The central theme of betrayal is converted into the metaphor of unjust theft which is merely hinted at the beginning of the play but whose implications spread until the hint becomes explicit reference.

The faithless Sheldon is substituted in Scene 4 by a new, silent telephonic interlocutor—the projection of a different, understanding listener who is also an accomplice. Her daughter Maxie's uninterrupted silence indicates, moreover, an unconditional acceptance of Stephanie/Wesker which sparks off Stephanie's series of recriminations and sarcastic comments about Sheldon, who is defined as a garrulous bore, ready to steal other people's language in order to use it as a pathetic means of seduction:

> And what conversation! He floated the debris of other people's battles. His thoughts would go on for so long his words would forget where they began. Dialogue like driftwood—sodden and cut off. He was a thief! What could you expect? He stole my youth and other people's arguments. A thief! (5:16)

The presence of the new and reassuring listener allows Stephanie/Wesker to confess her/his own deceptions: the mistaken choice of a pathetic interlocutor seduced by the stereotypes of the words ("And all because he said he loved me"). For the benefit of this new listener, the protagonist sarcastically calls to mind the setting of a standard erotic performance as she acts out the scene with the clichéd "curtain-raiser" approach and adopts a position which is clearly identifiable with the author's:

> "Tonight's the night" he'd announce. Subtly.
>
> "Faw what, honey?" I used to put on a shy, southern drawl and pretend I didn't know what he was on about.
>
> "What night's this, sugar plum? You all surely don't mean—oh, my, Sheldon, there's no stopping you I do declare." (5:16)

Just as Sheldon's abandonment is inscribed with betrayal and theft by the listener, the reader, and the critic, Stephanie's matrimonial choice reminds us of an insecure author in need of flattery who opts for a stubborn and unscrupulous audience, which cynically appropriates the language and uses it opportunistically. Similarly Stephanie's reactions as the betrayed wife and the abandoned writer—her attempts to "go on living" by visiting the exhibition of Hopper's paintings, the restaurant Serendipity in New York, a bookshop, and finally the sale of second-hand objects—signal the futility of taking refuge in things, objects, the products of a culture which is in any case always reified and economically quantified. Like Hopper's paintings of despair, new silent interlocutors of the voice in the monologue cannot credibly be substituted with real, live listeners. The listener's irretrievable disappearance sets up Stephanie/Wesker's futile search for meaning, which ends in the discovery of theft:

> What am I looking at such paintings for? I'm not lonely and desperate enough? Go out said my friends, visit places. But every place I go reminds me of him, of us, of our young years together. Stolen from me. Poisoned for me. (5:17)

Even the enormous ice cream, an incongruous dessert, ironically echoes yet another depressing sense of its meaning:

> For such large desserts I've got my just deserts—fat and abandoned and growing fatter by the hour. (5:18)

Having been robbed of the illusion of a listener, an empathic solidarity, Wesker's feminine gaze re-designs the objects and assigns them the function of reflecting his own sterile solitude, an abandonment which kills off imagination and forces one to face up to the reification of experience thinned out by consumption: ice creams, books, paintings, objects, love, and writing. In the last three scenes composed similar rhythms, these objects become so many fragments of a small universe which, having been obliterated by abandonment and futility, legitimates theft, indeed rendering it almost desirable:

> Who conceived so many editions? Who were they aimed at? Who's going to buy them for Christ's sake?
> There is something about abundance makes you feel a theft here and there wouldn't be missed. (Beat) What am I saying? Me! A remainder among remainders. (5:18)

Stephanie's voice is by now overshadowed by that of Wesker, a remainder among the remainders. Identified with the anonymous objects along the path to Stephanie's salvation, the voice presents the listener with the disconsolate notion of a culture made from scraps, emblematized by the courtyard where the sale of second-hand objects takes place.

The metaphor of stolen writing and love points to a discarded universe, made up of fragments and pitiful refuse, barely recalling worlds and certainties which have now vanished. The sale, which Stephanie arrives at with anxious punctuality (a reminder of her panic about getting home late at the beginning of the play), is not tended by any owner. As for the objects, the voice of the monologue, indignant about their up-rooting, names them with affection and tries to replace them in their context. The objects offer themselves unprotected and defenseless, as they are by now rejects:

> And what do we have here? A photo album. What kind of
> people throw away their relatives? In fact, come to think of
> it, what kind of people throw away their homes? You come
> to a sale like this and the question must be asked: why is all
> this discarded? Why should I want what someone else has
> discarded? What makes me think I could grow to love what
> someone else has squeezed all the love from? You come to a
> sale like this, the question has got to be asked. (5:19)

Prams, postcards, linen, records, and books make up a heterogeneous store of refuse from old worlds, picked out to make up new worlds at a low cost. All this forms an obvious metaphor for a postmodern and vulgarized consciousness in which the culture of abandonment and excess produces discarding and in which theft becomes "scavenging," a continuous stirring in the rubbish by tramps. The site of the sale, which will never take place, trivializes the sense of betrayal by emphasizing the stereotypes which substantiated it, by pointing to the vain futility of the language used by Stephanie's rival, who "talked Stephanie's husband into thinking he was tired of her," superimposed by the language of Wesker's literary rival who might steal the audience from the author with persuasive words. Both rivals coalesce into one single character, who is eventually presented as the sly expert exploiter of discarded fragments with which new writing full of the surprises desired by Sheldon is composed. Even the author, incarnated by the betrayed protagonist, must finally accept a "second choice" world. Abandoned by its owners, that world can be robbed with impunity because it has been devalued by refuse. Amid tears Stephanie concludes her monologue with a heartfelt and impotent plea for the appearance of an absent interlocutor:

> (*Calling*) Hey, mister! Come already! A half hour I've been
> here. (*Weeping*) I could steal things. (5:21)

Even Wesker, betrayed, robbed, and above all discarded, could be forced into stealing in spite of his own intentions.

∽

ENDNOTES

1. John Drakakis. *British Radio Drama*. Cambridge: Cambridge UP, 1981.

2. *Yardsale* had its stage premiere on August 12, 1985 at the Edinburgh Festival with Jeannie Fisher. Its first London performance was double-billed with *Whatever Happened to Betty Lemon?* on February 17, 1987. It was directed by Arnold Wesker at the Lyric Theatre Studio Hammersmith with Brenda Bruce as Stephanie and Betty Lemon.

3. Arnold Wesker. *One-Woman Plays: Yardsale, Four Portraits—of Mothers, Whatever Happened to Betty Lemon?, The Mistress, Annie Wobbler*. Vol. 5 Hammondsworth: Penguin, 1989.

4. All the quotations from *Yardsale* are taken from this edition of one-woman plays.

5. See, in particular, these statements by the author:

    "Why should an interpreter demand freedom to explore with his own experience the experience of another, when he himself has not taken the trouble to formulate his own experience into a responsible whole. There is about such ideas an element of *scavenging*" (my italics) (Arnold Wesker. *Distinctions*. Jonathan Cape, London 1985:25).
    "It can't be all that pleasant to devote a whole lifetime to earning a living—*scavenger-like* (my italics) from the dead flesh of a living litera-ture which you slaughter. You've made your contributions to the his-tory of theatre journalism. Don't wait for senility to set in and spoil it all" (*ibid.* p. 343).
    "I would like to comment on the censoring of plays by actors and directors round the world who *are scavenging* (my italics) the world of playwrights in order to make their opportunist mark in the theatre" (from an interview of Arnold Wesker by Barbara Lanati for *Panorama—*September 1988).

WORKS CITED

Esslin, Martin. *Meditations. Essays on Brecht, Beckett and the Media*. London: Methuen, 1981.

McLuhan, Marshall. *Understanding Media*. New York: McGraw-Hill, 1964.

Wesker, Arnold. *Distinctions*. London: Jonathan Cape, 1985.

——. *One-Woman Plays: Yardsale, Four Portraits—of Mothers, Whatever Happened to Betty Lemon?, The Mistress, Annie Wobbler.* Vol. 5 Hammondsworth: Penguin, 1989.

III. Historical Perspectives

The Modernity of *The Kitchen*

Kimball King

In a competition for playwrights sponsored by the London *Observer* in 1956, Arnold Wesker submitted a manuscript of *The Kitchen*, his first written work for the theater, which was subsequently rejected by the judges, mostly directors and managers, who read it. Therefore, the former restaurant worker's first work to be staged was *Chicken Soup with Barley*, the initial play in his famous *Trilogy*, which also includes *Roots* and *I'm Talking About Jerusalem*. Subsequently, *The Kitchen* was introduced as a one-act play at the Royal Court's small, experimental stage, Theatre Upstairs, in a Sunday afternoon performance in 1959. Two years later, the Royal Court staged a two-act version of *The Kitchen* for a six weeks' run. In its blend of socialism and humanism *The Kitchen* is thematically related to the Wesker *Trilogy*. However, Wesker in his earliest written theatre piece deliberately avoids the extended character motivation of his later plays and seems less concerned with narrative development and historical context. *The Kitchen* is an avant-garde work which blends many techniques of the absurdists, such as a minimal stage set, pantomime, elliptical and layered dialogue, and unexpected violence.

While I consider the Wesker *Trilogy* to be a brilliant and subtle work in its convincing psychological portrayals, complex intermingling of narratives, and strong ideological content, it is a more traditional blend of twentieth-century naturalism and realism than *The Kitchen*. The latter is a startling dramatic moment with poetic resonances.

In his youth Wesker was described by some English critics as an Angry Young Man like John Osborne. Others thought he was an old-fashioned socialist, a working-class writer, or a Jewish writer. Reade Dornan believes his strength lies in his particular blend of socialism and Jewish humanism, a faith in the old adage, "Love thy neighbor as thyself" and a champion of the individual, anti-authoritarian spirit (15–16).

Yet Alan Sinfield in *Society and Literature* virtually accuses Wesker of "resignation" to society's ills, suggesting that his defeated characters and their lost dreams are indeed a continuing fact of modern existence. Thus Sinfield, places Wesker closer to Samuel Beckett in his "hopeless" view of the human condition and contrasts him to advocates of change in the theater like David Mercer or John Arden (Sinfield 182–83).

Opposing Sinfield's view of a "defeated" Wesker, Heiner Zimmermann has argued that, unlike the nihilistic absurdists of the 1950s and 1960s, Wesker attempts to present a utopian view of life. In a rather intellectually cynical and discouraged era, Wesker stands alone as a champion of a society that deserves to exist. For example, Zimmermann, claiming that Wesker "advocates a revival of Utopian ideal" (186), describes the characters of *The Kitchen* in terms of their yearning for a society more sensitive to their needs. Dimitri, the Cypriot kitchen porter yearns for a "more creative job," and Michael, a young cook, seeks "a place of work closer to nature." In fact, Peter, the fish cook and main character, commits an anarchistic deed of despair when he explodes the line to the gas ovens. He "challenges fateful inevitability" and he "opens the possibility of an alternative" (Zimmermann 193). Most interestingly, Zimmermann concludes that the socialist Wesker believes that a true paradise contains "competition, ambition, struggle" (203), creating an overview of a playwright who refuses to resign himself to the world in its present condition.

While Wesker has preferred to call himself a "naturalist" (Morgan 31), Margery Morgan suggests that *The Kitchen* is in fact, an expressionistic work, although she acknowledges that the play's first director, John Dexter, may well have insisted on its "precisely drilled routines" (Morgan 42). Morgan emphasizes that "the collaboration at the Royal Court theatre between playwright, actors and directors fortuitously represented such a wedding of literature to stage practice as is necessary to all outstanding periods of dramatic history" (Morgan 42). She adds that in *The Kitchen* "the frenzied movement on a crowded stage—human bodies working together like the parts of a machine...[creates a]...vivid...image of industrial man's world" (Morgan 43).

Dornan, Sinfield, Zimmermann and Morgan emphasize very different characteristics of Wesker's work in *The Kitchen*, regarding him, respectively, as socialist-humanist, passive nihilist, utopian socialist, and romantic expressionist. Their varied reactions to the author's purposes illustrate his postmodern elusiveness. Wesker provides a series of apparent "truths" which are nevertheless contradictory, one insight undermining the assumption of another.

Although both Wesker and John Osborne belonged to the first wave of writers whose plays were examples of the flowering of the Royal Court Theatre in the late 1950s and early 1960s, the writer of *The Kitchen* is careful to distinguish between his own style and Osborne's. In Wesker's lengthy autobiography, *Arnold Wesker: As Much as I Dare*, Wesker implies that Osborne's early success with *Look Back in Anger* won for him a celebrity status somewhat daunting to his contemporaries at the Court, and by referring to Ionesco as "one of John Osborne's dreaded French writers" (Wesker 537), Wesker implies that he was himself more favorably disposed toward the theatricality of the French absurdist. Interestingly, too, Wesker, who praised Jocelyn Herbert for her stage designs for *Roots*, notes that previously Herbert had created a set for *The Chairs*. In *The Chairs*, the principal characters who are designated merely "Old Man" and "Old Woman" supervise the seating of a lecture attended by imaginary guests. Their pantomimed gestures become increasingly agitated as the audience is led to believe the lecture hall is bursting to capacity. Such a movement of characters (both real and imagined) in a small space resembles the feverish bustle of the large cast in *The Kitchen*, particularly at the fateful evening meal. Jocelyn Herbert once again designed a setting for Wesker when *The Kitchen* was presented in 1960. She credits *The Kitchen* for helping her discover her original style: "*The Kitchen* pointed me in the direction not of minimalism, that's the wrong word—but of provoking the audience to think for themselves and use their imagination" (Wesker, *As Much as I Dare* 538).

The abstract—absurd, if you will—quality of *The Chairs* apparently held no appeal for Osborne. While it would be far-fetched to call Ionesco an influence on Wesker, Wesker was surely vulnerable to the French playwright's continental whimsy. The mimed gestures of the cooks as they shape pastries and chop vegetables and the waiters bearing trays of empty plates to customers hidden from view, place *The Kitchen* more in a continental than English tradition.

Although the title of Wesker's first play linked it by implication to the "kitchen-sink" school of playwriting, which most frequently has been described as working-class naturalism, *The Kitchen*'s set design includes ovens, but not a sink, as major props. In contrast to Osborne's *Look Back in Anger*, which preceded and overshadowed Wesker's play, *The Kitchen* is clearly focused on working class life but its dialogue, setting, and action are not naturalistic by any traditional definition. There are far too many minor characters to permit naturalistic dialogue in the tradition of Chekhov. Fragments of speech are interrupted by the physical labors of the actors, are frequently "layered" so that one must choose and follow a single thread of conversation, and occasionally the technique produces absurd results (as Reade Dornan has pointed out).[1] There is only the visual suggestion of a restaurant's kitchen counter and serving space; we never see any customers; the plates are empty, and the hum of the ovens is portentously symbolic, more expressionistic than believable.[2] finally, the playwright insists in a note that the cooks "will mime their cooking" (2:10), that no actual food is seen as prepared and that the pacing of the actors becomes increasingly frenetic, building to the crescendo of violence which concludes the play. Even the uniforms of the restaurant staff make the characters more interchangeable and symbolic of workers in general than of individuals. Jimmy Porter and Cliff in *Look Back in Anger*, as well as Alison and Helena, dress in a manner that locates them in a social hierarchy. Porter's wearing boxer shorts on stage may have scandalized audiences in 1956, but his attire is appropriate for a rebellious (and physically fit) young working man lounging in his own flat. Alison's ironing board is real, and she actually presses Jimmy's clothing on stage rather then miming the activity. Cause-and-effect conversations take place as Jimmy's acrid pronouncements goad Alison into making statements which he, in turn, will ridicule.

Perhaps to bourgeois audiences trained to hear the educated speech and to see the more elegant costumes of pre-war salons, both Osborne's and Wesker's plays offered the same opportunity to view a segment of society foreign to theatre (and often their own) experience. Yet as Dornan has noted, Osborne despite his antipathy to the rich was not a working-class playwright, and the Porters' marriage, a union of an alienated university graduate and the genteel daughter of a retired civil servant is a sado-masochistic game about two people choosing a lowly social status rather than a comment on everyday relationships among the poor.

Look Back in Anger for all its innovative vitality and snarling has a somewhat conventional plot, including a symmetrical relationship between Alison and her social peer, Helena, who replaces her temporarily in Jimmy's affections; a minor character, Cliff, who unsuccessfully acts as a buffer between the antagonists; a miscarriage which is a long-time secret; and a tentative, last-minute reconciliation between husband and wife. *The Kitchen*, on the other hand, is relatively plotless, and the unstable young German cook's destructive attack on the gas lead to the ovens is only partly a reaction to his frustrating love affair and is more likely the unexpected result of circumstances he never fully understands and which the audience only comprehends in retrospect.

In his stage directions Wesker specifies that the initial action of his play is the night-porter's lighting of the gas ovens and notes that "as he lights each oven, the noise grows from a small to a loud, ferocious roar. There will be this continuous babble between the dialogue and the noise of the ovens"(13). These authorial directions compare to O'Neill's description of the furnace which fires the engines of Yank's steamship in *The Hairy Ape*:

> ...there is a tumult of noise—the brazen clang of the furnace doors as they are flung open or slammed shut, the grunting, teeth-gritting grind of steel against steel, of crunching coal. The clash of sounds stuns one's ears with its rending dissonance...the roar of the leaping flames of the furnace, the monotonous throbbing beat of the engines. (1)

In both plays, technology is viewed as a potential enemy to the working man, overpowering him and trapping him in a dehumanizing existence. O'Neill did not learn Marxist principles from an articulate communist mother like Wesker's, but the atavism of Yank, O'Neill's "hairy ape," and the near-bestiality of Yank's co-workers as well as his satirical disdain for the guilt-ridden capitalist socialite, Mildred Douglas (a self- proclaimed "waste-product of the Bessemer process") have tempted more than one critic to view *The Hairy Ape* as a political statement. In fact, a striking production of this 1922 classic mounted by the (East) Berliner Ensemble in England's National Theatre (a short while prior to the breakdown of the Berlin wall), presented a classic Marxist interpretation of the American playwright's expressionistic tour de force.[3]

However, O'Neill was not politically sophisticated, and the aesthetic impetus of the New York Armory exhibit of expressionist painting in 1915 contributed more to the playwright's conception of his *Hairy Ape* than any social philosophy.

Nevertheless, Wesker, who had clearly structured *The Kitchen* as a metaphor for society with its workers and managers, also created a play which is more effective as an expressionistic piece, and so it has been staged by Ariane Mnouchkine (France) Koichi Kermera (Japan) and John Dexter (England).

Contrasting Wesker to two American playwrights whose careers made a significant impact on the theatre of the 1930's, Lillian Hellman and Clifford Odets, reveals the modernity of Wesker's dramaturgy. All these playwrights share a Jewish background and have been influenced by Marxist philosophy. However, Wesker's plays are distinctly more modern than his "predecessors'" in America. For the most part Hellman's techniques resemble Ibsen's, and her plays are classically "well made." They are based on sequential action, the revelation of secrets, and they contain elaborate exposition and a symmetrical structure. For example, in Hellman's *The Little Foxes* (1939), a "good" daughter and her principled father are contrasted to a manipulative, greedy mother and her unscrupulous brothers. Regina, a strong woman, overshadows her high-born but weak sister-in-law, Birdie. (Gentle but ineffectual aristocrats are no match for rapacious upstarts.) When Regina discovers her nephew's embezzlement, she blackmails her brothers into submitting to her business plans, but the play ends with the suggestion that her brother, Ben, may, in turn, blackmail Regina for having deliberately withheld medicine from her dying husband. Odets's plays are somewhat more loosely plotted than Hellman's. A rationale of political action is built up in progressively purposeful dialogue, which leads to the taxi strike in *Waiting for Lefty* and the creation of a social hero in *Awake and Sing!*, both written in 1935. Odets provides us with the believable dialogue of urban American Jews in the 1930s, but the construction of his theatre pieces varies little from other political writers who share his conventional fourth-wall technique.

By contrast, Wesker is a product of post–World War II theatrical sensibilities. Not only Osborne's explosive *Look Back in Anger* with its raw emotions but also the absurdism of Beckett and Ionesco blend curiously with Anglo-Saxon naturalism. Both Harold Pinter in

England and Edward Albee in America share this same mixture of symbolic exaggerated action and earthy, everyday detail. In his auto-biography Wesker notes that Ann Jellicoe and N.F. Simpson, fellow Royal Court dramatists of the era, were writing plays with strong absurdist elements. He says he believes Pinter, on the other hand, "seemed to me a naturalist who wrote about the absurd" (514). Wesker himself appears to be a naturalist capable of incorporating hints of the absurdist style into his work.

Glenda Leeming and Simon Trussler have observed that the char-acters in Wesker's plays "can only live in the kitchen"(28). In the same way Ionesco's characters in *The Chairs* appear to have no life outside the empty lecture where they and their imaginary guests await the deaf-mute orator. At the play's conclusion, the Old Man and his wife jump out of windows. While some may see a bitter comic irony in the suicide of nonagenarians, I believe the couple have merely jumped from the stage set. Their only "life" is their participation in a non-event. Outside the room they cease to exist. Similarly, one recalls the conclusion of Tom Stoppard's *Rosencrantz and Guildenstern Are Dead*. The two anti-heroes step off the stage rather than "die" as their proto-types in *Hamlet* had done. Rosencrantz whispers "now you see me, now you—" and disappears(126). For characters like Rosencrantz and Guildenstern, the stage provides their only opportunity to exist.

The action of *The Kitchen* is presented straightforwardly. In a London restaurant called the Tivoli a large and busy staff of cooks, waiters, and porters prepares first for the noon meal and later for supper as the restaurant's owner and manager supervise operations. There is a descending hierarchy within the staff—from the owner to the cooks to the waiters and finally the porters. Peter, the fish cook, and Paul, the pastry cook, have the largest speaking roles. Peter, a German, is the lover of one of the waitresses, Monique, who is preg-nant with his child (again, we are told) yet married to another man. All of the play's characters, save owner Mr. Marango, lament the te-dium of their jobs, which they consider unimportant and unreward-ing. Paul, who is Jewish, philosophical, and articulate is probably a spokesman for the playwright, decrying the self-centeredness and political apathy of his neighbors and co-workers. Various scenes in-volve bigotry toward minority workers, petty grumblings, and veiled hostilities in the work force, waitresses overworked and additionally burdened with unwanted pregnancies. Peter continually argues with

Monique not to abort their child and to leave her husband. But her husband has promised her he will buy a house, and ultimately she rebuffs Peter. This personal frustration added to his general discontent with his job drives him to an act of violence so that he destroys the lead to the ovens that are cooking the evening meal. As the restaurant is evacuated, the owner complains that he is a fair employer who doesn't deserve disloyal and destructive workers:

> Why does everybody sabotage me...I give work, I pay well, yes? They eat what they want, don't they? I don't know what more to give a man. He works, he eats. I give him money. This is life, isn't it? (2:78)

Robert Wilcher believes the conclusion of *The Kitchen* "reverberates with...general and political significance" (31), and Leeming and Trussler consider the activities in the restaurant kitchen to be a "dramatic metaphor for industrial capitalist society" (31), implying that rebellion against a confining—and dehumanizing—society is inevitable and that Wesker's play proffers strong warnings of imminent social upheavals. Of course, it is impossible for audiences after World War II to see a backdrop of gas-fired ovens without recalling the Holocaust, the supreme example of man's inhumanity to man. Humanism and Marxism vie for the playwright's attention, and he hints at man's terrible capacity to destroy himself.

True, Wesker clearly illustrates the dangers of a society which neglects the myriad yearnings of its people, but he does not suggest that such disregard of the "immaterial" is exclusive to capitalism. In an age when few families employ personal servants, the service industry, as it is called (restaurant workers, cleaning services, shop clerks, etc.) provide a new type of "servant" that Wesker astutely observes. But it is a mistake to believe he singles out capitalism as the sole evil. Mr. Marango, though obtuse in his way, is a fair and honest man. He truly wants to know what more people expect of him. Interestingly, he is not a member of the traditional English establishment but an entrepreneur from an ethnic and uneducated background. The dilemma of *The Kitchen* is not easily resolved. Audiences are left with tentative, existential questions. For Wesker a system worth sustaining must combine humanity with practical politics. He is sufficiently realistic to understand the problematic nature of social harmony. The playwright's earliest work reflects the contradictory nature of experience and the unreliability of "definitive" interpretations. It combines stark, naturalistic prose with expressionistic background devices and dark metaphorical actions; its humor often derives from juxtapositions which create an aura of absurdity. *The Kitchen*, therefore, becomes a lightning rod of twentieth-century theater, attracting and dispersing powerful currents.

❧

ENDNOTES

1. Dornan points out the droll non-sequiturs produced by commingling personal and professional talk in a conversation between Peter and Monique. Peter (tenderly): "Listen, do you want to know where I went this afternoon? To buy your birthday present." Monique: "A present?" Winnie (to Hans): "One veal cutlet." Winnie (to Kevin): "Two plaice" (71).

2. This contrasts with *Roots*, the second play of the Wesker *Trilogy*, where the setting's naturalism is emphasized by the sight and smell of real liver and onions cooking on a stove.

3. This production was filled with ironies, both intentional and unintentional. The play was performed in German so that one of the few English-speaking roles was given to the German sailor. financing for the Ensemble's attack on capitalism was provided by Mercedes-Benz Inc., the motorcar company which symbolizes for many capitalistic excess. And at the close of a limited engagement, the elaborate multi-million pound set was dismantled and sold as scrap metal.

WORKS CITED

Dornan, Reade W. *Arnold Wesker Revisited*. Boston: Twayne Publishers, 1994.

Herbert, Jocelyn. *A Theatre Workbook*. London: Art Books International, 1993.

Leeming, Glenda, and Simon Trussler. *The Plays of Arnold Wesker: An Assessment*. London: Gollancz, 1971.

Morgan, Margery. "The Celebratory Instinct," in *Essays on Contemporary British Drama*, ed. Hedwig Bock and Albert Wertheim. Munich: Max Hueber, 1981.

O'Neill, Eugene. *The Hairy Ape, Anna Christie, The First Man.* New York: Boni and Liveright, 1927.

Sinfield, Alan. *Society and Literature. 1944–1970.* London: Holmes and Meier, 1983.

Stoppard, Tom. *Rosencrantz and Guildenstern are Dead.* New York: Grove Press, 1967.

Wesker, Arnold. *As Much as I Dare: An Autobiography.* London: Century, 1984.

——. *The Kitchen.* Penguin, Vol. 2, 1976 reprinted with revisions in 1990.

Wilcher, Robert. *Understanding Arnold Wesker.* Columbia: Univ. of South Carolina Press, 1990.

Zimmermann, Heiner. "Wesker and Utopia in the Sixties." *Modern Drama* 29 (1986): 185–206.

Wesker's One-Woman Plays as Part of a Popular Tradition

Margaret Rose

The present essay aims at placing Wesker's cycle of one-woman plays[1] in a tradition of one-person sketches and plays, which take their starting point in the popular entertainment of illegitimate theater during the late eighteenth century. Later monologistic forms, which come closer to being plays, were performed in both illegitimate and legitimate theater. The earliest monologue sketches were written by men for male characters; only in the second part of the nineteenth century did women writers join their male colleagues, and subsequently both male and female characters took center stage.

The tradition I am concerned with is, of course, a very different one from that in which Beckett's one-person plays are to be situated.[2] In the case of Beckett, the disintegration of dialogue and the isolation of the individual derive from radical changes which came about at the end of the nineteenth century with the symbolist theatre movement. On another level, Beckett's monologue plays represent modern-day soliloquys, or, as Enoch Brater has perceptively noted, they come closer to being performance poems than drama, given their emphasis on diegesis rather than mimesis.[3]

The following chronology represents a brief account of a heavily fragmented history.[4] Popular entertainment has been traditionally deemed an inferior theatrical form, unworthy of academic analysis, and only in recent decades has this attitude begun to change. In the latter part of the chronology, history becomes a herstory of women writers and performers, whose work has likewise tended to be neglected by academic criticism.

Probably the earliest show that came near to being a one-man play—*The Diversions of the Morning*[5]—was written and devised by Samuel Foote (1720–77) and performed in 1747 at the Little Theatre in the Haymarket, London. In order to avoid the restrictions of the Licensing Act, this actor-dramatist combined a number of sketches with music. Foote, with the help of a couple of actors in minor roles, interpreted a series of monologue sketches, satirizing real-life characters, such as a quack doctor, the Chevalier Taylor; a popular educator, the Orator Henley; an auctioneer, Christopher Cock; and a magistrate, Thomas De Veil.

Alexander Stephens (1710–84), an actor with Garrick's Company, created a remarkable one-man show, entitled "The Lecture on Heads," first performed at the Little Theatre, April 30, 1774.[6] It proved an enormous success, having more than a thousand performances in Great Britain alone. Stephens also traveled to the United States and around the world, where his show was so popular that it was pirated, adapted, and revised. Like *The Diversions*, Stephens' sketches are satirical in tone, with their satire aimed at both historical figures and well-known personalities from contemporary society. Two hundred years before Wesker used dummies in *The Mistress*, Stephens employed a number of busts. These were placed on a table at the side of the stage, and with each sketch, Stephens brought forward the appropriate bust, with which he interacted, exploiting his ventriloquist's skills.

Charles Mathews (1776–1835) enjoyed two successful careers since he was a well-known actor in legitimate theaters, such as Drury Lane and Covent Garden, where he worked with leading figures, like Edmund Kean and Charles Kemble. He also performed his own one-man shows in London and around the country. In 1808 he made his debut with the one-man show, *The Mail Coach Adventure*, which premiered in Hull and then had a second production at the New English Opera House, in London, in 1817.

Mathews created a more complex dramatic structure than that of his predecessors by dividing the show into three sections: parts one and two were entitled "table acts" and "sequences with music and narrative," and the third part, "monopolylogues." The last part is particularly interesting for the development of the monologue play, since structurally speaking the "monopolylogue" resembles a farce with a simple plot of absurd adventure, development and various characters.[7] Mathews, moreover, interpreted the different roles—both male and female—exploiting his talent as a ventriloquist to create the illusion of different characters both onstage and offstage.

Mathews's *A Trip to Paris*, a series of rapidly paced character impersonations, is held together by the simple story of an Englishman's trip to the French capital. The work ridicules the Gallomania rife in eighteenth-century England. Unlike his predecessors, Mathews adopted a variety of costumes and realistic scenery for his "monopolylogues": a real diligence was placed onstage in *A Trip to Paris.* Another innovative work was *Mr. Mathews's Memorandum Book* (1825), in which Mathews tells the heavily fragmented tale—without a strict chronology—of his own life, inventing a number of minor characters.

The first woman to devise and perform a one-woman show was the actress and opera singer, Frances Maria Kelly (1790–1882). When she retired from a distinguished stage career in 1835, she diversified by founding a drama school for women, in Dean Street, Soho. With the help of song writer, John Hamilton Reynolds, she also created a one-woman show, comprising songs and sketches. *Dramatic Recollections and Studies of Character* was first staged at the Royalty Theatre, London, in 1841. In the work Kelly impersonated a number of female characters, who are listed in the playbill as follows: Miss Betty Rattle (a desirable inmate for unfurnished apartments), Mademoiselle Jejeune (a governess and aspiring actress), and Mrs. Parthian (as well as her memory serves her). The sketch, entitled *Mrs. Parthian,* is particularly interesting since Kelly ingeniously combined autobiography and invented facts. In the show, Kelly took center stage as Mrs. Parthian, an aging actress, but also interpreted minor characters from the protagonist's past and present, whose stories are anecdotal and gossipy.

Beatrice Herford (1868–1952) divided her time between writing, acting and directing her own monologue plays.[8] She made her stage debut at the Salle Herard in London in 1895 and enjoyed an immediate success. Leading figures of the day, such as George Bernard Shaw, William Archer, Ellen Terry, and Henry James, appreciated Herford's talent. She moved to America in 1895, and in 1904 she founded her own theater, the Vokes Theatre, in Wayland, where she regularly performed her repertoire.

Herford is to be considered the pioneer of a new genre "the one-woman play."[9] Differently from the sketches previously described, she developed a single female protagonist. Her women are realistically depicted and come from all walks of life. Herford practiced a gentle satire concerning all forms of hypocrisy and human foibles.

Herford's plays in miniature possess the basic elements of drama having a minimum of plot, development, action, interaction, conflict, and pseudo-dialogue. She innovated in the area of language by creating clipped dialogue, in which the monologuing protagonist is "interrupted" by invisible characters, whose lines are indicated in the script by a series of dots. The high-society lady in *Piazza Ladies* is seen outside a hotel talking to a large, albeit invisible, company. The spectator is therefore called upon to imagine what the other women are saying in the pauses. Herford used a minimum of costumes and scenery, relying on her skill to create the protagonist and the invisible characters, through carefully planned movements and gestures as well as her extremely versatile vocal range.

The American Ruth Draper (1884–1956) took her one-woman shows on frequent tours to Britain and the rest of Europe.[10] She insisted that she was a character actress and a writer of miniature dramas as opposed to a *diseuse*, mimic, or impersonator as early critics labelled her. Draper warmly acknowledged Herford's influence on her work but at the same time created a more complex dramatic form in her own plays.

Draper's dramas in miniature travel a wide range of emotions from tragic to comic, with the creation of fairly complex female characters who are involved in a sustained dramatic action, marked by conflict, development, and a climax. The Miner's wife in the homonymous play is shown courageously coping with her hard life in a Scottish mining village, while, at the end, she is seen waiting for her husband who has been trapped down the mine. She uses her sharp sense of humor to deal with what are tragic circumstances.

Like Wesker later, Draper divided many of her plays into sections, with a different protagonist in each: *Three Women and Mr. Clifford* contains three female roles, while *In a Church in Italy* has five parts. Draper concentrates on a single theme, moreover, which is explored from different points of view.

Draper's women are realistically depicted and come from a range of social backgrounds and countries. The women are usually involved in a realistic action like the secretary in *Three Women and Mr. Clifford* who is seen busily working in Clifford's office as she answers the phone, talks to her boss, and deals with the mail. The dramatic language is wide ranging and perfectly characterizes the protagonist. Draper innovatively used foreign languages within the same play (in *A Church in Italy*, the German, the two Italians, the British and American woman, all speak in their mother tongue).

The clipped dialogue invented by Herford is also present in Draper. The stage is therefore populated with invisible characters who interact and enter into conflict with the protagonist(s). In *Three Women and Mr. Clifford*, each of the three women, in the three consecutive monologues, interact with the invisible Mr. Clifford, while the play reaches a climax through the conflictual situation between him and his wife.

Joyce Grenfell (1910–1979), a distant cousin of Draper's and a great admirer of the older woman, produced a number of one-woman shows featuring what can be best defined as monologue sketches, given their brevity and the limited development of the central character.[11] Like the previous one-man shows, Grenfell combined these sketches with songs and music.

Grenfell was a gentle satirist, a role which is well described in her obituary "a gently mocking and affectionately amused commentator on English manners and social customs." Grenfell's women are often English eccentrics whose monologues touch upon the absurd. In *English Lit*, the Vice Chancellor's wife relates a fanciful tale about her grandmother's passion for a small squirrel whom she believes to be a reincarnation of a distant cousin, and, at the same time, she keeps a conversation going with a television producer who is interviewing her.

Grenfell depicted lower-class women, too, like the village mother in *Mothers* who relates the tale of her son's illness, in language colored by dialect, suggesting the "earthiness" of this particular human scene. In the tale, the woman represents her own voice as well as that of her son's, so bringing the story of his illness vividly into the present.

With the cycle of one-woman plays, Wesker continues to show his faith in the realist mode—albeit of a stylized kind—which links his plays to the popular tradition. Like his eighteenth- and nineteenth-century precursors, he sometimes bases his protagonists on real-life characters: Annie Wobbler (in *Annie Wobbler*) was inspired by a washing woman his family employed in the thirties. On the other hand, he has said that Betty (protagonist of *Whatever Happened to Betty Lemon?*) is an older female version of himself, linking this play to the autobiographical tradition mentioned with respect to Mathews and Kelly.

As in the popular tradition, Wesker creates female characters whose social class, education, and linguistic register make them readily identifiable figures in contemporary society. Wesker's females are ordinary women, who are most frequently middle class, like Samantha (*The Mistress*) or Ruth (*Four Portraits of Mothers*), and less often working class, like Annie Wobbler and Betty Lemon. They live out their monologistic hour, moreover, in settings— invariably rooms—which clearly signal their social status. Samantha's workshop indicates her profession, while Betty's kitchen cum-sitting-room in an Edwardian mansion flat shows she has climbed the social ladder and become a member of the middle class.

Wesker is the exponent of a tragi-comic style which is found in Ruth Draper and Grenfell (to a lesser degree), whose female characters possess a strong sense of humor and irony which help them to face the direst of circumstances. All the mothers, with the exception of Deborah, in *Four Portraits of Mothers* are unhappy and frustrated, but keep going thanks to their sense of humor.

Like Draper before him, Wesker has been insistent that his solo works are plays as opposed to monologues. They are, he has said, "plays for one performer" which feature "a person responding to a situation or involved in an action and engaged in an exchange of conflict." Here Wesker mentions the elements of situation, action, interaction, and conflict which are basic ingredients of drama with more than one character. This represents another important link with Herford, Draper, and Grenfell, where emphasis is on mimesis as opposed to diegesis.

Situation and action are carefully planned in Wesker's one-woman plays: we watch Betty going through her morning routine of collecting the newspaper and post and making her morning coffee. That particular morning she is busy preparing the speech she has been asked to make at the award ceremony which will honor her with the title of "Handicapped Woman of the Year"; we are shown Samantha at work in her atelier while waiting for a phone call from her lover. Interaction may occur on various levels given the absence of other characters: the protagonist may engage with others who are offstage (Ruth talks and interacts with her daughter who is offstage); with invisible people on stage (in an interview about her latest book, Miriam, a writer, talks to an invisible journalist [*Annie Wobbler*]); with inanimate objects onstage (Betty to her wheelchair and noose or Samantha to her tailor's dummies).

Even in Wesker's one-woman plays, dramatic language still seems to represent a way of building bridges as Beatie Bryant defined it in *Roots*. Like his precursors in the present study, Wesker has created a kind of pseudo-dialogue which allows the character to interact with others and may also create conflict. Betty Lemon, for example, represents a polyphony of voices which animate the reported dialogues from her past life, and in the process she enters into conflict with the people from her past. At other times, Wesker's characters talk on the phone (Naomi in *Four Portraits*) or to offstage characters (Ruth in *Four Portraits*), or to inanimate objects (Betty's wheelchair and noose), inviting the spectator to imagine the implied passages of the pseudo-dialogue.

From the above discussion, Wesker can be seen to be a late twentieth-century proponent of what is essentially a popular tradition dating back to the late eighteenth century. An important step in the development of one-woman plays was taken when a woman first took center stage with Frances Maria Kelly's *Dramatic Recollections and Studies of Character*. Subsequently, women like Herford, Draper, and Grenfell continued and developed the one-woman form.

While the one-woman play has continued in the work of women dramatists in the late twentieth century—Pam Gems, Nina Rapi, Sue Frumin, Janet Cresswell, Niki Johnson, Berta Freistadt, and Franca Rame are just a few of the better-known names—Wesker stands as an important male exponent of this dramatic form in miniature.

℮ℨ

ENDNOTES

1. Wesker's one-woman plays (*Yardsale, Whatever Happened to Betty Lemon?, Four Portraits of Mothers, The Mistress* and *Annie Wobbler*) are published in Volume 5, London: Penguin, 1989.

2. For Beckett's one-person plays see Samuel Beckett, *The Collected Shorter Plays by Samuel Beckett.* London: Faber and Faber, 1984.

3. Enoch Brater, *Beyond Minimalism, Beckett's Later Style in the Theatre.* London and New York: Oxford University Press, 3.

4. I am indebted to Barbara Castelnuovo and Alexandra Mossi for their valuable help in my research on the popular tradition.

5.   Two Acts of *The Diversions* can be found in Tate Wilkinson, *Wandering Patentee*, vol.. 1, York: 1795: 285–298.

6.   *The Lecture on Heads* was first published in Dublin, 1765. The text is re-published in Gerald Kahan, *George Alexander Stephens and "The Lecture on Heads."* Athens: Univ. of Georgia Press, 1984.

7.   Richard Klepac, *Mr. Mathews at Home*. London: The Society for Theatre Research, 1979.

8.   Beatrice Herford's monologue plays are collected in two volumes: *Monologues*. London: Scribner and Son, 1908; and *Beatrice Herford's Monologues*. New York: Samuel French, 1937.

9.   For details concerning Beatrice Herford's life and works, see *The Historical Files*, held at the Vokes Theatre, Wayland, Massachusetts.

10.   See Morton Daubel Zabel, *The Art of Ruth Draper. Her Drama and Characters*, London: Oxford Univ. Press, 1960. The volume includes a long essay on Draper's life and works and thirty-five of her character dramas. Draper's letters (*The Letters of Ruth Draper*, ed. Nella Warren, foreword by Sir John Gielgud, London: Hamish Hamilton, 1979) provide a wealth of information concerning Draper. For further details about Draper, see Iris Origo, *A Need to Testify*, London: John Murray, 1984; and Muriel McKenna, "The Art of Ruth Draper," in Helen Chinoy and Linda Jenkins, eds., *Women in American Theatre*, New York: Theatre Communications Group, 1987, pp. 114–19.

11.   For details of Joyce Grenfell's life and works, see the three volumes of autobiography: *Joyce Grenfell Requests the Pleasure*, London: Macmillan, 1976; *In Pleasant Places*, London: Futura Books, 1979; *The Time of My Life*, edited and introduced by James Roose Evans, London: Coronet Books, Hodder and Stoughton, 1989.

Histories of the New Left
Arnold Wesker and the Angrier Young Men
Meenakshi Ponnuswami

Without revisiting the specific ideological debates between Arnold Wesker and later socialist playwrights of the 1960s and without attempting to assess the exact extent of Wesker's "influence" upon those playwrights, this essay will offer some suggestions for ways to reconsider the factional divisions within postwar socialist theatres in Britain. Wesker is usually associated with the "first wave" of postwar British theatre, which is said to have emerged after John Osborne's *Look Back in Anger* was performed in 1956—Wesker's comment that he saw Osborne's play and "immediately went home and wrote *Chicken Soup*" is frequently quoted. He is therefore typically grouped with such playwrights as Harold Pinter, John Arden and Margaretta D'Arcy, Edward Bond, David Mercer, and Osborne himself, that is, with those whose articulation of dissent is understood to have paved the way for an angrier, more radical "generation" (a term inappropriate not only because it describes writers who were born within ten years of one another). A central line of contention between these two waves of postwar dramatists appears to have been drawn between those who argued, like Wesker, for a cultural revolution in which "high art" would be made available to working-class audiences and those others who questioned the politics of such a program, drawing attention to the elitism and paternalism of its assumption that working-class communities suffer from cultural deprivations. With the exception of Arden/D'Arcy and, to a lesser extent, Bond, the earlier generation is often, and often erroneously, alleged to have produced formally conventional plays, to have been susceptible to ideological compromise and fuzziness and to have been inadequately concerned with historical or material contexts. The later and more politically explicit generation, on the other hand, is said to have challenged all aspects of contemporary culture and politics, to have sought new audiences and new ways to address those audiences, and to have formulated new strategies with which to confront the contemporary crisis of spectacle and representation: these would include Howard Brenton, David Hare, David Edgar, Trevor Griffiths, John McGrath, Caryl Churchill, and the myriad of artists and groups which constituted the socialist theatre's avant-garde from the mid-1960s onwards.[1] The apparent polarity of these positions, however, masks significant ideological continuities between the New and Newer Left, between those who were mobilized in 1956 and those who were first politicized, often while at University, in 1968.[2] By tracing some of these continuities, I propose to suggest there may be some new ways of contextualizing Wesker's work.

I will focus particularly on the historical drama of postwar socialist theatres, and hence on Wesker's *Trilogy*, because it is in the New Left's rewriting of history that its ideological negotiations are at once most visible, heterogeneous, and unpredictable. Only a year before the pivotal Prague Spring of 1968, Stuart Hall, E.P. Thompson, and Raymond Williams suggested in *The New Left May Day Manifesto*— a document which Wesker signed—that the fragmentation and subsequent regrouping of the British Left in the aftermath of 1956 had evoked a "sense of failure—a new kind of failure, in apparent victory" (Bull 6). An important consequence of such self-criticism seems to have been a renewed interest in the history of British socialism, particularly in the evolution of radical consciousness and collective mobilization. As Alan Sinfield has observed, attempts to find examples of authentic indigenous resistance had been launched by historians in the 1940s but later "had the advantage" of allowing communist historians to evade "the embarrassment of Stalinism." New Left historians therefore sought to "uncover...a story of utopian ideals and resistance to oppression that predated the Soviet revolution" (237–38).

Both the New Left's "sense of failure" and its resulting critical retrospection are reflected in post-1956 theatrical reconfigurations of the English history play. Like Russian agitational propaganda of the 1920s and workers' theatres of the Depression, New Left theatres have recognized that the interrogation, reconstruction, and redistribution of knowledge, particularly of historical knowledge, are central goals in oppositional cultural production. Although postwar historical drama has often looked to the past to find inspirational narratives of working-class agency, the New Left's analysis of *contemporary* history has more typically been characterized by what Kobena Mercer

has provocatively called a "mood of mourning and melancholia" (424).
As John Bull has convincingly argued, the avant-garde theatre of the
60s and 70s "was more a product of [Left] despair" than a manifestation of the radical political consciousness which was, by the late 70s,
disappearing "with more than a suspicion of a whimper" (8–10).
Narratives of the inevitable compromising of Left idealism and criticism of Left opportunism and hypocrisy have therefore been vastly
popular among New Left playwrights.

It is here that the lasting effects of Wesker's *Trilogy* seem to be
most clearly visible. The narrative of Left history in *Chicken Soup
with Barley* (pf. 1958) and *I'm Talking About Jerusalem* (pf. 1960)
legitimates the utopian fervor of postwar socialisms at the same time
that it grimly details the betrayal of such idealism by socialist ortho-
doxy, by the new imperialisms of the Soviet state, and, ironically, by
disillusioned young socialists themselves. Thus, when *Chicken Soup*
opens in 1936, the youthful idealism and energy of Dave Simmonds
and Ada Kahn is able to fuel and revitalize an older generation of
socialist activists, but this promise for a viable future socialism in
England is seen to be destroyed by the war. By 1946, Ada lashes out
at what she perceives as the inadequacies of her mother's political
philosophy, specifically at Sarah's unshakable faith in "an industrial
society":

> You have *never* cried against the jungle of an industrial
> society. You've never wanted to destroy its *values*—sim-
> ply to own them yourselves. It only seemed a crime to
> you that a man spent all his working hours in front of a
> machine because he did not own that machine. (1:43)[3]

Here, Ada challenges the conventional socialist formulation of proletarian control of the means of production by questioning its faith in
industrialism. Her reaction seems in part to be predicated on her
wartime experience of working-class life, which she dismisses conde-
scendingly as six years of "auditing books and working with young
girls who are…lipsticked, giggling morons" (1:42). Questioning the
narrowness of the received socialist conceptualization of "progress" as
well as its conviction in working-class self-consciousness or agency,
Ada projects a personal alternative, a retreat into the pastoral (the
history of which adventure Wesker initiates in the last scenes of *Chicken
Soup* and traces more fully in *I'm Talking About Jerusalem*).

By the end of the play, Ada's disgust with Left politics has been confirmed by Wesker in several ways, most tangibly in his depiction of the now-completed deterioration of the armchair socialist Harry. By 1956, although Sarah defiantly proclaims that she is "still a communist" in spite of "the news about Hungary," she is unable to rouse her tired son Ronnie as he lapses into nihilism. *Chicken Soup with Barley* concludes, of course, with Sarah's impassioned defense of the socialist vision:

> You think it doesn't hurt me—the news about Hungary?...
> But all my life I've fought. With your father and the rot-
> ten system that couldn't help him. All my life I worked
> with a party that meant glory and freedom and brother-
> hood. You want me to give it up now?... If the electrician
> who comes to mend my fuse blows it instead, so I should
> stop having electricity? I should cut off my light? Social-
> ism is my light, can you understand that? A way of life.
> (1:73–74)

But the point seems to be that Sarah stands willfully alone among the postwar rubble of a former truth. The blown fuse of revolutionary socialism, Wesker suggests, can no longer generate or sustain any meaningful potential for social transformation, radical or otherwise. The play thus ends on a note of unreconciled skepticism, hovering insecurely between Sarah's desperate, irrational affirmation and Ronnie's apparently imminent decline into the chronic spiritlessness which his father suffers.[4]

Wesker's analysis of Left failure in the *Trilogy* epitomizes a central narrative in Newer Left histories of postwar socialism, apparent in later plays as varied as Trevor Griffiths's *Occupations* (1971) and *The Party* (1973); David Hare's *The Great Exhibition* (1972); Howard Brenton and Hare's *Brassneck* (1973); Brenton's *Magnificence* (1973), *The Churchill Play* (1974), and *Weapons of Happiness* (1976); and Caryl Churchill's *Light Shining in Buckinghamshire* (1976).[5] A paradigmatic analysis of postwar socialist failure is detailed in David Edgar's celebrated 1982 epic *Maydays*, one of the most nuanced histories of the British Left to be found in postwar theatre. *Maydays* documents "how the much publicized shift to the right looks from the insides of the skulls of people in mid-flight" (Edgar 172), tracing this ideological journey from the pivotal moment of Hungary in 1956—where Wesker's *Trilogy* leaves off—to the somewhat more quiet moment of

Greenham Common in the early 1980s.[6] An older generation of communists, represented by the academic Jeremy Crowther, becomes (like Dave and Ada in some respects) disenchanted with socialism after 1956. Increasingly disgusted by what he sees as the cultural decadence of welfare socialism, Crowther joins a Conservative group—the Committee in Defence of Liberty—which claims to be dedicated to correcting the "sickly and corrosive culture of appeasement" (Edgar 312). But the postwar generation radicalized by 1968 (among others, Crowther's student Martin Glass), although dismayed by the increasing conservatism of its elders, also shifts gradually to the political Right. Martin, who is hired by Crowther's group to write pamphlets for the committee, eventually develops a proto-nationalist affiliation to old Englishness: he buys his childhood home, joins a church which distributes soup "only to the conspicuously needy," and completely dissociates himself from his former allies, whom he now calls "malcontents" (321; 300).

Maydays and other New Left histories advance arguments similar to Wesker's: that socialism cannot be achieved within the framework of a capitalist society, that both passion and logic are necessary preconditions of socialist commitment, that the Soviet example, tainted by Stalinist authoritarianism, offers little inspiration for the manifold forms of postwar socialism, that the industrial proletariat has been seduced into fetishizing the commodity and therefore lacks potential as a revolutionary force. In other words, blame for Left failure is targeted in several directions: at the larger socio-economic context, at the allegedly co-opted proletariat, and at New Leftists themselves, fragmented and dislocated by their own disparate priorities.

Socialist self-admonishment, however, has often been qualified by critiques of self-doubt itself. It is significant that Wesker signed *The New Left May Day Manifesto* (and indeed was the only playwright to do so), a document which, in 1967, reminded the Left of the urgent need to "build...a new kind of movement" and specifically advocated the formulation of extra-parliamentary democratic socialisms. In the *Trilogy*, Wesker seems to seek some form of spiritual regeneration in specific actions, in the Zen of working with one's hands. For later socialist playwrights, confirmation seems on the one hand to be easier; the projected means of revival, which tend to sidestep tricky problems of psychology or metaphysics, are more predictable and concrete. On the other hand, the Newer Left was confronted by a more complex and less easily resolvable state of crisis: a hardened, more cynical, and more powerful state, and the new, uncharted terrain of multinational, post-industrial consumer capitalism. The quest for a radically reconfigured socialism, which Wesker articulates with force and passion in the *Trilogy*, appears by the late 1960s as a quest for survival, not only for the Left itself but for all humankind. The note of urgency and despair which underpins much New Left writing can be traced to the inadequacy of proposed solutions, while the solutions themselves sometimes appear as an act of faith.

But the terms on which affirmation is achieved can be revealing. Wesker's plays do seem to be more concerned with the inner workings of ideology—its impact upon behaviors and relationships—than with materialities, with the concrete historical process of building new movements. As Edgar observed in a 1982 essay, "the New Left did not share the old left's hostility toward the individual, moral impulse in politics"; rather, "it believed firmly that the outcome of the revolution was present in the means of its making" (1988, 180). In *Chicken Soup*, Sarah's continuing devotion to socialism is both problematized and redeemed by the fact that she is seen to remain "a simple, old-fashioned humanist" (to quote Wesker's description of himself in a 1977 interview [1981, 153]), one who is convinced that socialism will fail unless it remains firmly grounded in a humanist commitment to other human beings. Even the cynical Monty in *Chicken Soup* treats Sarah's maternalistic politics with sentimental fondness:

> It was all so simple. The only thing that mattered was to be happy and eat. Anything that made you unhappy or stopped you from eating was the fault of capitalism. Do you think she ever read a book on political economy in her life? Bless her! Someone told her socialism was happiness so she joined the Party. (1:135)

More importantly, the only difference between Sarah's humanist socialism and that of her children is merely that Sarah is unable to live without urban working-class people while Dave and Ada are unable to live with them. Their concepts of Jerusalem are, of course, separated by differences which at first sight appear irreconcilable: by incompatibilities of generation and personality, and also, more importantly, by conflicting aesthetics. Dave high-handedly deplores "foam cushions" and "jerry" houses, in much the same manner that Ada had sneered at the "lipsticked, giggling morons" with whom she had worked during the war. Nevertheless, it is precisely the clarity and simplicity of Sarah's vision, the reaffirmation of human connectedness signified by chicken soup, which Sarah's children seek after the war—when affiliation to the industrial proletariat has, for them, lost its sentimental appeal, and when the conditions of work and home have rendered obsolete the old harmonies of community or family (such as those which Wesker details in the early scenes of the play and which are throughout a source of nostalgia and familial self-definition).

In *I'm Talking About Jerusalem*, Dave and Ada seem to seek not only a new socialism but entirely different relations of labor and community. For Dave, this quest entails the enactment of a new work ethic, one based on "an old truth" he claims to have learnt from boat-makers in Ceylon: "that a man is made to work and that when he works he's giving away something of himself, something very precious" (1:163). When Sarah accusingly asks them why they have chosen to run away from socialism "to an ivory tower," Dave explains that "Nothing's wrong with socialism": "only," he adds, "we want to live it—not talk about it" (1:164). The failure of this experiment seems guaranteed from the start, but Wesker's purpose is not to trace the causes for this failure in specifically material or historical terms. Rather, he seems to search, like Ada and Dave themselves, for new ways to conceptualize and live socialism: for a new work ethic as well as for new kinds of work, for renewed connections to land and people, for new social relations and ways of thinking about class, culture, and community.

Later New Left playwrights articulate this quest in different terms but, like Wesker, address a crisis of spirit as much as of history, material, or circumstance. Edgar claims to have written *O Fair Jerusalem* (pf. 1974) specifically as an "attack on...fashionable despair" and as a critique of the notion that "we live in an eternal cycle of ghastliness" (1979, 11). Even Howard Brenton, whose work has been criticized for its unrelenting negativism, suggests at the end of several plays that the revolutionary spirit remains (to borrow Frantz Fanon's words) subdued but untamed. Recognizing the futility of attempting to break out of prison (because there is "nowhere to break out to"), trapped political internees in the futuristic *The Churchill Play* (pf. 1974) vow to "survive" but "not at any cost" (Brenton 1986, 176), and the notorious critique of English involvement in Northern Ireland, *The Romans in Britain* (pf. 1980), concludes with an act of self-determination, the colonized Celts' formulation of the legend of Arthur.

However, Newer Left playwrights are concerned not only with the remaking of subjectivities—with the evolution of new kinds of spirit or new self-definitions—but also with the means and materials of such change. Edgar's *Jerusalem*, for example, celebrates "the immense adaptability of the human spirit" at the same time that it expresses "amazement at the resilience of the status quo" (Edgar 11), a perspective which seems to blend humanist reverence for heroism with a rather more skeptical socialist view of historical process. The play draws upon the interesting coincidence of four apparently unrelated events: that the bubonic plague struck Britain in 1348, exactly six hundred years before the establishment of the National Health Service in July 1948; that, also in July 1948, the first U.S. atomic weapons arrived on British bases; and that, about the same time, the recently discovered antibiotic streptomycin was found to cure tuberculosis. Edgar's purpose, as he describes it in a 1979 interview, is to demystify the process of revolutionary change by suggesting that it is measured and prepared, not achieved in sudden outbursts of unplanned activity:

> ...perhaps one needs to look for change to rather more mundane processes than hitherto: because perhaps we've tended to view the revolutionary *moment* as being much more important than the revolutionary *process*. It does seem to me, for instance, that the abolition of tuberculosis was by no means solely caused by the great moment of the discovery of penicillin, but much more by better drains. (1979, 11)

In a similarly subdued vein, attempting to trace the actual, gradual process of change, David Hare's *Fanshen* (pf. 1975) pays tribute to the power of grass-roots organization during the Chinese revolution and finds some hope in the idea of continual self-revaluation and self-reinvention.[7] Discourse and conference are also applauded in Edgar's 1990 *The Shape of the Table*, in which the most startling feature of the 1989 restructuring of Eastern Europe is the non-event: Perestroika occurs as two groups (as in Hare's *Fanshen*) write and re-write each other's drafts of the future until one group suddenly, and anti-climactically, wins. As a character in *Maydays* had explained, those who have never had the opportunity to participate in a political process must "work out how to do it as they [go] along" (Edgar 1991, 198). What interests Edgar, then, what he sees as significant in the progress of momentous change, is the necessary detail, the fact that the Vietnamese and the Americans spent seven months at peace talks in Paris arguing "quite literally," as a character in a recent play puts it, about "the shape of the negotiating table" (Edgar 1990, 37–38).

It is also interesting that *Maydays* itself ends not with the disheartening if unsurprising spectacle of Martin's conservatism but with a scene which seems to search for the beginnings of a new order. As he wrote *Maydays*, Edgar found himself reaching for a sense of "unambiguous, untrammelled confirmation" and found it, significantly, on "our side of the Greenham Common wire" (1988, 175). When Martin threatens to issue an injunction against the women who are setting up a peace camp on a part of his property, he learns that he is dealing with new forms of subversion:

> 1ST WOMAN: Injunctions require names. We have no names…No membership.
> 2ND WOMAN: And no committees.
> 3RD WOMAN: No printing press. No postal code. No phone.
> 2ND WOMAN: And I assure you—nobody "in charge…." (1991, 323)

Edgar's suggestion that the meek may inherit the earth after all marks an important divergence from traditional Left suspicion of informal or underground radicalism. In *Light Shining in Buckinghamshire* (pf. 1976), which depicts the counter-cultural movements within the English Revolution of 1640, Caryl Churchill similarly qualifies an otherwise pessimistic account of left failure with a tacit celebration of the anarchic, subversive energies which are released by the revolutionary underground. Both Churchill and Edgar seem to harbor some hesitant sympathy for counter-cultural radicalism even as their plays comment upon the inability of Coca-Cola revolutionaries to operate within concrete political frameworks. As Edgar suggests towards the end of *The Shape of the Table*, rock groups singing Bob Dylan songs and young agitprop groups who dub themselves the "Special Operations Unit…for the Rooting Out of Self-Importance" may have some usefulness after all, at least to the extent that they enable, in parody, a form of national self-criticism and inventiveness.

Such attempts to applaud carnival subversiveness do contradict the New Left's more frequent criticisms of the disorganized Left, that is of vaguely defined rebel groups which lacked serious or systematic connections to existing political organizations and which often functioned at random rather than in cooperation with any broader strategy or plan. As early as 1974, Brenton had argued that the "fringe," both in the theatre and in politics at large, had "failed" and located the roots of this failure specifically in the activities of those Left group which had broken away from traditional Left associations:

> Its failure was that of the whole dream of an "alternative culture"— the notion that within society as it exists you can grow another way of life, which, like a beneficent and desirable cancer, will in the end grow throughout the western world, and change it. What happens is that the "alternative society" gets hermetically sealed, and surrounded. A ghetto-like mentality develops.... Utopian generosity becomes paranoia as the world closes in. (1981, 91–92)

Although he claims to lament the failure of the quest for a "gentle, dreamy, alternative society," Brenton advocates more revolutionary strategies: "If you're going to change the world, well, there's only one set of tools, and they're bloody and stained but realistic. I mean communist tools" (1981, 92).[8] For Edgar, at least in 1982, the problem was not merely that such "alternative" radicalisms had locked themselves into a dreamy ghetto. He shares Brenton's reservations concerning the paranoiac tendencies of the underground counter-culture, but his retrospective analysis argues that "the maze of political contradictions" in which the New Left found itself by the late 1960s was a consequence of its attempt to apply "materialist models of ideology and organization" to a political philosophy "based in personal life":

> ...the old organisational imperatives of Leninism combined with the New Left's own hidden determinism and elitism to create a network of tiny, conspiratorial vanguards, of a tightness and zeal that might have frightened the Bolsheviks themselves. (1988, 181)

Edgar, like Brenton, refers specifically to the formation during the late 60s of highly publicized militant fringe constituencies (such as the First of May Group or Angry Brigade). Within ten years, by the late 70s, the critique of "alternative society" solipsism would become a standard way for the Left to articulate the failures of New Left politics and for the political Right to define the dangers of radicalism generally.

In other words, there are important differences between Wesker's approach to the idea of an "alternative culture" and that developed by playwrights who were politicized during the more volatile years of the late 1960s: as we can see, the later playwrights share Wesker's skepticism concerning the Dave/Ada variety of socialist experimentation but seem more critical than Wesker of its immanent self-absorption and vanity. In Wesker's account of the failures of "alternative" socialisms, the counter-cultural fringe does not decline inexorably into "tiny, conspiratorial vanguards"; Dave and Ada return to London before they can evolve into a murderous little band of Charles Manson followers. However, the *Trilogy* reflects similar suspicions concerning hermitage and draws attention to the often unhappy conjunction of materialist and individualist ideologies which characterizes the political philosophy of the younger postwar socialists.

The pessimism and mistrust with which so many of these plays treat counter-cultural radicalism, and postwar socialism generally, signal the New Left's frustration not only with the difficult task of building a revolutionary movement in a late-capitalist society but also with its own inability to imagine the means to radicalize what it regarded as a consumerist working class. In light of the vehemence with which the Newer Left chastised the counter-cultural fringe and the zeal with which it asserted its support for the Parisian student-labor coalitions of 1968, one could reasonably expect that both New and Newer Left plays would be committed to organized labor politics and to specific strategies for the radicalization of the proletariat. Ironically, New Left theatres, unlike the workers' theatres of the 1930s, were unable even at their point of greatest productivity to participate in working-class politics and the labor movement at large. As Edgar has perceptively observed, "the centre of revolution…shifted" after 1968 "from the factory-floor to the supermarket"; young New Leftists understood "revolutionary politics" to be "much less about the organization of the working class at the point of production and much more about the disruption of bourgeois ideology at the point of consumption" (1988, 26). The New Left theatre, in other words, concentrated on exposing what it saw as the vacuity of consumerism to what it arrogantly thought of as a brainwashed proletariat. Edgar's representation of New Left disenchantment with the industrial proletariat's alleged seduction by postwar consumerism echoes almost exactly the terms of Dave and Ada's rejection of the foam cushions and lipstick which they seem to believe are emblematic of working-class life: "'False consciousness,'" writes Edgar, "was an altogether too feeble description [for the New Left] of the condition of the masses in the age of the electric toothbrush and the vaginal deodorant" (1988, 182).

The problem of the New Left's dissociation from organized working-class politics as much as from popular mass culture was central to several vociferous debates concerning the aesthetic methods and ideology of postwar socialist theatres. Having worked at the Royal Court and witnessed firsthand the rapid growth and institutionalization of the post-Osborne generation, McGrath came to the conclusion that "this famed New Era" of theatre was simply transforming "authentic working-class experience into satisfying thrills for the bourgeoisie" (1981b, 11). A serious "oppositional" theatre, he argued, should participate in the "social, political and cultural development of the working class toward maturity and hegemony" by "searching...for those elements which point forward in the direction of a future rational, non-exploitative, classless society" (1981b, 21). With the 7:84 theatre company, so named as a reminder that 7 percent of the population owned 84 percent of the wealth, McGrath sought to avoid the theatrical establishment altogether and to seek an authentic "popular audience" in working-class venues. The enormous success of 7:84's *The Cheviot, the Stag, and the Black, Black Oil* in 1973—a play which has with good reason been called "a paradigmatic radical popular play" (van Erven, 1988, 109)—confirms McGrath's belief that radical political theatres can play to appreciative audiences in capitalist societies if such plays remain rooted in the values and culture of working-class communities.

Central to the debates between Wesker and McGrath, and also to the crossing of pens (as Edgar puts it) by Edgar and McGrath on several occasions, were purportedly divergent views on the uses and constitution of popular culture.[9] As Baz Kershaw has observed, McGrath's work conceptualizes "working-class counter-culture" by linking two concepts "that have usually been seen as distinct, even in opposition"—namely the concept of the urban industrial proletariat and that of the disorganized, ideologically plural, cultural avant-garde (1992, 149). At least in principle, Wesker's vision corresponds with McGrath's; after all, the idea was that Centre 42, a movement to promote the arts for the working classes, would restore or institute a cultural project at the centre of working-class political organization:

> Centre Fortytwo, with a Council of Management consisting of leading trade unionists and artists, aims to establish a cultural centre to exist not merely in its own right—to play to audiences not merely in the area where it is situated—but in such a way as to be able to assist, for example, trades councils to mount something more than a recruiting drive.... [A] movement of people's festivals seems possible. The artist co-operating with the trade unionist could easily prove a meeting out of which is built the new tradition. (Wesker 1970, 47–48)

Wesker and McGrath had in fact been among the originators of Centre 42, and McGrath worked in the movement for a brief time, seeking the company of others who wished to engage in theatrical work outside the dominant cultural apparatus of the southeastern parts of England (Dornan 1988, 50–51). Both 7:84 and Centre 42 sought to bring into the theatre the millions of working-class people who were thought to be sitting at home in front of television sets. The quest for this authentic "popular audience," for the real revolutionizable proletariat, was in many respects the cornerstone of the cultural theory of the New Left theatre: this was the audience pursued energetically not only by both Wesker and McGrath but also by several playwrights who, by the mid-70s, abandoned the earlier agitprop venues of the street or factory floor and began to seek larger stages.

At stake in such debates concerning the constitution of the audience for socialist theatre is the difficult question of how working-class life may or should be represented. It is, for example, partly in response to Wesker's representation of working-class characters in *Roots* that McGrath accused Wesker of displaying "a lamentable ignorance of the strengths and values of the working-class itself" (qtd. in Itzin, 1980, 104). In a telling statement during a late-60s interview, shortly after describing his enjoyment of the East End and "the street life," Wesker interestingly traces his admitted unease of what he constructs as "lumpen" brutality to his consciousness of being Jewish:

> One of the things I've inherited from my parents is an
> intense fear of brutishness—of the *Lumpenproletariat.*
> That's why characters like the boys in Edward Bond's *Saved*
> affect me in a very particular way. I curl up at them...this
> is what links [my] plays to Centre 42 and this is why I
> have always thought of *Roots* as a Jewish play—it's a fear
> inherited from the community of that brutish quality and
> the feeling that something needs to be done against it.
> Because it's dangerous. (Hayman 4)

It is significant that Wesker mentions Bond's *Saved,* the notorious
play in which a baby in a perambulator is stoned to death by a group
of young men (pf. 1965). The full violence of *Saved* is manifest not in
the isolated incident of the stoning of the child but in the careless
ease with which a culture of violence inhabits the entire universe of
postwar urban life. Wesker's anxieties about lumpen brutishness are
implicit in Bond's own analysis of why "people who pass most of
their lives as spectators" may resort to violence: "human violence,"
writes Bond, "occurs in situations of injustice. It is caused not only by
physical threats, but even more significantly by threats to human
dignity" (13).

Bond's attempt, of course, is not to express a fear of what Wesker
would call lumpen aggression but to explain how capitalism has made
that sort of violence inevitable. This problematically Orwellian conception of proletarian bestiality appears in various forms in Newer
Left accounts of working-class anger: "if men make you live like an
animal," resolve the fugitives in the opening scene of Howard Brenton's
The Romans in Britain, "Be an animal" (1989, 6). Joyce in Caryl
Churchill's *Top Girls* advances a similar argument when her sister
Marlene reminds her of their father's alcoholism and physical violence towards their mother: "Their lives were rubbish," protests Joyce,
"They...were treated like rubbish.... [W]hat sort of life did they have?"
(1990 139). Consider also McGrath's own representation of "the
suffering of the urban industrial working class of the north of England":

> the brutality, the violence, the drunkenness, the sexism, the
> authoritarianism that have been part of its life since the In-
> dustrial Revolution. On the other hand,...[t]hese are the
> people who may well be making revolution. (1981b, 25)

Elsewhere, McGrath uses similar terms to describe the conditions
under which the urban working-class audiences addressed by *The*

Cheviot, the Stag, and the Black, Black Oil (pf. 1973) live: "the architectural degradation, the raw, alcohol-ridden despair, the petty criminal furtiveness, the bleak violence of living in many parts of industrial Scotland" (1981b, 71). What is particularly interesting about this account is that it details what *The Cheviot* had ignored; McGrath himself acknowledges that the play was never performed in such venues of organized labor as "miners' clubs, Trades Council clubs, [or] the union halls of central Scotland" (1981b 71).[10] The play's silence about such concerns does, of course, seem appropriate to its rewriting of Highlanders long stereotyped by English colonizers as "lazy, shifty dreamers" (McGrath 1981a, vii). But the association of "petty criminal furtiveness" with urban industrial life is a central problem in the New Left's often-confused imaging of the urban proletariat.

A fundamental irony here is that Wesker's *urban* working class (as opposed to its rural counterpart in *Roots*) seems by comparison with McGrath's Highlanders to be the more full-blooded, complex, and vital. This is a consequence, I would argue, not only of the old-fashioned naturalism of Wesker's work (McGrath's *ceilidh* and Brechtian fragmentation leave little room for extended character analysis) but also, significantly, of the *Trilogy's* autobiographical basis in "authentic" working-class experience. *The Cheviot*, however, also claims to represent an authentic *volk*, and in this sense both plays pose similar problems concerning the curating of the national popular. Because "people's history" plays like *The Cheviot* rewrite history "from the bottom up" (historian Christopher Hill's frequently-quoted phrase), they develop a form of integrationist propaganda, incorporating the local histories and cultural practices of target audiences into broader polemics concerning imperialism and capitalism. Such plays attempt to produce a "shareable and common history" clearly linked to organized political struggle within working-class communities (Samuel, 1981, 28), and to use this sense of shared history to effect mass radicalization as much as local grass-roots community-building. At the same time, because many have been forced to rely on state subsidy, New Left theatres have functioned in a dual capacity, both as self-proclaimed guardians of the dangerous radical past and as performing museums of the state, staging and conserving the national-popular on the margins of a society in which historical knowledge is distributed primarily through film, television, and textbook. The quest to recover an authentic "popular" past can, as such, operate in the interests of the dominant classes, insofar as both the state and the capitalist machinery seem to encourage projects, such as museums or art fairs, which make a spectacle of, and thereby relegate to the perpetual past tense, the cultural production of what is assumed to be the true folk of a nation.

It is partly for this reason that Edgar remains skeptical about the idea of folk culture, which, he argues, has become assimilated into consumer culture to such an extent that it has lost any meaningful popular appeal it may once have had:

> the real problem with McGrath's project...is the notion that there is a genuine, rooted popular culture out there, and that if you take variety shows, club entertainment and pantomime and inject them with socialist content, then...you're part of a lived tradition that stretches back, and...you can place workers' contemporary experience within the contexts of their history. Well, I'm sorry, but I still don't buy it. I think the forms that have survived the televisual onslaught—including poor old panto—have been so extensively corrupted that they no longer have any usable relationship with autochthonous folk forms at all.... Everywhere there is rupture, and even in the countryside the folk song, the morris dance and the mummers' play are not remembered but reclaimed, an act of social archaeology. (1988, 233)

It is interesting that both McGrath and Wesker seek alternatives to mass culture in precisely the sorts of folk traditions which Edgar dismisses in this statement. Wesker's 1960 lecture, "O Mother Is It Worth It?" (which later became the pamphlet Wesker sent to the general secretaries of all trade unions) specifically targets the Labour Party and trade union movement for having neglected working-class culture:

> Why has the trade-union movement not erected its own theatres up and down the country—*they* should be responsible for the erecting of a National Theatre—what a monument to their struggles that would be. But they haven't looked into their own ranks to see even a folk culture, and a whole wealth of ballad and song is filtering away as the old members die out. (Wesker 1970, 18)

McGrath similarly calls for a recognition of the continuing popularity in working-class communities of such folk forms as the *ceilidh*, and in doing so he implicitly disputes Edgar's contention that whatever survives of folk culture has been "corrupted" in the process of its reclamation by mass culture. McGrath notes that the Highlands *ceilidh*, as it was incorporated into performances of *The Cheviot*, was received "with recognition and pleasure" not only within Highland communities but also by the "much-maligned industrial proletariat" of the industrial belt of Scotland.

Unexpectedly, however, McGrath seems to applaud the appropriation of folk-music by the music industry:

> There is, and has been for some time, a massive boom in music loosely termed "folk," particularly in Scotland. This contributes a tremendous amount of music from the history of the people to the generally available pool of cultural experience, music with all kinds of beauty, expressiveness, meaning and, above all, potential. Rescued from the Victorian drawing-room by A. L. Lloyd, Ewan MacColl and many other singer-entertainers, popularized by Joan Baez, and developed by many hundreds of talented groups of singers and musicians in Scotland, Ireland, America, Brittany, even in England…it now makes its way into the record rack of the young car worker, into the repertoire of the pub singer. The biggest smash hit on the entertainment scene is, after all, a folk singer: Billy Connolly. And Scotland's current contribution to the ratings battle on British TV is another folk-singer, Isla St Clair. (1981b, 71)

At first sight, McGrath's celebration of the increasing popularity of folk music would seem to suggest that he is indifferent to the politics of cultural usurpation, in this case of Scottish authenticity by English capital (of course, a single glance at *The Cheviot* would immediately demonstrate otherwise). McGrath's point here may be that the evident marketability of folk arts is clear indication that such forms are far from being obsolete. His interest is in the ways in which such forms have continued to survive in spite of the onslaught of postwar consumerism. For Edgar, the point of entry into the entertainment industry is in itself the point at which folk culture is rendered inauthentic and, more importantly, "corrupt." McGrath on the other hand does not appear to be concerned with the process by which popular culture, whether folk or rock, can be consumed by capitalism; rather, he seems willing to draw upon all manifest examples of popular culture in order to draw in his audience.

It should be noted that Wesker, unlike McGrath, makes little effort to incorporate "folk" culture in his plays; the authenticity of the *Trilogy*'s cultural framework, I would argue, stems from Wesker's attention to naturalistic detail of dialogue and characterization rather than from what Edgar calls "social archaeology." The question of authenticity is, in any case, troubling not only because of the potential for artifacts of national identity to be colonized by the state or consumer culture. The broader issue here concerns the self-limitations which are tacitly agreed to by both the New and Newer Left in constituting the popular, folk, or proletariat. This is not to suggest that there are no differences within New Left imaging of the people-nation: on the contrary, it seems clear that McGrath would contest Wesker's distinction between the TUC or organized proletariat and the "lumpen" elements of *Saved*, while Edgar seems more at home with the *Marxism Today* family of Left intelligentsia than with the audiences whom he addressed early in his career while he was a member of the touring agitprop group General Will. Edgar, who has been accused by McGrath of "ignorance of the complexity of the nature of popular culture" and "profound but automatic elitism" (McGrath 1981b, 62–63), has described, in terms strikingly similar to McGrath's own account of 7:84, General Will's attempts "to draw upon traditions culled from popular culture, most notably the music hall and folk music, either as total formal structures, or at least as cultural reference points" (Edgar 1988, 35–36).

However, while the exact scope and constitution of the rural and urban working class has been extensively debated, there has been an astonishing consensus about who or what will *not* be included in New and Newer Left histories of Britain. In the first place, because the New Left self-indulgently writes itself as an authentic revolutionary force, it limits its own ability to provide a holistic context in which to view postwar history and, as a result, uncritically affirms an Anglo-European narrative in which the Cold War continues to occupy center stage, and in which socialism and capitalism are seen to be the only significant conflicting forces shaping all history.[11] More precisely, it seems to be an unself-conscious anglocentrism in New and Newer Left versions of history which produces this kind of analytically self-centered preoccupation with the Cold War and consumer capitalism.

An important consequence of such historical astigmatism has been that British New Left historians, at least on the stage, have ignored postwar revolutionary socialisms situated in other parts of the world. Accordingly, the processes of decolonization are virtually erased from theatrical representations of postwar history, as though the loss of the colonies and attendant shifts in global immigration patterns had no impact upon British politics, economy, or culture. The effort, in other words, seems to be to write histories of the Left, or Left histories, in which Englishness can be treated as an autonomous or independent figure, separable not only from the "official" history written by the ruling classes but also from the history of the rest of the world. The Spanish Civil War in Wesker's *Chicken Soup with Barley* appears only in its capacity as an *effect* upon young British socialists, and the up-heavals in the shape of the rapidly decolonizing postwar world are presumed to have had no impact whatsoever on the lives and fortunes of the British working class: after all, if 1956 was the moment of the Soviet invasion of Hungary, it was also the moment of the Suez crisis, arguably one of the final nails in the coffin of British imperialism. In general, the events of Hungary in 1956, of Czechoslovakia and Paris in 1968, are reduced in the New Left history play to metaphors of awakening and disillusionment, and, most predictably if also most emphatically, Ireland appears only in its capacity as a problem which confronts England.

Although the history of British colonialism has not been entirely ignored, New Left criticisms of the imperial past (and indeed of its present, especially in relation to Ireland) have too often, in Conradian manner, reinvented colonialism as something which happens to the colonizer. David Edgar's 1976 *Destiny* is one of very few plays which directly confront the politics of race in working-class communities, and even here the question of the postcoloniality of the new racisms is subordinated to what is seen as a more pressing problem, the evolu-tion of neo-fascist ideologies among the English working class. In *The Romans in Britain*, Howard Brenton's 1980 polemic against En-glish involvement in Ireland, the history of the oppression of the Celts is juxtaposed against the idealistic crisis of conscience experienced by a British Army agent sent to Ireland to assassinate a "Republican" leader. The second narrative eventually subsumes the first in a manner which positions the British spy as the author of the Celtic history developed in the play, granting him a tragic insight and heroic centrality not available to any of the Celtic characters. This ideological shift, from the colonized to the colonizer, is also apparent in Caryl Churchill's 1979 *Cloud Nine*, which traces the contemporary crisis of sex and class—"You can't separate fucking and economics," as one character puts it (1985a 309)—back to Victorian constructions of English national character. To do so, Churchill situates the first act, a sex farce, in an unnamed African colony during the nineteenth century, briefly accounting for the existence of twentieth-century imperialism in a later scene in which the ghost of a soldier killed in Belfast returns to participate in an orgy. Once again, what little the play has to say about the experience of the colonized (specifically, from Jean Genet, that the colonized internalize racism—to the extent that the only African character in *Cloud Nine* is played by a white man) is less significant to the play's account of imperial history than is the crisis of sexual identity experienced by the colonizers, apparently as a result of their ventures into the unknowable.

More damagingly still, New Leftists have ignored the challenge posed by the radical underground at home. As Kobena Mercer has argued in a perceptive analysis of the ways in which the idea of 60s radicalism has been historicized in the United States and Britain, it is significant that recent anniversaries of "1968" have been characterized by "nostalgia for the good old days when the good old boys could act out their heroic identities as student revolutionaries":

> What makes matters worse is the legitimation provided by ex-leftist intellectuals eager to repudiate the oppositional fantasies of the past…, or more importantly, the inability of the left to produce a more pluralistic account of the past which recognizes the diversity of movements and actors implicated in the democratic revolutions of the 1960s. (1992, 426)

This "selective erasure," argues Mercer, "serves to disarticulate…the rhetorical vocabularies of the various "liberation" movements within the New Left and the new social movements that once defined themselves in opposition to it" (425). Such criticism had been advanced earlier, on somewhat different terms, by some New Leftists themselves. In 1989, for example, ten years into Thatcher's tenure and some time before the dismantling of the Soviet bloc, Edgar alerted fellow socialists of the urgent need to regroup and reconfigure Left priorities: "The left," he cautioned, "has got to embrace genuine political pluralism, not out of lip-service, nor out of a vague, residual anti-Stalinism, but as part of the very warp and weft of its politics":

> And surely there will be no chance (as well as no point) in a socialist victory in the early 1990s unless by then the left has managed to integrate the priorities of the new emancipatory movements into its central political platform, a project which will involve, among other things, the greening of its theory and the feminising of its practice…. What is certain is that the effort to bring about a synthesis of the new cultural movements with a viable economic agenda is the left's most urgent political task. (1988, 21–22)

What is curious about this statement (and, indeed, perhaps the reason that there was no socialist victory in Britain in 1990) is that it should have been considered requisite in 1988, by which time most of the "*new* emancipatory movements" which Edgar cites—"the women's, peace, green and anti-racist movements (including apartheid)"—were, after all, well over the age of consent. Further, Edgar's suggestion that the Left embrace pluralism and "integrate the priorities" of these fringe constituencies leaves little room for any radical reconstitution of the Left itself: implicit in Edgar's recommendation is the unfortunate if unintentional suggestion that the Left, as a spent force, should expropriate and indeed colonize the transformative energies of the new radicalisms.

Wesker's vision of Centre 42 acquires a particular relevance and urgency when we consider the vast scope of the emerging refashionings of postwar British society. Wesker asks us as early as 1960 to think carefully about whose culture is going to be preserved and on whose terms. The answers he proposes do often seem to be those of an old-fashioned humanist, and they are indeed couched in a language which may be unlikely to appeal to a more trendy Left. But it may be useful to consider whether some recent political and cultural coalitions—the "new emancipatory movements" Edgar describes, for example—are centered on the types of principles which Wesker outlines in his program for Centre 42. "Fortytwo," writes Wesker, "was seen as an attempt to enable works of art to be communicated to as many people as possible—especially those to whom the experience of art was unfamiliar" (1970, 114). Leaving aside the tricky question of pedagogy (whether is it still possible to speak uncritically of who has had "the experience of art," what might be said to constitute "art" in the first place), the issue of *access* to culture, which is implied in Wesker's comment and which both Wesker and McGrath have raised frequently, is a pressing concern. Recall Wesker's original notion that Centre 42 would function not only as a fixed location for the arts but also as a portable festival which could assist in organized political activity (such as trades councils recruitment drives). It may be interesting to ask whether such large public festivals as (most notably) the annual Notting Hill Carnival or the women's peace camp on Greenham Common have in some ways attained what Wesker hoped the Centre would. If so, a preliminary step in the reconstruction of the political theatre movement would need to be a reconceptualization of such ideas as "popular" or "theatre," one that at the least recognizes Britain's pluralism and stretches beyond anglocentric folk art to a more representative mass culture.

ᥱↃ

ENDNOTES

I would like to thank my colleagues Glynis Carr and Linden Lewis for their careful criticism of preliminary drafts of this essay. I am also grateful to Reade Dornan for her invaluable advice, encouragement, and camaraderie. Parts of this essay have appeared earlier in my article "Feminist History in Contemporary British Theatre," *Women and Performance* 7,2 (May 1995).

1.   State censorship of theatre in Britain was abolished in 1968, so the "generational" differences can be useful in distinguishing between various forms of political and sexual explicitness in plays produced before and after 1968.

2.   The term "New Left" refers broadly to the various forms of democratic socialism which developed in Europe and the United States in the aftermath of World War II, when the radical intelligentsia sought to break away from Soviet communism, especially from the legacy of Stalinism. The years 1956 and 1968 are often identified as pivotal moments in the formation and re-formation of New Left ideology. Following the failure of the British Communist Party to condemn the Soviet invasion of Hungary in 1956, seven thousand members, notably those associated with the Communist Historians' group, left the Party (see Heinemann 1976; Saville 1976). As Alan Sinfield argues, it was at this point in British history that "an independent left became feasible" (1989, 238). Subsequent New Left activism was consolidated in the politically momentous year of 1968, following (most

significantly) the Soviet suppression of student demonstrations during the "Prague Spring" in Czechoslovakia and the French suppression of student-labor agitation in Paris. For a useful overview of such postwar socialisms and their relation to British political theatre of the period, see Itzin 1980 and Bull 1984.

3.   All references to *Chicken Soup with Barley*, *Roots*, and *I'm Talking About Jerusalem* are taken from Volume 1 of the Penguin edition of *The Wesker Trilogy* (Wesker 1964).

4.   As Glenda Leeming and Simon Trussler have noted, it is, of course, too easy to argue that "Wesker wants to prove in *Chicken Soup with Barley* that socialism can never work." It is certainly true that Wesker carefully constructs "internal qualifications and problems" and that the play is "characteristically open-end[ed]" (Leeming and Trussler 1971, 14). However, I would still argue that the narrative in the *Trilogy* as a whole reinscribes the conventional version of the decline of socialist idealism in postwar British history—even if Wesker presents a complex, qualified, and open-ended account of this trajectory.

5.   (All dates mentioned here are dates of first performance). It is no coincidence that so many of these narratives of socialist decline and fragmentation were written and performed in the early- and mid-1970s, not only in the aftermath of the political excitement of the late 60s but also in response to the industrial crisis of 1970–74. In 1970, Harold Wilson's Labour Party government unexpectedly lost the General Election to the Conservatives, who formed a new government under Edward Heath. The Heath years were marked by widespread labour agitation, which came to a climax in December 1973, when Heath declared a state of emergency during a crucial miners' strike.

6.   "Greenham Common" refers to a famous women's peace camp which was established in the fall of 1981 outside the United States Airforce base in Greenham Common. For years, the camp attracted thousands of anti-war protesters and became (for peace workers as much as for feminists) an inspirational example of the power and tenacity of grassroots activism.

7.   However, as Catherine Itzin notes, it is only in this play that Hare treats "revolutionary social change" with any optimism (1980, 336).

8.   Brenton, who is unlikely to have much sympathy for the pastoral retreat attempted by Dave and Ada, draws an absolute line of distinction between communist groups and more ideologically fuzzy, quasi-anarchist associations which tried to maintain a distance from more strictly organized politics. In practice, these groups overlapped both in actual membership and in ideological affiliation.

9.   The most comprehensive accounts of this debate have been provided by Catherine Itzin (1980, 102–128) and Reade Dornan (1988).

10.   The group's next play, *The Game's a Bogey* (pf. 1974) addressed precisely this audience, but my point here is that McGrath never acknowledges the contradictions implicit in *The Cheviot*. Upon receiving an invitation from the Scottish Nationalist Party, the group warned that it out "would attack bourgeois nationalism," a threat which apparently did not deter the SNP. After 7:84 agreed to accept the SNP's commission, McGrath responded to critics on the left by declaring that they "had not read James Connolly or John Maclean, or even...Lenin on 'The Right of Nations to Self Determination'" (1981a, xxvi). I would argue that he ignores the possibility that the play simplifies the relationship between nationalist and capitalist interests. See McGrath 1981b, 70–77.

11.   Even the restructuring of Eastern Europe since 1989 has been wistfully interpreted on the British stage as a return to a "true" pre-Stalinist socialism and as an affirmation of the instinctive, idealistic, and youthful radicalism of the baby-boom generation: note the subdued self-congratulation which underpins Tariq Ali and Howard Brenton's *Moscow Gold* (pf. 1990) and (to a lesser extent) David Edgar's *The Shape of the Table* (pf. 1990).

WORKS CITED

Ali, Tariq, and Howard Brenton. *Moscow Gold*. London: Nick Hern, 1990.

Bond, Edward. *Saved. Plays: One*. London: Methuen, 1977.

Brenton, Howard. "Petrol Bombs through the Proscenium Arch." Interview with Simon Trussler. *New Theatre Voices of the Seventies*, 85–97. *See* Trussler.

———. *The Churchill Play. Plays*. London: Methuen, 1986.

———. *The Romans in Britain. Plays: Two*. London: Methuen, 1989.

Bull, John. *New British Political Dramatists*. London: Macmillan, 1984.

Churchill, Caryl. *Cloud Nine. Plays: One*. London: Routledge 1985 (a).

———. *Light Shining in Buckinghamshire. Plays: One*. London: Routledge, 1985(b).

———. *Top Girls. Plays: Two*. London: Methuen, 1990.

Dornan, Reade. *Committed Theatre in Post-War Britain: The Approaches of Arnold Wesker and John McGrath*. Unpublished dissertation. East Lansing: Michigan State University, 1988.

Edgar, David. "Towards a Theatre of Dynamic Ambiguities." Interview with Clive Barker and Simon Trussler. *Theatre Quarterly* 9,33 (Spring 1979): 3–23.

———. *The Second Time as Farce: Reflections on the Drama of Mean Times.* London: Lawrence and Wishart, 1988.

———. *The Shape of the Table.* London: Nick Hern, 1990.

———. *Maydays. Plays: Three.* London: Methuen, 1991.

Hare, David. *Fanshen. The Asian Plays.* London: Faber & Faber, 1986.

Hayman, Ronald. *Arnold Wesker.* London: Heinemann Educational, 1970.

Heinemann, Margot. "1956 and the Communist Party." *The Socialist Register*, 43–57, 1976.

Itzin, Catherine. *Stages in the Revolution: Political Theatre in Britain since 1968.* London: Methuen, 1980.

Kershaw, Baz. *The Politics of Performance: Radical Theatre as Cultural Intervention.* London and New York: Routledge, 1992.

Leeming, Glenda, and Simon Trussler. *The Plays of Arnold Wesker: An Assessment.* London: Victor Gollancz, 1971.

McGrath, John. *The Cheviot, the Stag, and the Black, Black Oil.* London: Methuen, 1981.

———. *A Good Night Out: Popular Theatre: Audience, Class and Form.* London: Methuen, 1981 (b).

Mercer, Kobena. "'1968': Periodizing Postmodern Politics and Identity." *Cultural Studies*, eds. Lawrence; Grossberg, Cary Nelson, and Paula Treichler, 424–49. New York: Routledge, 1992.

Samuel, Raphael, ed. *People's History and Socialist Theory.* London: Routledge & Kegan Paul, 1981.

Saville, John. "The XXth Congress and the British Communist Party." *The Socialist Register*, 1–23, 1976.

Sinfield, Alan. *Literature, Politics and Culture in Postwar Britain.* Berkeley and Los Angeles: Univ. of California Press, 1989.

Trussler, Simon. *New Theatre Voices of the Seventies: Sixteen Interviews from Theatre Quarterly: 1970–1980.* London and New York: Methuen, 1981.

van Erven, Eugene. *Radical People's Theatre.* Bloomington: Indiana Univ. Press, 1988.

Wesker, Arnold. The Wesker *Trilogy*. Baltimore: Penguin, 1964.

——. *Fears of Fragmentation*. London: Jonathan Cape, 1970.

——. "A Sense of What Should Follow." Interview with Simon Trussler. *New Theatre Voices of the Seventies*, 145–56. *See* Trussler, 1981

IV. Critical Approaches

Whatever Happened to Betty Lemon?[1]
Theatre Translation: Theory and Practice
Rossana Bonadei

I. A "Squared" Text

The destiny of the dramatic text is to change guise continuously, to interact with many codes and systems of writing, voices, sounds, and visual images. This is what Luigi Pirandello expressed in a 1908 essay, "Illustratori, attori e traduttori." The text, he said, is written, read, acted, put on, listened to, seen, and is never identical to itself: the fact that it is ductile, "promiscuous," that it yields immediately to others, means that the theatrical text immediately loses its aura, it becomes an orphan ("in search of an author" as he suggested shortly after). In Pirandello's essay, which is surprisingly full of modern suggestions, the dramatist expresses his "nostalgia" for his own text while explaining that he finds himself sharing the responsibility for its performance on stage with others. The essay in question is aptly entitled "Illustrators, Actors and Translators." These are special readers who have the difficult task of turning their own reading and aesthetic judgment into something public and "performable."

> All three of them are faced with an already expressed work of art, i.e., one which has already been conceived and performed by others, which the first must translate into another art; the second into material action; the third into another language.... The same can be said, although to a lesser degree, of the translation which each one of us makes of the works of others, if not exactly during the act of reading ...then when we report back to others or to ourselves the ideas and expressions received from our reading, that is when we re-evoke the work we have read. Once the transfer from one spirit to another has taken place, the changes are inevitable.... It may happen, indeed it often happens, that as we read we re-evoke better that which the writer has evoked, we express better inside

> ourselves that which the author has expressed badly or
> has not expressed at all…in short that we achieve that
> which the author did not succeed in achieving.[2]

This essay sustains Pirandello's idea that translation is a natural part
of theatrical art, so much so that the theoretical consideration and
comprehension of both could move along parallel lines. Our discussion is based on this idea, remembering that, in his famous essay on
translation, "On Linguistic Aspects of Translation," Roman Jakobson
also identifies the genesis of certain aesthetic expressions within the
act of translation: that is why the "interpretation of linguistic signs
through non-linguistic signs" is called "inter-semiotic translation," as
opposed to endo-linguistic and inter-linguistic translation.[3]

And is not this precisely the case of theatre? Is it not true that
theatre lives on a necessary transmutation of codes, an endless translating and re-translating within a complex interaction of languages
and semiotic conventions? Dramatists, unlike poets, often have certainties regarding the "how it has to be" of their own texts and often
recriminate directors and actors for "not having understood," or for
performances which actually prevent the audience from "really understanding." It has happened that dramatists have decided to direct
their own work, or even to perform it, thus removing any space for
interpretation. However, this practice of gathering all the functions
together, which is no guarantee of greater expressiveness for the text,
does not cancel out the basic characteristic of the theatrical event: to
paraphrase a well-known argument by S.T. Coleridge, it belongs simultaneously to the domain of "the text and the execution," of the
written work and the performance. As Pirandello reminds us in his
essay, even the performance of a playwright-director-actor is only a
translation, close to the original but never the same.

If we move into the field of inter-linguistic translation, the possibilities for contention are endless. Foreign directors and actors are an
even greater danger for playwrights, however authors are often
unqualified to judge the accuracy of a translation into a foreign language. There are even some playwrights, though not many, who translate their own works into other languages. However, even in these
cases the suspicion remains of an inevitably painful divide between
the original work and the translation. This can be illustrated by the
comments made by Samuel Beckett, the most illustrious example of
this practice, while working on the translation of *Fin de partie*:[4]

> I have not even begun the translation. I have until Au-
> gust to finish it and keep putting off the dreaded day....
> It seems funny to be making plans for a text which doesn't
> yet exist and which, when it does, will inevitably be a
> poor substitute for the original. (The loss will be much
> greater than from the French to the English *Godot*).
> (Beckett 107)

Beckett's case brings us to the crucial problem of the double expressive potential of the theatrical text: a written text, *script*, submitted for publication, which is also a dramatic script conceived for performances that will take place in other languages, other cultures, and
before other audiences, none of which will ever be identical. This
dual role brings us back to the question of the relation between the
"origin" of the theatrical text with respect to the linguistic-cultural
context, which is evidently a relationship of necessity much more
than it is for other literary texts.

Only recently has literary criticism investigated the inter-semiotic
reality of the theatrical text. The implications of this investigation
have had repercussions within the non-systemic debate concerning
the translation of theatrical texts, and this has led to the re-inclusion
of the questions and hypotheses about theatre translations within the
wider problem of "how theatre communicates."[5]

Critical debate, which is too vast and lively to be sufficiently dealt
with here, has mainly concentrated on the extraordinary potential of
the theatrical word. The word manifests itself as a place of tension
between its presumed fixity—word fixed by writing—and its ever-
changing oral and kinetic destiny for ever-changing voices and spaces
for ever-changing audiences: "theatre texts being literary texts created
for the page to be read off the page."[6] Moreover, it is correct to insist
on the idea of the tension between writing and acting, which alone can
create the difference between theatre text and canvas or score for mime.

Alessandro Serpieri speaks evocatively of "squared" words, as opposed to "linear" words of a text in prose or poetry, in order to underline spatial, gestural, and performance volumes inscribed within the
sign, which dilate beyond measure the potentialities of its consumption. Temporarily immobilized on the page, the theatre word already
contains the information for its translation into something other than
itself, its imminent "disguising" as bodies, voices, sounds, visual effects,
where the specific nature of theatre consists in organizing the word as

if movements of the characters in reciprocal relation or in respect with objects and spaces of the stage."[7] We may also speak, as does Paola Pugliatti, of "latent signs," or we may, like Franco Ruffini, consider the performance potentialities of the theatrical word as "submerged" texts which surface with the stage performance, but which then sink back down with the passing of the play from the stage.[8] Otherwise a text cannot be considered dramatic without being performed (think of the inevitable sense of incompleteness of the never-performed "dramas" by P.B. Shelley).[9]

The word written for theatre is bound to lose much of its ambiguity once it is embodied on stage. It is chained more or less allusively to one context, and it follows more or less humbly the diachronic parabolas of spoken language: for this reason the theatre word, more than any other literary word, is subject to the usury of time; it is time-bound. Indeed owing to its pragmatic destiny the theatre word travels materially between spaces, objects and flesh and blood people, it "adapts" more or less docilely to them—to their tastes and to their languages. These languages, including those tightened and refined by verse, imitate the dialogues and the dialogue rhythms of individuals and groups with a historical and social collocation. They are full of information but also of allusions, which are not included and decoded in all languages. And as we know at the theatre there is no time for slow tasting or deferred reading; there is no time for consulting the dictionary or encyclopaedia or to stop the scene and think over it or think back on what has passed. The only interruption is when one leaves: thus the text on stage must communicate reasonably immediately and explicitly and its survival in *other* eras and other cultures will be proportional to its ability to be re-written, to adapt from *that* into *this*.

If the "origin" of a text is determined by a strong historical context, it may produce a functional hyper-determination or a harmful "stability" which is incompatible with the "extended time" of literature. Thus the stronger the "origin," the less the text can withstand the usury of time. On the contrary, the text which is written and then immediately re-written will continue to live throughout all its re-writings, through the various stages, directors, actors, and audiences. As we know, nothing is the same twice in the theatre, not even one line. In spite of what playwrights think, the intrinsic instability of the theatre sign is not compatible with the values of "fidelity," but rather with the "felicitousness" of its performances.

But what, then, is the concern of inter-linguistic translation? Literature? Fidelity? Felicitousness? And what is its object? The literary text or its performance? In short, if we accept the hypothesis that the dramatic text is in fact a pretext, a "domain" of inter-linked re-writings, each of which is limited by specific conventions of idiom, stage, and acting, what then are the repercussions for the theory and practice of translation? It is not by chance that the most productive contributors to the Anglo-Saxon debate on translation, for example, those identified in the most recent work by Susan Bassnett-McGuire,[10] have emphasized and developed within Theatre Semiotics the concept of the "tension" of the dramatic sign, as opposed to the exaggerated "instability" whereby "anything goes" in theatre and other kinds of translations. A strong hypothesis of "tension" treads the difficult ground of the "double life" of the dramatic text, juggling both with the rights of the text and the script, of the literary word and the stage performance, of the autonomy of the text and of its ideological functions. In short, even within the framework of accepted instability, the structural and rhetorical margins which *belong to* the text and which can resist the many forces of on-stage re-writing are not omitted. Any removal of these is to be considered as sign of the irreversible transition into a truly "other" text, by "others" ("remaking" is common practice in the theatre, and may refer both to cases where the playwright re-reads works from the past or to directors who decide to impose their stamp on the work). We could perhaps think of using margins of constancy on which to base both the stage translation and the inter-linguistic translation, and with which to measure the tension, the play of yield/resistance between text and codes.

Like the director, the translator enters into this field of tension but perhaps with a more complete literary responsibility. His/her position is one of textual evaluation which responds to criteria which are not only dramatic and which are less concentrated on the reality of the context and communicative function. The translator is concerned with a word which is above all literary. All that belongs to the text as a written form can legitimately be described as a distinctive trait of that text and can function as an "original" nucleus—a primary reference system on which to base a strategy of interpretation and translation. According to a line of thought shared by many contemporary critics, the dramatic text, no less than other writings, offers itself as poetic text, and as such is subject to the same treatment as poetry rather than theatre in terms of interpretation and translation. The ambiguity is not necessarily removed; the metaphor is not necessarily recreated; the phonic and syntactic scores compete to produce sensory effects. In short, paraphrases, periphrases, clarifications, solutions, hyper-interpretations can destroy the unity of a text, thin out the rhetorical depth, and flatten the dramatic profundity. We may at this point conclude that, at this stage in the comparison, the tension which the translator must deal with concerns the literariness of the "linear word" and its semiotic potentialities.

Outside of this position, the translator enters into the field of the tension produced by the "squared" word. Here "that which has to be translated is not just the visible words of the written text, but also one or many invisible texts."[11] This is the reality of the words "for the theatre," subjected to centrifugal tensions "off the page" and to requirements which are more purely communicative in nature: "performance centred" requirements which take into account the realities of space, voice, diction, and rhythm, and "foreign-culture centred" requirements, i.e., aimed at satisfying, under different guise, the tastes, needs, and the ideologies of different communities. From this point of view the "dominant structure" is more easily eroded when faced with the needs of performance and exportation. Thus, just as a director is called upon to satisfy the expectations of a given audience at a given time, so the translator must commit himself to rendering the text as readable as possible for the actor and comprehensible for the audience, possibly at the price of major formal or functional alterations. Just as the performance is timebound, so, too, is the translation which results from it, made as it is of a verbal immediacy which is "datable" and soon "dated," and probably destined to perish with the stage production from which it originated. It is for this reason also that translating and re-translating are continuous in the theatre, and as in the cases of direction and acting, the most important criterion for translations is that of a "felicitous execution."

And yet, as Susan Bassnett-McGuire suggests, and as various translations in circulation in theatres testify, the two positions—a valorization of the literary text or the needs of the stage performance—are not totally alternative, nor is the "felicitousness" of the solutions so rigidly proportional to the coherence with which the rights of the written text or the performance are respected. There are margins of compromise, precisely because every text is a unique system, because the proportions of poetry and ideology from which the texts take life vary, and the perspectives of comparison with different codes are also variable. Thus if a text is dense with poetic material, and the director and translator decide to keep this and succeed in rendering it, then that text may pass through many codes without sticking too much to ideological and historical specifications. It may also happen that "dominant" aesthetic functions in that text—its being conceived as "tragic," "comic," "grotesque" or otherwise—are included in one code and excluded in another, except when there are substantial changes, where in order to save the function the content is lost and vice versa. Or it may be that a text is full of ideological implications which cannot be translated functionally into other codes but which can continue to play a testimonial or admonitory role, whereby, even though the original coordinates have been modified, it still succeeds in communicating emotions. In short the yield/resistance mechanisms of a text to a code and of a code to another code can lead to interventions which are dishomogenous, sometimes conservative, sometimes of creative transposition, sometimes of adaptation. The important thing is that everything follows a plan of reasoned "violation."[12] Thus one unity is exchanged for another, for an "alternative" expression. Thinking herself of Pirandello, but above all the effort which has to be made by directors and translators faced with the problems of coming up with words in other languages, Bassnett-McGuire suggests "co-operative translations," collaborations which put different readings and sensibilities together, and with performances which involve a number of collaborators. This certainly implies compromises, but these serve to curb interpretational radicalizations and to gather the many facets of the work into a whole.

II. Arnold Wesker's *Whatever Happened to Betty Lemon?* Dominant Elements of the Text, and the Resistance of a Context.

> What about those handicapped by their impoverished imaginations, eh?
>
> —*Whatever Happened to Betty Lemon?*

From the original published script[13] in English up to the performance in Italian, our work on Wesker's text was the result of both co-operation and many compromises. The text was pored over by all those involved: the author, called upon to speak about his work, the two translators, native speakers of both languages involved, and the actress who had to struggle with lines which were not always fluent within her own verbal and performance system. Each of these, moreover, brought along their own linguistic, cultural, and historic context which would in some way influence the reading, the interpretation, and performance.

The physical presence of the author could not but emphasize the problem of the original intentions and essence of the work. However, the translation onto a foreign stage and into a foreign language proceeded according to criteria of homogeneity, in the sense that the modifications imposed by performance and translation requirements were integrated within the system, on the basis of the new textual hierarchy imposed by the act of translation.

The structure of the theatre seminar-workshop itself, which was the backdrop to the Wesker event, helped create a strategy of "cooperative translation." In line with this, the inter-semiotic and inter-linguistic journey of *Whatever Happened to Betty Lemon?* began with analytical and descriptive considerations based on the structural features of the script. Margins of commutation onto an Italian stage were then defined. In the early stages we also used interpretative suggestions which arose from other specific contributions to the seminar. The analysis which follows, based on contrast, obviously does not deal with all the problems which arose from the text: rather it highlights those textual "nodes" where reading and translation ran across particular difficulties, those passages where "violations" had to be made, and therefore choices which we realized might have weakened the original felicitousness of the text.

Speaking of "dominant elements" of the text, Angela Locatelli was correct in identifying "recursiveness" as the dominant principle on which *Whatever Happened to Betty Lemon?* is built, thus "dialogues, memories, movement and action are structured recursively" and move within the text ordered by an "evident strategy of parallelism." Dramatic movement comes from and is swollen by "the repeating of lines which are almost identical but with few precise references, related to every changed situation,"[14] which are produced and re-produced around four semantic nuclei: a) handicap, as an occasion for reflection by the character on herself and others ("What about those handicapped by..."); b) memory of or contact with the family, which is verbalized in the repeated "advice" which relatives give to Betty and in the mechanical speech of the daughter's answering machine ("I had an uncle...who declared to me," "I had a father...who advised me," "I am not here. If you want to leave a message..."); c) the political and ideological self-characterization ("As a socialist...", "Let them win!"); d) the private and existentialist self-characterization ("I didn't fucking plan it this way!" and "Ollymollycollywolly...").

It is clear how recursiveness, as an aesthetic function in the text, serves to order the chaos of an erratic and aleatory monologue[15] and contains the disorienting effects of a "naturalistic" simulation which moves from the verbal muttering of Betty (with the post, the television, advertisements, the childhood voices). If this function is removed from the design, the dramatic situation risks falling into a verbal incongruousness difficult to act or listen to, an involuntary absurdity which is not of the text. For this reason we decided to keep the function and to leave its verbal contents almost intact, like a kind of obsessively repeated trace, in keeping with the obsessive nature of the character. This was a difficult decision both in terms of performance and translation if we think of the abhorrence Italian has for repetition. However had we resorted to *variatio*, the use of lexical synonyms or periphrases, it would in this case have destroyed a major aesthetic function which we preferred to keep. It was therefore particularly difficult to resolve the condition of the actress, who could do nothing but vary the intonations strongly, never establishing a rhythm which was in some way repeatable and with the risk of ending up over-acting.

Betty's language is not however simply a domain of obsessive repetition and more or less aleatory interference from the private and public languages of others. It is not just made up of childhood echoes and media codifications: there is something which is *truly Betty's*, and it is produced in a sort of "poetic" speech which goes beyond the context. This language, which is already fragmentary and incomplete, has also moments of joyous self-proliferation and non-sensical euphoria. Betty plays with words, plays at mangling her name with obscene allusions; she abandons herself to obscure propitiatory formulas and to kinds of liberating ejaculations with which to crush anxiety and exorcize the baseness of men. It is clear: Betty who is no longer able to dominate objects or people deludes herself that she can dominate words, like Humpty Dumpty she twists them with her witty imagination, nonsensical caprices, and idiosyncratic meanings. In order to deal with these micro-texts of "linguistic mythology," which Jakobson defined as untranslatable as they are inextricably linked with the distinctive features of the code which carries them, we followed the criteria of "creative transpositions": it was mainly up to the actress to "imagine" those ditties and bawdy verses in Italian and to recreate Betty's euphoria. Thus in this case we maintained the function, but the contents of the function were radically modified. An important use of a "creative transposition" was made in the translation of the "battle cry" which Betty uses in moments of great excitement: "Ollymollycollywolly OUT OUT OUT Thingymeejig and wadjamacallim OUT OUT OUT." The actress followed some advice from the author (who suggested taking inspiration from political slogans) and threw herself into a courageous "imaginative philology." She invented a game of literary and rhythmic decomposition and recomposition. Eventually on the basis of vague semantic shadows ("OUT"; "JIG") and simulations of words she reconstructed an aggressive and obscene slogan.[16]

So far we have spoken of "dominant" structural elements and possible tensions between text and word on stage; let us now see what happens to those functions which more entirely take their substance from a precise language, culture, and history. We have noted that the text oscillates very clearly between naturalistic aspiration and metaphysical suspension. The entire environment of physical and verbal space within which the character is imagined to move will depend mainly on how the director and translator deal with these oscillations.

How far does Betty's essence derive from her being an eccentric English working-class woman of Jewish extraction, with all that this historical and social collocation implies ("née Rivkind," "a socialist." married to a "Sir" Labour M.P., etc.). Or rather, how much should Betty be read as a kind of "everywoman," bearer of traits which can be easily translated into various contexts? Is not Betty essentially a courageous individual who is able to maintain her dignity in spite of her being different—female, aged, handicapped, Jewish, and anarchic? In trying to imagine an "exportable" Betty, and the words with which she could be expressed in Italian, we opted for a studied compromise, by the Italian equivalents which would be otherwise incomprehensible (Rivkind = Coen, Dalston Junction = London ghetto). We then gave new contexts to some cultural references but maintained some effects of the Englishness wherever this could contribute to producing ideological emphasis (like the irony of hearing herself called a "Lady").

Returning to contextual functions, I would like to conclude with a reflection upon the dramatic and iconic node around which *Whatever Happened to Betty Lemon?* is constructed: physical handicap. Physical handicap qualifies and radicalizes the existential condition of the character Betty, "an old woman crippled by everything old age brings." This physical handicap is "real" when it is represented on stage "naturalistically": the presence of the wheel chair, the drama of the difficult movements, the falls, the suspicion of arteriosclerotic delirium.... But there is more: Betty's lines project handicap back onto the others ("And what about those handicapped by...?"): if she is physically handicapped (but is she really?) the others are spiritually and mentally handicapped, from which we deduce that her heaviest handicap is having to put up with the more serious handicaps of others—their stupidity, moral unworthiness, and the general blindness which afflicts human kind. But her "let them win" is no sign of acceptance or resignation: on the contrary, Betty never stops speaking out or denouncing.

Thus physical handicap itself is suspended between "reality" and metaphor and therefore can be read in one of two directions: either one can create a play which is a social indictment, provoking thought on the condition of old and handicapped people in modern society, or on the contrary create a timeless "icon" not dissimilar to certain solutions offered by the Theatre of the Absurd.

The "naturalistic" simulation of physical handicap is in fact underlined in the text by unusually meticulous stage directions and by the dramatic presence of the wheelchair, a privileged interlocutor within that community of objects which are Betty's new family. This is a huge, noisy and shiny chair which the author would prefer to be operated electronically and which careful lighting should keep always visible: in short it is a true mechanical monster which Betty imagines is to be fought against and tamed, a prosthesis which is added to a body in which "nothing works the way it should." (Betty actually appears to be surrounded by technological prostheses—the answering machine, the television set, the coffee machine—which give her a contact with the external world which would otherwise be impossible, with notable science-fiction-type grotesque effects.) The text itself does not restrict itself to evoking Betty's handicap verbally as a possible result of her neurosis, rather it places it on stage, to be seen: it is the "reality" of the handicap which forces Betty to "fight" every day, to suffer, shout and cry with pain. It is physical handicap which has crushed her life ("I wasn't always like this.... Once I could run, I could swim, dive.... I used to drive a car believe it or not.... My life was spent on many battle-fronts..."), and which marks her body with the signs of a progressive degradation, a living death. The obviousness and the demonstration of this handicap are in this sense dramatically functional. It becomes the occasion for a discharge of energy and collective exorcism in the face of an anxiety which belongs to all of us. The stage reflects daily life.

But it is precisely here that the text goes off on a different communicative path: the anxiety seeks to amuse. Betty is funny in her awkwardness and unscrupulous in her verbal aggression. In moments of desperation she curses obscenely "like a child"; she receives a letter which elects her "Handicapped Woman of the Year." Here then is the comic intention of the text: the attempt to joke about physical handicap, to laugh sympathetically with Betty (Betty after all reveals to us a scene which could well be our own future: any one of us might be Betty sooner or later!), and at the same time to deride a puritanically meritocratic and efficient culture, which by awarding a prize to someone who overcomes adversity with their strength of will, runs into unheard-of stupidity, a society which turns a "fucking" condition into an occasion for public celebration. Thus even for Wesker in this play, tragedy, comedy, self-irony and irony, death, and carnival blend inextricably in accordance with traditional styles and characteristics of British theatre. And it is precisely here that the major problems of "exportation" arise. It is that specific linguistic, cultural and historic context which allows such a functional blending to happen: once transformed into an Italian context the function only works partially, and its original ideological and aesthetic contents suffer. The level of moral and social development of our context is not the same as that in which the text was created: in Italy there is little modern "culture" of old age and handicap to tap into; thus, the subject is avoided or treated differently. It is certainly not put on show, nor is it acceptable to laugh at it in public. Our society does not boast, like the British welfare state, an efficient health service, committed to normalizing the lives of old people and the handicapped; and our widespread Catholic background prefers an image of passivity and placated resignation for old people and the sick. It does not make social "heroes" of them and "piously" abstains from turning them into clowns. Just how much this traditional framework holds, in spite of the centrifugal forces which our culture has recently experienced, became clear to us through our own resistance to transferring intact certain aspects and attitudes of the character and to laughing at them, which the playwright considered natural backed up by the experience of the English stage.

How would an Italian audience react faced with a repugnant "old bag" who, seated on her handicapped person's throne, shouts, swears, has obscene memories and gestures, making reference to a body altered by the years but still alive and cumbersome? Within this crisis the "naturalistic" simulation, which we decided to keep, penalized us a great deal, so we eventually opted for some adjustments. In order to make the dramatic situation plausible in the new context, without losing its dramatic impact, we partly "adapted" the character. We kept Betty's verbal exuberance and argumentativeness, and, where possible, we accentuated her rather neurotic militancy. We increased her gesticulation and had her move in agitation on stage. We toned down her vulgarity and her coarse poses, however, not through censorship but rather for reasons of "credibility": we did not want the audience to see Betty as a "tart," or worse, an arteriosclerotic who has lost her judgment and decorum, or to hear her words as an unpleasant blathering rather than as a painful and lucid madness.

But we have to admit that the comedy within the piece did not surface: with the conditions listed above it was difficult to laugh— one could smile perhaps but not laugh: the audience was actually more (melo) dramatically than comically involved in Betty. As a matter of fact, comedy is not easily translatable, the comic discourse being deeply rooted in a specific language, culture, and society or, rather, one has to decide to translate either the comic function or its contents. It is very difficult to succeed in passing to another code, another context, while keeping both function and contents intact. Comedy can usually only be heavily recreated. And it is significant that when it came to ending his comic treatment of physical handicap, Wesker himself, who is usually so precise in his requests, put down his pen and handed it over to the director and actress, calling upon their "power for comic invention" and their stage imagination.

಄

ENDNOTES

1. *Whatever Happened to Betty Lemon?* was performed on November 12, 1986, at the Theatre du Rond—Point, Paris, with Judith Magre, directed by J. Michel Ribes. Its first London performance was in a double bill with *Yardsale* on February 17, 1987, at the Lyric Theatre Studio, Hammersmith, with Brenda Bruce, directed by the author and designed by Jackie Prefold. The text, originally published in German (München: Englisch-Amerikanische Studien, 1986) is now included in Arnold Wesker. Vol 5. *One Woman Plays*, Penguin ed., 1989. Like the other Wesker one-woman plays, so characteristic of his most recent dramatic production, *Whatever Happened to Betty Lemon?* stages a fragment of a woman's daily life by means of an uninterrupted monologue which lasts approximately ninety minutes. In this case the protagonist, Betty Lemon, is an old and aggressive Jewish woman, wife of a former Labour Prime Minister, who struggles with the problems of old age and her difficult personality.

    The Italian translation and staging, from which this article takes inspiration, were part of a Theatre Workshop project hosted by the University of Bergamo in 1987 and organized by the lecturers of English together with the Bergamasco-Alasjarvi Theatre Company of Turin at the Donizetti Theatre in Bergamo. Arnold Wesker participated in the Workshop, the rehearsals and the staging. The contributions to the Workshop were reproduced in the proceedings of the conference, "Arnold Wesker. Past and Present," published in *Quaderni* del Dipartimento di Linguistica e Letteratura Comparate dell'Università di Bergamo, Bergamo: Vol. 4, 1988. *Betty Lemon* (in the Italian title) was performed on June 12, 1987, in Bergamo and on the 28th of June in Turin. The Italian translation, by Rossana Bonadei, Maggie Rose, and Ulla Alasjarvi, was published in *Sipario*, July–August, 1992.

2. Luigi Pirandello, "Illustratori, attori e traduttori," *Nuova Antologia,* January 16, 1908.

3. Roman Jakobson, "On Linguistic Aspects of Translation," *On Translation*, ed. R.A. Brower (Cambridge: Harvard U.P, 1959).

4. Samuel Beckett, *Disjecta: Miscellaneous Writings and a Dramatic Fragment* (London: J. Calder, 1983). The note comes from a letter from Beckett to Alan Schneider, dated April 30, 1957. The premiere of *Fin de partie* was performed at the Royal Court Theatre on April 3, 1957. Cf. the introductory note to *Endgame* (London: Faber and Faber, 1958) 5.

5. Alessandro Serpieri. "How Theatre Communicates," *Collected Essays*, ed. Alessandro Serpieri (Firenze: Il Formichiere, 1974).

6. Susan Bassnett-McGuire. "Ways Through the Labyrinth: Strategies and Methods for Translating Theatre Texts." *The Manipulation of Literature*, ed. Theo Hermans (London: Croom Helm, 1985) 87–102.

7. Interesting reflections on theatre texts and the problems of translation can

also be found in the preface to William Shakespeare, *Amleto* (Milano: Rizzoli, 1980).

8. Paola Pugliatti, *I segni latenti. Scrittura come virtualità scenica in King Lear* (Messina-Firenze: D'Anna, 1976); and Franco Ruffini. *Semiotica del testo* (Roma: Bulzoni, 1978).

9. This refers to the writings in verse which Shelley himself called "tragedies" or "experimental tragedies" as Harold Bloom defines them more precisely, "conceived in the Shakespearean shadow." Yet they are tragedies only in a very peculiar sense and have little in common with the stageplays they ostensibly seek to emulate. Their true companions and descendants are Browning's giant progression of dramatic monologues, *The Ring and the Book*, and certain works of Hardy that share their oddly effective quality of what might be termed "dramatic solipsism." Cf. Introduction to Shelley, *The Selected Poetry and Prose* (New York: Signet Classics, 1966) xxix.

10. Susan Bassnett-McGuire. "Translating Spatial Poetry: an Examination of Theatre Texts in Performance." *Literature and Translation*. Eds. James S. Holmes, José Lambert and Raymond van den Broeck (Louvain: ACCO, 1978) 161–76.

11. Susan Bassnett-McGuire. "Problems in the Translation of Theatre Texts." *Interazione, dialogo e convenzioni. Il caso del testo drammatico* (Bologna: Clup Bologna, 1983).

12. In "On Linguistic Aspects of Translation," Jakobson speaks of "creative transpositions" as an alternative practice to translation in the case of texts where "the grammatical categories have an elevated semantic content." In poetry, and in the same way in popular and day-to-day "linguistic mythology" of proverbs, magical formulas, and idioms, "verbal equations are promoted to the rank of constructive principle of the text and thus become vehicles of a proper meaning." Regarding the idea of "violation" as "the essence of translation, like a systematic taking away and adding in which an original corresponding hierarchy is lost and another is created, see the theoretical essay of Anton Federov, "The Problem of Verse Translation," (1927) in *Linguistics* 137 (1974).

13. At the time of our workshop, the Penguin edition was not yet available. Both textual analysis and translation followed a script kindly provided by the author (a second revised version, dated 1987). All quotations here are from that version.

14. Angela Locatelli, "Recursività dialogica e dell'azione in *Whatever Happened to Betty Lemon?*" *Arnold Wesker. Past and Present, Quaderni del Dipartimento di Linguistica e Letteratura Comparate dell'Università di Bergamo* (Bergamo: Vol. 4, 1988).

15. On the "fragmentedness" of the text and the language which expresses it, see in particular Alessandra Marzola, "Funambolismi Weskeriani," in *Arnold Wesker, Past and Present*, Bergamo Conference, 1988.

16. For this and other reflections, see Ulla Alasjarvi and B. Bergamasco, "Betty Lemon, Note a margine della messa in scena," from *Arnold Wesker, Past and Present*, Bergamo Conference, 1988.

Works Cited

Alasjarvi, Ulla, and B. Bergamasco. "Betty Lemon, Note a margine della messa in scena." *Arnold Wesker. Past and Present, Quaderni del Dipartimento di Linguistica e Letteratura Comparate dell'Università di Bergamo*, Bergamo: Vol. 4, 1988.

Bassnett-McGuire, Susan. "Problems in the Translation of Theatre Texts." *Interazione, dialogo e convenzioni. Il caso del testo drammatico*. Bologna: Clup Bologna, 1983.

———. "Translating Spatial Poetry: an Examination of Theatre Texts in Performance." *Literature and Translation*, eds. James S. Holmes, José Lambert and Raymond van den Broeck. Louvain: ACCO, 1978, 161–76.

———. "Ways Through the Labyrinth: Strategies and Methods for Translating Theatre Texts." *The Manipulation of Literature*, ed. Theo Hermans. London: Croom Helm, 1985, 87–102.

Beckett, Samuel. *Disjecta: Miscellaneous Writings and a Dramatic Fragment*. London: J. Calder, 1983.

Federov, Anton. "The Problem of Verse Translation," (1927) in *Linguistics* 137 (1974).

Jakobson, Roman. "On Linguistic Aspects of Translation." *On Translation*, ed. R.A. Brower. Cambridge: Harvard Univ. Press, 1959, pp. 232-39.

Locatelli, Angela. "Recursività dialogica e dell'azione in *Whatever Happened to Betty Lemon?*" *Arnold Wesker. Past and Present, Quaderni del Dipartimento di Linguistica e Letteratura Comparate dell'Università di Bergamo*, Bergamo: Vol. 4, 1988.

Pirandello, Luigi. "Illustratori, Attori e Traduttori," *Nuova Antologia* 16 January 1908.

Pugliatti, Paola. *I segni latenti. Scrittura come virtualità scenica in King Lear*. Messina-Firenze: D'Anna, 1976.

Ruffini, Franco. *Semiotica del Testo*. Roma: Bulzoni, 1978.

Serpieri, Alessandro, "How Theatre Communicates." *Collected Essays*, ed. Alessandro Serpieri. Firenze: Il Formichiere, 1974. The volume includes essays by Elam, Kemeny, Pagnini, Pugliatti and others. More recent developments of this theoretical approach are in *Interazione, dialogo e convenzioni. Il caso del testo drammatico*. Bologna: Clup Bologna, 1983.

Wesker, Arnold. *One Woman Plays*. Vol. 5. Harmondsworth: Penguin, 1989.

Dialogic and Monologic Contexts in Arnold Wesker's Monologues and Monodramas

Klaus Peter Müller

> Existence is not only an event, it is an utterance. The event of existence has the nature of dialogue in this sense; there is no word directed to no one. (Holquist 27)

> More than binarism, dialogism may well become the basis of our time's intellectual structure. (Kristeva 89)

Theatre in its most ancient form is generally regarded as a rather monolithic event, comparable to a religious festivity or a mythical ritual, with the function of honoring the gods and interpreting and justifying life connected with the deity.[1] The form was solely choric, before, in the Western world probably in the sixth century B.C., the first actor was introduced as "hypokrites," the one who gave answers to the chorus (Leo 1). This dialogic element was reinforced by Aeschylus and Sophocles who added a second and third actor and decisively expanded "the possibilities of drama by allowing for interplay between individual characters" (Harwood 45). Dialogue has been a basic element of drama ever since, with monologue used only sparingly and for specific purposes, such as the expression of strong emotions or individual reflections about vital problems.[2]

Contemporary drama, however, is characterized by an increase in monologues and monoplays (dramatic pieces for single performers). The "crisis of modern drama" (Szondi 20ff.) is closely connected with the "crisis of language," the fact that characters in plays act less and talk more, while language itself has become a matter of dispute, doubt and refutation. Distrust in humankind's ability to act, and thus to shape human history, has brought along distrust in all means of communication and identification. If "I am another," and when it is language that speaks me,[3] who am I to talk to, who am I speaking with, by what means, and for which reasons?

While there may be a reason to communicate after all, because there is always a certain "desire in language" (Kristeva), it is hardly anything definite outside one's own personality, it is rather something that is always already within the individual, such as the language s/he uses and the culture s/he is part of. The conflict of modern life as depicted in literature and drama is again and again that between an individual and an overpowering system which infiltrates the individual, so that it ultimately becomes a conflict within the individual him- or herself. The question of whether a human being can still exert a certain freedom and independence or whether s/he is completely submerged in all-encompassing systems, such as language and culture, is answered in different ways by postmodernists (such as Lacan or Derrida) and modernists (such as Gadamer, Habermas, or George Steiner). While the postmodernists (implicitly) underline the importance or even the complete dominance of the system by abolishing concepts such as identity or selfhood, the modernists argue in favor of preserving at least a relatively reasonable margin of human self-determination. It is only in the latter case that real dialogue is possible. Although postmodernists put great emphasis on the importance of the other, their discourse—being largely influenced or even determined by the dominant system—is rather monologic, even though they maintain that it leads to "always different, always postponed meanings" and is therefore polyphonic (Derrida lxv). Gadamer, a modernist, however, makes the point that dialogue is a precondition of understanding.[4]

Monologue does not depend on just one person being present or speaking, of course. Both linguists and literary scholars have stressed the fact that monologue is defined by the unilateral direction of what is being said: "in dialogue we have the semantic changes of direction between each of the utterances and in monologues one unified semantic direction" (Pfister 128). Jean Piaget (18f.) characterizes the monologue as egocentric. For Friedrich Kainz (172) dialogue alone establishes social contact, the most important effect of language. Mikhail Bakhtin defines a monologic text as "one unitary and singular belief system," as "a single, unitary authorial discourse" (334).

Bakhtin's attempts to categorize certain genres, such as drama and poetry, as mainly monologic, and others, especially the novel, as basically dialogic, have, for good reasons, been refuted as one-sided, as not very useful for typologies of genres, and not corroborated by the literary evidence.[5] His emphasis on the ultimately dialogic nature of language, however, has yielded a number of important insights into the ways in which language functions, how meaning is established, and why human truth, value, and identity can only be relative. Bakhtin's dialogism provides an entire epistemology, including linguistics, axiology, and "a general aesthetic," or "an architectonics, a science of building" reality and meaning.[6] It is in this context that the first epigraph to the present article must be understood. One can also express the dialogic nature of meaningful life in this way: "Language, when it means, is somebody talking to somebody else, even when that someone else is one's own inner addressee" (Bakhtin xxi).

For Bakhtin each human being is always in dialogue with somebody else. Bakhtin sees everybody as responsible for the creation of his or her identity, for giving value and meaning to one's own life. As "'we have no alibi in existence,'...we must, we all must, create ourselves, for the self is not given to any one of us" (Holquist 28f.).

Whatever genre one may choose for the creation of one's self, it is quite obvious that for Bakhtin any discourse consists of three elements "having a structure very much like the triadic construction of the linguistic sign:...an utterance, a reply, and a relation between the two. It is the relation that is most important of the three" (Holquist 38). The basic form of language is, therefore, dialogic, whereas in a monologue speaker and listener, or rather their positions or points of view, are no longer really distinguishable from each other.[7]

What determines whether a text is monologic or dialogic, is not simply the direct meaning of the words uttered, but above all the concrete situation, the individual, and historic conditions of the utterance: "Who speaks and under what conditions he speaks: this is what determines the word's actual meaning" (Bakhtin 401). This is also how ultimately genres are defined: "by the object, the goal, and the situation, of the utterance" (Todorov 84). Bakhtin's distinction between monologic and dialogic texts specifically underlines the importance of historical, social, and individual contexts of discourse.[8] It is these contexts that define the meaning(s) of an utterance; they create the dialogue of understanding. There is already a dialogue at work within each single text which always consists of two poles: the language as such, as a reiterative system of signs, and the concrete historical situation in which these signs are used and which gives particular meaning to them.

New contexts provide new meanings, new interpretations, and new dialogues. Such contexts will also help determine the meanings and qualities, the values of Wesker's monologues and monodramas. We are here, of course, in the very realm of the human sciences, including literature, described by Bakhtin in the following way:

> The shorthand record of the human sciences. It is always the record of a dialogue of a particular kind: the complex correlation of the text (object of study and reflexion) and the context that frames it and which is being created (as questions, objection, etc. are raised), where the scholar's knowing and evaluating thought accomplishes itself. It is the encounter of two texts: the already-given text and the reacting text being created, and therefore, it is the encounter of two subjects, of two authors. (Todorov 23)

In the context of contemporary drama, Arnold Wesker's writing of monoplays is not a unique event. The increase in monologues and monodramas has already been noticed and commented upon by a number of critics.[9] One of the functions of monodrama is a particular response to drama in a difficult crisis. It has time and again been seen as offering new perspectives for drama or at least as an outlet for things for which there seemed to be no alternative form of expression.[10] In addition to the general crisis in language already referred to, the English theatre, which had flourished in the 60s and 70s, went through its own crisis in the 80s, with a resulting upsurge of monodrama.[11]

Wesker's development is representative of the growing concern in contemporary drama with the individual. This concern has always been especially strong after experiences of failure or frustration with society as a whole or as a collective social force. Playwrights who still believe in social forces and hope for solidarity are, therefore, less inclined to use the monologue. Edward Bond, for instance, who is said to have become "increasingly radical and didactic" (Innes 156), has a very definite opinion about the monologue: "The individual is no longer a metaphor for the state and his private feelings can no longer be used to express cause in history or will in politics....Hamlet's soliloquy has withered into the senile monologue of *Krapp's Last Tape*" (Bond 136). So whereas in Shakespeare the individual expressed the social, while the personal was also the political, contemporary (bourgeois) theatre has put an end to this dialogue and become monologic for Bond. His evaluation, of course, also depends much on the contexts used and is not shared by those such as Michelene Wandor who still claim that "the personal is political" and that its forms of expression are socially relevant.

Arnold Wesker has been called "a 'socially realistic' playwright" himself. It is a definition he has always resented, because it has made people blind, as he puts it, to all the other aspects in his work, "the paradoxical, the lyrical, the absurd, the ironic, the musical, the farcical, etc." (Wesker 1986, 367). There has always been a certain amount of individualism in him, "which perhaps runs counter to his 'social' image" (Leeming 1983, 4).

It is easy to see how the "social" image came about. In his early plays Wesker was mostly concerned with the lives and struggles of social groups and with individuals in such groups. There was usually a long cast of characters, and only a small number of monologues. Wesker was known as "a playwright who knows how to write dialogue" (Leeming 1985, 17). On the other hand, there has been in his plays, right from *The Kitchen* onward, the kind of monologue for which he has also become famous, indeed "a master of this art" (Leeming 1985, 30). These monologues are sometimes called "set-piece speeches" or "educational set-pieces" (Leeming 1983, 87f. with reference to *The Friends*).

An early example of this type of speech, which is particularly interesting as it is a metaphoric description of a monologic situation, is the "story" told by Paul in *The Kitchen* (2:51f.) about the wall between people who do not care to understand each other. This motif is taken up again in *I'm Talking About Jerusalem* and presented in the same type of speech by Dobson. He describes the lack of communication in his two marriages where any effort to make oneself understood failed, because everybody seemed to be using "a foreign language" (1:184).

From the very beginning of his writing, therefore, Wesker is fully aware of the conditions in which language becomes monologic. Such conditions occur whenever people do not listen to each other, when they do not want to understand, and when they try to avoid becoming really involved in life, in having to find a justification for their existence, in giving reasons for their actions and meaning to their way of living. Dave in *Jerusalem* is such a person who refuses to listen to others, who calls Dobson a "cynic," a trouble-maker, and a disturber of the peace desired by these people. He clearly avoids becoming involved in dialogue and categorically says: "We are not going to go around apologizing for the way we live. Listen to people and we'll go mad. Enough now!" (1:185).

Wesker not only shows that language becomes monologic when the addressee refuses to listen or interact but also that language is used monologically when there is too great a discrepancy between the world people live in and the world described by language. Any utopia which has nothing to do with ordinary lives is, therefore, also monologic. This is expressed by Ronnie in the wider context of his speech about *Jerusalem*, the war in Spain in 1936, the end of World War II, and Labour's victory in 1945 when he realizes: "As soon as I say something, somehow I don't believe it. Don't you find that with things? As soon as you pronounce something it doesn't seem true?" (1:212). Ronnie is ultimately "mad" (1:218), because reality has caught up with him and his utopian ideals. He has been the one to "say all the right things" and "think all the right things," but he has not been able to combine his thoughts and statements with reality, and he, therefore, has failed "as a human being" (1:216f.). The ending of Jerusalem underlines the fragmentary nature of human life, which has to be accepted, because, as Ada says: "Whose life was ever a complete statement?" (1:215). Ronnie's madness has been brought about by his one-sidedness, by the monologic quality of his utopia. He (like the spectator or reader of the play) is now forced to begin a new dialogue.

Language, as we have learned from both Bakhtin and Wesker, becomes monologic when there is no (open-minded) listener or when there is no world to which the language refers. But Wesker also shows how a monologic situation arises when the speaker and the listener do not really differ from each other. Andy's speeches and ideas in *Their Very Own and Golden City*, e.g., have the effect of monologues, because people only hear what they want to hear. "Men need leaders" (2:196), and in that case they do not care about the individual person, but only about his/her function or ideas. After his monologue, which expresses his emotional turmoil, Andy tells Kate about a girl who came up to him after one of his lectures and said: "I don't believe you. You said all the things I believe in but I don't believe you" (2:197). Andy understands that in this way there is no real dialogue, but only an identification with one's own ideas: "We don't really like people, do we? We just like the idea of ourselves liking people" (2:197). In a much more fundamental sense than Jessie assumes when she says to

Andy that he is talking to himself again and "always did" (2:197), Andy has lived and worked monologically. People have only ever accepted him for their own ideas in him, not because of his own individual qualities. Young Andy's conviction, "Aye—and people are good" (2:199), is actually the article of faith for the dialogic communication needed for real human emancipation and liberation: a communication which acknowledges not only a common basis for everybody in abstract ideas, but also individual qualities and differences in human beings. The play ends, according to Wesker, in an atmosphere of "sad irony" (2:199), but not in hopelessness. It has become evident that the characters live monologically. The dialogue which could improve their lives has not yet begun.

Monologue is thus a substantial and essential formal as well as thematic element in Wesker's plays. The opening of *The Friends* has not only "Wesker's two strands of monologue but three" (Leeming 1983, 87). Esther, Manfred, and Roland are speaking to themselves. Only Esther is aware of this, and at the end of her first speech, she points out the fact that people do not listen to each other (3:75). Manfred is monologic again and again in that he repeatedly quotes from books, but for him the words are not related to concrete things, or actions, nor does he really believe in them: "Terrible, isn't it? I can't bring myself to believe any of that. Lying there it sounded so logical and right; but saying it, actually using the words—nothing. Stale" (3:97). That is why for Esther he is not effective, simply a rabble-rouser, "a rebel," not "a revolutionary" such as herself (3:106).

Whereas for Manfred "words act like dams" (3:85) shutting people in and locking out action, feelings, and passion, for Macey they are gates helping to understand the world. But Macey also realizes that people do not listen ("It's like talking to a brick wall"), they do not even have the "grace" to "say hello or ask about people" (3:84), nor have they really understood anything of what has been written since the invention of print. People like that, he says, are "crippled" (3:85), they are "children" who do not know what they are doing (3:94), they are "weird" and "unnatural"(3:112). But Macey himself cannot communicate with others either. One reason is that he is not listened to, another, equally important, is that he is so full of "self-hatred" that he shuts himself in this way (3:113).

Roland's monologic predicament makes him say: "I can't find words; and words I find I don't want to use, and words I use I don't believe in." Ultimately, while Tessa is "*in a fever of distress,*" "*he is in a catatonic state*" (3:115). None of these characters can "comfort" each other (3:115), because they are all too concerned with themselves, with their personal lives, individual fear, and guilt. Both Macey's and Crispin's monologues (3:112f., 116) are traditional emotional reflections and confessions. They are also both spoken in a monologic situation where others do not listen or respond.

The characters are only vaguely beginning to listen at the end of the play. After Simone's speech they "*seem chastened and mellow, though more touched than convinced.*" Manfred again voices their reluctance to listen: "Yes, Simone, we've listened. But that's not the half of it" (3:125). He is right, it is not enough to just listen. In order to get out of the monologic, death-like situation they must all try "*to overcome their fear of death,*" their sense of failure and isolation. Their "love for the dead" must ultimately be combined with love for the living. That new dialogue has not yet begun, though. In *The Friends*, the characters are "*forced to accept the presence of the dead among them*" (3:126). At the end of the play, it is up to the audience to decide whether to carry on a dialogue with the living.

Wesker is concerned with liberating people, with making them see that language should be used like "bridges" (1:90) to make connections, not like "walls" or "dams" to shut people in. Beatie Bryant in *Roots* learns that this is difficult and requires "much effort," but it is also the only way of finding one's identity, one's "roots" (1:146). One will never find a fixed identity, or a predetermined one, or one that provides complete peace and happiness. On the contrary, "it's asking questions, all the time" (1:147); it is a permanent quest for meaning and value.[12] Beatie at the end of the play has liberated herself from Ronnie. She no longer quotes him anymore; she speaks for herself. But, again, nobody listens. She is "articulate at last," no longer an infant, but she "stands alone" (1:148). Thus the play again ends in an atmosphere of sad irony, not with a cozy resolution but with a conflict that leaves the spectator or reader pondering. It is a new dialogic situation.

Whereas Beatie is only "beginning" (1:148), Betty Lemon is determined not to end the dialogue. Betty does not quote anybody, in fact, she is her own woman, "an old woman crippled by everything old age brings" (5:25). She stands opposed to everything that cripples people and takes away their freedom to be responsible for and to create their own lives: age, sex, diseases, bad teachers, hypocritical parents, lying politicians, false beliefs, bad marriages, despair, lack of creativity, and want of love.

Whatever Happened to Betty Lemon? is one of Wesker's monodramas, the plays he explicitly refuses to call "monologues," because they involve not simply "one person merely speaking and not engaged in any action," but rather a character "responding to a situation or involved in an action and engaged in an exchange of conflict" (5:7). These plays were mostly written, performed, and published in the 1980s. But Wesker's concern with individual lives and their presentation on stage began much earlier. He has, in fact, discussed this theme in connection with *The Four Seasons* as something that is ultimately far more important than the class struggle and social issues: This, he said, was "a play about love, I was not going to be touching upon social issues, and I had to ask myself the question: 'Could I do this? Is this valid in—not merely in theatre, but is it valid as part of a socialist concept of art?' And I believe I decided it was, since…once the economic battle is over there is still the battle of being alive, of being a human being" (Leeming 1985, 28f.).

Being alive and human implies being involved in a real dialogue with others. *The Four Seasons* again shows that in order to be "generous and understand," one has to listen to the individual person one is with, and that very often people hear only what they want to hear (2:95). When people cry for their "own misery" only, there is no love left, no warmth to drive away the cold, just "sadness and waste and neglect and suffering" (2:108, 111). For Wesker, art has always had at least three basic purposes: "If compassion and teaching the possibility of change are two of the many effects of art, a third is this: to remind and reassure people that they are not alone not only in their attempts to make a better world but in their private pains and confusions also" (2:113).

In Wesker's monodramas there is no abandoning "of concern for socialist principles nor a turning away from a preoccupation with real human problems" (2:114). Betty Lemon indeed addresses many of the vital questions of our age. But are we listening, or do we only hear what we want to hear or what we have heard so often before? There is a problem with the monoplays in that the situations depicted in them do not perhaps always provide the basis for a real dialogue with the spectator or reader. The danger is that a too-ready identification with the character can stifle any dialogue at all, as can a complete lack of identification.

Dialogue underlines the importance of the other. In dialogue the other is not neglected, usurped, or denied; it is, on the contrary, acknowledged in its own right and accepted as "'the most powerful factor in understanding'" (Holquist 26). Dialogue is in fact, "Bakhtin's metaphor for the unity of the two elements constituting the relation of self and other, the simultaneous unity of differences in the event of utterance" (Holquist 36). The speaker in Wesker's monodramas is often too much like the spectator, the otherness, the differences and oppositions needed for a real dialogue are not sufficiently presented. There is an epistemological basis for this problem, which Bakhtin expressed very much like Charles S. Peirce: "experience exists even for the person undergoing it [the 'I'] only in the material of signs [the other]"(Holquist 49). The characters in the monodramas are too much like the "I" and too little the other.

Wesker, who clearly sees that there must be a certain amount of freedom whenever there is to be a dialogue, does not always give enough imaginative freedom to the spectator in his monodramas. Annabella Wharton says "the smaller a work of art, the greater should be the co-efficient of expansion" (5:101). But there is always the danger of entropy in such a case, of too many possible interpretations, or of its opposite, the reduction of a text to a single interpretation, of a character to a familiar stereotype: the abandoned wife in *Yardsale*, the lonely elderly person in *Betty Lemon*, the mother figures in *Four Portraits—Of Mothers*, the frustrated eponymous lover in *The Mistress*, or the personae chosen in *Annie Wobbler*.

Wesker's skillful use of language gives his monodramas the "poetic relationship" he wanted to achieve (Leeming 1985, 44), but they do not really constitute dramatic art; they do not create the kind of dialogue the spectator is involved in in Wesker's other plays. The monodramas are too devoid of a context that would make them specific individual historical conflicts and provide them with value and meaning in the way defined by Bakhtin above. The spectator is too easily inclined to adopt a stereotypical response; he is intrigued by the language and the characters but not aroused to indulge in a dialogue with the characters or their problems.

In the monodramas, the characters are shown from the inside and present things from their point of view. Their views are not really "contradictable" (5:108). The monologues in the other plays, on the other hand, are put into contexts which give them a certain profile, a concise individuality and meaning. Thus the spectator or reader is aware, like Shylock in Wesker's play by the same title, of "how causes work their effects—but *within their time*" (4:231). Shylock's own monologue here (4:230–33), the Weskerian set-piece speech, is about the progress of knowledge in human life and the importance of language. It is instantly contradicted by the situation in which Shylock lives, "*as though [this] is evidence to refute all he's said*" (4:233). But the whole play shows that what is expressed in the monologue is important in the world, that it is, however, also idealistic, and will take a long time to become reality. Portia understands this: "Wisdom, inconsiderately, does not translate in a moment" (4:263).

A key element in Wesker's monologue, which is also reflected in Portia, the "new woman" (4:197), is the knowledge that things change and nothing remains the same. The possibility for change which includes the hope for the intellectual and emotional growth of humankind is alive through Portia. This hope is necessarily connected with human intelligence and free dialogic communication:

> *I* am not a thing of the wind, but an intelligence informed by other men informed by other men informed! *I* grow. Why can't they? What *I* thought yesterday might be wrong today. What should I do? Stand by my yesterdays because *I* have made them? I made today as well! And tomorrow, that I'll make too, and all my days, as my intelligence demands. (4:263)

Portia's idea of what might nowadays and in the wake of Bakhtin be called "intertextuality"[13] is just another version of Shylock's concept of the history of knowledge. Both imply change and continuity, an intelligent creation of meaning in a never-ending dialogue. But most people will not listen nor learn from history. Thus they do not grow, they remain immature infants, imprisoned in their fears, their utopias, their self-inflicted or adopted confines, shutting themselves and others in. Arnold Wesker is a modernist, like Bakhtin.[14] He still has some faith left in human intelligence, and he wants to enlighten his audience and readers. He wants them to see and make use of their freedom, even if it is as limited as in the monodramas. Wesker still hopes for human dialogue to begin, because, as he said in connection with *The Merchant*: "The free spirit implies the supremacy of the human being over the state, over repressive authority, over that which aims to frustrate initiative, cripple imagination, induce conformity" (Leeming, 1985, 59).

But his work, just like reality, is full of monologic speakers who are not listened to, who talk about things that are not real, or who simply repeat what was said by others and what they neither understand nor believe in. Whether they speak in what are traditionally called monologues is not so important. What really counts is the exact context which reveals whether it is a dialogue or a monologue that is taking place. The traditional form is only a part of the reiterative language system. We have to listen to the individual utterance in order to understand the language against its contextual backdrop. Only then will we be able to evaluate it as monologic or dialogic and thereby become involved in the endless dialogue of understanding and of (re-)creating reality and meaning.

ଏ

ENDNOTES

1. Hunningher; Nicoll; Eliade.

2. Monologue was already used for these purposes by Homer. For the development of monologue in ancient drama, especially in the new comedy, cf. Leo.

3. Rimbaud's famous dictum "Je est un autre" in his letter to Georges Izambard in 1871 (Rimbaud 200) and Lacan.

4. Gadamer, 447 and Jauß. See also Holquist 25 for the same difference between Derrida and Bakhtin.

5. Keyssar; Lachmann, 51–62; Pechey; Todorov, 90f.

6. Holquist 33: "Although, then, dialogism is primarily an epistemology, it is not just a theory of knowledge. Rather, it is in its essence a hybrid: dialogism exploits the nature of language as a modeling system for the nature of existence, and thus is deeply involved with linguistics; dialogism sees social and ethical values as the means by which the fundamental I/other split articulates itself in specific situations and is thus a version of axiology; and in so far as the act of perception is understood as the patterning of a relation, it is a general aesthetic, or it is an architectonics, a science of building." See also Holquist's definition of "dialogism" in Bakhtin 426.

7. Bakhtin as quoted in Todorov 44; Sartre; Lodge 97f., and Todorov 63ff. are doubtful about the existence of an absolutely monologic text.

8. Todorov (34 and 46) quotes Bakhtin with these statements on literature: "every literary work is sociological" and "It is the axiological horizon that assumes the most important function in the organization of the literary work, and especially in that of its formal aspects." Quite generally this means that "the speaking subject, taken from the inside, so to speak, turns out to be wholly the product of social interrelations. Not only external expression but also internal experience fall within social territory. Therefore, the road which links the internal experience (the 'expressible') to its external objectification (the 'utterance') lies entirely in social territory" (Bakhtin in Todorov 33).

9. Cf. Goetsch; Müller 1982; Müller 1993, 6f., Weiss.

10. Szondi 1975, 17; Demmer 2f.

11. Müller 1993.

12. For questions and answers in Wesker, in hermeneutics and in dialogism cf. Müller 1993 8; Jauß 23; Todorov 53f.

13. Holquist 49 quoting Bakhtin: "understanding comes about as a response to a sign with signs. Since, therefore, there is no sign in itself, every given sign is a link in the great chain comprising all other signs: 'And nowhere is there a break in the chain, nowhere does the chain plunge into inner being, non-material in nature and unembodied in signs.'" This, again, is very much like Peirce (1933, 551; 1955, 594).

14. There are, of course, also important similarities with Martin Buber. Cf. Buber 1973 and also Dembo 1988.

Works Cited

Bakhtin, Mikhail Mikhailovich. *The Dialogic Imagination. Four Essays*. Ed. M. Holquist. Austin: University of Texas Press, 1981.

Bond, Edward. *The Worlds with The Activists Papers*. London: Methuen, 1980.

Buber, Martin. *Das dialogische Prinzip*. Heidelberg: Lambert Schneider, 1973.

Dembo, Lawrence; S. *The Monological Jew. A Literary Study*. Madison: University of Wisconsin Press, 1988.

Demmer, Sybille. *Untersuchungen zu Form und Geschichte des Monodramas*. Köln/Wien: Böhlau, 1982.

Derrida, Jacques. *Of Grammatology*. Baltimore: Johns Hopkins University Press, 1976.

Gadamer, Hans-Georg. *Wahrheit und Methode—Grundzüge einer philosophischen Hermeneutik*. Tübingen: Mohr, 1960.

Goetsch, Paul. "Die Tendenz zum Monologischen im modernen Drama:

Beckett und Pinter," in Horst Groene, ed., *Hörspiel im Englischunterricht.* Paderborn: Schöningh, 1980, 73–98.

Harwood, Ronald. *All the World's a Stage.* London: Methuen, 1984.

Holquist, Michael. *Dialogism. Bakhtin and His World.* London: Routledge, 1990.

Innes, Christopher. *Modern British Drama 1890–1990.* Cambridge: Cambridge University Press, 1992.

Jauß, Hans Robert. "Zum Problem des dialogischen Verstehens," in Lachmann, *Dialogizität.* München: Fink, 1982. 11–24.

Kainz, Friedrich. *Psychologie der Sprache.* Vol.1. Stuttgart: Enke, 1962.

Keyssar, Helene. "Drama and the Dialogic Imagination: *The Heidi Chronicles* and *Fefu and Her Friends.*" *Modern Drama* 34.1 (1991): 88–106.

Kristeva, Julia. *Desire in Language. A Semiotic Approach to Literature and Art.* New York: Columbia University Press, 1980.

Lacan, Jacques. *Ecrits: A Selection.* London: Tavistock, 1977.

Lachmann, Renate. *Dialogizität.* München: Fink, 1982, 51–62.

——, ed. "Dialogizität und poetische Sprache," in Lachmann, 1982, 51–62.

Leeming, Glenda. *Wesker the Playwright.* London: Methuen, 1983.

——. *Wesker on File.* London: Methuen, 1985.

Leo, Friedrich. "Der Monolog im Drama. Ein Beitrag zur griechisch-römischen Poetik." *Abhandlungen der königlichen Gesellschaft der Wissenschaften zu Göttingen* X, 6, 1908. 1–119 (repr. Göttingen: Vandenhoeck & Ruprecht 1970).

Lodge, David. *After Bakhtin. Essays on Fiction and Criticism.* London: Routledge, 1990.

Müller, Klaus Peter ed. "Theater als Sinnsuche und Geschichtsschreibung: Signifikante Entwicklungen im englischen Theater der Gegenwart." *Englisches Theater der Gegenwart. Geschichte(n) und Strukturen.* Tübingen: Narr, 1993, 3–58.

Müller, Wolfgang G. "Das Ich im Dialog mit sich selbst: Bemerkungen zur Struktur des dramatischen Monologs von Shakespeare bis zu Samuel Beckett." *Deutsche Vierteljahresschrift* 56 (1982): 314–33.

Pechey, Graham. "On the Borders of Bakhtin: Dialogisation, Decolonisation." *Bakhtin and Cultural Theory.* Eds. Ken Hirschkop and David Shepherd. Manchester: Manchester University Press, 1989, 39–67.

Peirce, Charles S. *Collected Papers.* Eds. C. Hartshorne and P. Weiss. Vol.4. Cambridge: Harvard University Press, 1933.

——. *Philosophical Writings.* Ed. J. Buchler. New York: Dover, 1955.

Pfister, Manfred. *The Theory and Analysis of Drama.* Cambridge: Cambridge University Press, 1988.

Piaget, Jean. *Le langage et la pensée chez l'enfant. Etudes sur la logique de l'enfant.* Paris: Delachaux et Niestlé, 1976.

Rimbaud, Arthur. *Poésies. Une saison en enfer. Illuminations.* Paris: Gallimard, 1977.

Szondi, Peter. *Das lyrische Drama des fin de Siècle.* Frankfurt: Suhrkamp, 1975.

——. *Theorie des modernen Dramas.* Frankfurt: Suhrkamp, 1973.

Todorov, Tzvetan. *Mikhail Bakhtin. The Dialogical Principle.* Manchester: Manchester University Press, 1984.

Wandor, Michelene. "The Personal Is Political. Feminism and Theatre," in *Dreams and Deconstructions: Alternative Theatre in Britain.* Ed. Sandy Craig. Ambergate: Amber Lane Press, 1980, 49–58.

Weiss, Rudolf. "Form und Funktion des Monologs im englischen Gegenwartsdrama: Bond; Shaffer; Keeffe, Edgar." *Studien zur Ästhetik des Gegenwartstheaters.* Ed. Christian W. Thomsen. Heidelberg: Winter, 1985, 225–39.

Wesker, Arnold. *The Wesker Trilogy. Chicken Soup with Barley. Roots. I'm Talking About Jerusalem.* Vol.1. Harmondsworth: Penguin, 1964 (repr. 1977).

——. *The Kitchen. The Four Seasons. Their Very Own and Golden City.* Vol. 2. Harmondsworth: Penguin, 1976 (repr. 1990).

——. *Chips with Everything. The Friends. The Old Ones. Love Letters on Blue Paper.* Vol.3. Harmondsworth: Penguin, 1980.

——. *The Journalists. The Wedding Feast. The Merchant.* Vol. 4. Harmondsworth: Penguin, 1980.

——. *One Woman Plays. Yardsale. Whatever Happened to Betty Lemon? Four Portraits—of Mothers. The Mistress. Annie Wobbler.* Vol. 5. Harmondsworth: Penguin, 1989.

——. "The Nature of Theatre Dialogue." *New Theatre Quarterly* 8 (1986): 364–68.

Arnold Wesker and Women
His Later Plays

Glenda Leeming

In his introduction to the Penguin volume of his *One Woman Plays*, which contains five short plays for a solo actress, Arnold Wesker is concerned to point out that during the five years in which these plays were written, he had also written several others for mixed casts and large numbers; the impression that he had written nothing else over this period was thus mistaken.[1] Several critics have commented that these plays retrospectively highlight a special interest in women's experience that was always present in Wesker's work, in that they develop the use of long speeches by early women characters such as Sarah and Beatie in the Wesker *Trilogy*. While this is true, it is not the whole truth, as long speeches by male characters are equally frequent and striking in his plays—the reminiscences of Pip in *Chips with Everything*, and Manfred's set piece speech in *The Friends* are examples that spring to mind.

Nonetheless, from Wesker's ten published plays since 1978, a period that also includes *Caritas*, a play centered on the life of a medieval anchoress, it appears that the five *One Woman Plays* illustrate an increasing concern with the experience of women. Although as I shall suggest later there are dominant men in some of the mixed plays, the only play which structurally foregrounds a male character to a similar extent is the radio play *Bluey*, in which the protagonist is also the narrator, other male and female characters appearing briefly as part of his memories. Moreover, Wesker has since 1989 written three further plays (the two earlier have been performed), all again centering mainly on women characters.[2]

I hope to explain how Wesker presents a convincing picture of certain aspects of women's experience, showing women's attempts to struggle against constraints which are not biologically innate but are imposed by society. Because of his focus on language, Wesker exposes the way society supports or rejects individuals according to their relation to discourse: in the plays we see how the women characters' identity, their sense of self, is affected by their control or lack of control of the dominant discourse, which in turn is affected by their social environment (upbringing, education, social position, relationships with men, and so on). So far, Wesker thus is in tune with other modern schools of thought which emphasize the way in which masculinity, femininity, and individuality in general are culturally constructed: these schools of thought also propose, roughly, that individuals are molded by the conditions, norms, expectations, assumptions, values of their time and place to acquire many characteristics that are then often wrongly labelled "innate," typical, essential but, in fact, are not so. Much human conflict stems from the mismatch between society's stereotypes and the residual, varied and different human drives and potentialities, good and bad, which can never be fitted in to any single formulation. Theorists in feminism, psychology, and sociology make the same point in different ways, for example, de Beauvoir's "One is not born, but rather becomes a woman,"[3] or Lacan's rejection of the "anatomy is destiny" dictum.[4]

At the same time Wesker retains a traditional liberal humanism which asserts the centrality of the individual and the existence of free choice, against all the odds, a sort of freedom which is denied as impossible by many adherents of the determinist schools of thought. Nonetheless, his liberalism is qualified: even though Beatie Bryant in *Roots* breaks from her limited background and learns to become a newly thinking and articulate subject, Harry Kahn states, and Ronnie repeats, in the *Trilogy*, that "You can't change people. All you can do is offer them some love and hope they'll take it" (1:56; 1:210).

Wesker's sense of the pressure of social factors is extended by his insight into the experience of decentered groups in society. As a Jew, Wesker's own experience of various levels of antisemitism in Britain was reinforced by more extreme persecution suffered by older generations of his family in Europe and by the genocide of Jews by Hitler's Germany. He is sensitive to the treatment of Jews by British society as perpetually "other," alien, to be regarded with suspicion, however successful or accepted they may externally seem to be. Wesker's work thus shows interesting parallels between the female subject position and that of other marginalized and decentered groups, such as that of Jews in non-Jewish society, and of artists in what he sees as a mainly philistine society.

Wesker therefore treats with sympathy the gap between the stereotypes society sets up, and the amorphous, changing, struggling, if limited, human being who must always differ from the simple stereotype. At the same time, while perceiving women's difficulties, he does not see them as a peculiarly feminine problem but as the problem of any thinking subject caught in the web of social expectations. The constraints of stereotyped femininity are felt particularly in individual male-female relationships, but outside such relationships the women tend to struggle with the constraints of the social order as the disadvantaged men characters do.

In the *Annie Wobbler* plays, the first and last sections can be seen as demonstrating this common human plight, where the women characters struggle as thinking human subjects in ways which could equally be experienced by men; the middle example is the only one which refers to gender-specific female experiences. The three characters are each searching for a sense of identity, and all three find that identity is fluid and elusive, slipping and reforming according to the other identities that confront them, and is particularly related to their control of dominant discourse. Annie, the old charwoman, reveals her lack of understanding and, thus, control of her life and herself through her imperfect and inadequate control of language. She has been pushed to the margins of society and does not feel that she belongs anywhere, aware of her position among a class of outsiders, like the "foreigners," the Jewish East End family she now works for: "All sorts live here. You'd think because all sorts live here they'd leave you alone. But they don't, madam, they don't" (5:85). She has come to think that she was nothing:

> Because I was a nothing, madam, and I knowed I was a
> nothing. That's knowledge for you. I wasn't told, I wasn't
> treated bad, but it come to me. Nothing! A nothing Annie
> Wobbler. Nothing brains and nothing looks and nothing
> grace. A serving-maid for other people! A bag of rags and
> bones. Sack of old coal, that was me. (5:87)

She has no image of herself, merely a void. When she looks in the mirror, as all three women characters do, she sees "this face, but I don't know nothin' about it 'cept it's growing old.... Funny feeling, looking at yourself and not knowing what you see. So I don't do it much" (5:84). Her formation of a self-image has not fully taken place. Annie is aware that there is something missing in her consciousness:

"Always felt full of holes. They left bits out when they put me to-gether, see, I couldn't never understand nothing, madam. All a for-eign language to me" (5:89). The lack of control over her life, and even over her own image, is related to her lack of verbal concepts. Because she cannot explain herself, other people cannot label her in social terms, and she cannot label herself. Her entry into the social order has never been complete, and she remains an extreme example of the dangers of being caught in an imperfectly controlled, inarticu-late world.

In Wesker's plays, however, this is seen as equally dangerous to men and women; as noted above, he does not present irrationality and inarticulacy as peculiarly feminine problems—for every Mrs. Bryant there is a Mr. Bryant; for the "lipsticked giggling morons" Ada refers to in *Chicken Soup*, there are also "men who...behaved like animals" (1:42).

Anna, the second character, a clever young woman newly gradu-ated with first-class honors, on the other hand is involved in a more recognizable confusion between her sexuality and her claims to intel-lectual dominance. She is seen asserting her sexuality by conforming to the stereotype of the "over-fleshed tart" in black underwear, while being quite aware that she could be criticized for this conformity; "What do you think you're doing, Anna? And in black!" she asks herself, "My God! You're so corny" (5:92). As she dresses for an evening out with her boyfriend, she alternately denigrates her appearance, as not beautiful enough, and her intelligence—she keeps assuming, then rejecting, the pose of being less knowledgeable than she is, the "te-dious English habit of boasting ignorance" (5:92). She considers the convention that she should assume socially acceptable femininity by pretending to be less intelligent: "He can be modest about his clever-ness, but I will have to hide mine." Here, however, she goes on to relate the convention to a generally human struggle for dominance—"Why don't men like their women to be clever? They like them to be clever, but not cleverer than them. Still, I don't suppose anybody en-joys anybody being cleverer than them. It's so undemocratic" (5:94), and although this refers to a constant theme of Wesker's work—the mean-spirited inability of most people to admire and honor the achievements of others—Wesker does not allow her to remark fur-ther on the distinction she began with, that is, the social expectation that the man need only assume modesty but the woman should adopt total silence. Here his insistence on common human experience seems to overshadow and interfere with his emerging theme of sexism in social behavior.

The dialogue displays Anna's comic indecision, as she looks in the mirror seeking her identity, about the various conventions of femininity and her confusion about whether to hide her intelligence, or conversely to avoid the conventions of glamour because these are unworthy of her intellectual powers. The resolution shows her deciding aggressively to choose both the "corny" black underwear and glamour dress that express her sexuality and at the same time to display her intellect, her "cultural references," without concealment—she is a language student, and her assertiveness proposes overtly to take the form of control of social discourse. Like many other outsiders, Anna is preparing to compete in the male-dominated world, represented by her pleasant, civilized, but opinionated boyfriend, and intends to succeed on society's own terms.

> You've broken the stranglehold of those century-old genes
> of crass ineptitude and supplication and you've unknown
> muscles to flex and a lot of intimidating to make up for
> and he's just the size and texture your teeth need sharpen-
> ing upon! (5:97)

Here she is asserting ("*With mounting triumph*") her intelligence but without denying her sexuality, even if this too is expressed in conventional ways.

In the final tripartite section of the play, Annabella Wharton, the character expresses many important themes and preoccupations that Wesker has argued both inside and outside his plays; Annabella is herself a writer, and shares Wesker's initials AW—with more opportunity for identification with the author than Annie Wobbler the charwoman. (In *Their Very Own and Golden City*, the protagonist was to have been called Andrew Wadham, changed to Andrew Cobham when it was pointed out that the initials would too closely identify him as the author's mouthpiece. With Annabella Wharton, Wesker seems to accept the identification.)

In the first two of three interviews which Annabella gives, she deliberately chooses a persona and ends the interview with contempt for the interviewer (a recorded "voiceover") and "sadness, it seems, for the performance she has just now put up" (5:102). Her first persona is a modest, humble, absent-minded, scatty woman whose incompetence and unpretentiousness are clearly no threat to anyone. Her "performance" here protects her with the camouflage of ordinariness, denying that there is anything to envy or to attack. It parallels the "don't make trouble" maxim of Jewish communities, seeking to avoid attention, because of the experience that attention always leads to persecution, an attitude which Wesker has often referred to.[5] At the same time it again acknowledges the envious sniping at any exceptional talent by the ungenerous mediocrities—"lilliputianising," in the phrase Wesker coined in *The Journalists*.

So the first Annabella Wharton spins a rationale for her work, pretending that no skill or talent or hard work goes into her writing: "Used! I'm not responsible for what I write, Good Lor' no! Merely the medium through which they bring themselves to life." Even less would she claim the implied superiority of being in a position to give other people a message: "Terrible word! A message? God forbid! They'd have my guts for garters!" And she goes on to deny any assertiveness on her part—"That's their prerogative to interpret, take what they want, what they need. A good piece of literature is open to many interpretations.... God forbid I should mean one thing"(5:100–101). In his writing and lecturing against the misinterpretation of his work by critics and directors,[6] Wesker has repeatedly argued against this kind of opinion. Annabella, then, fears being attacked by the literary establishment, just as Wesker has been attacked by the theatrical establishment, and her experience is that of an artist, not specifically that of a woman although her placatory "niceness" is also a front often adopted by women to avoid hostility. This constructed identity itself is a matrix in which the stereotype of the impractical, helpless, woman duplicates that of the impractical, helpless artist.

Her second persona however is much more assertive, not unlike Anna in her triumphant phase. This is the Annabella who looks in the mirror, "checking"—not interrogating—her appearance: she knows what her image is supposed to be. She claims to have entered the power struggle and won it:

> Fucking Empress of China! Nothing like it!
> High! I'm high all the time. To come to that dinner table throbbing with power from those detestable powerful people and have them begin to treat you with respect— nothing like it! It's cleansing, as though before—you were diseased, and now you're cured. (5:103)

Annabella is emphasizing that control of discourse (as a writer and at the social level) is power and that power reinforces her sense of identity. She also rejects "messages," and says that "Themes are for Ph.D.s and the Germans" (5:104). This Annabella is defending herself too, this time by offering the image of the tough, practical, self-seeking cynic. It is an appeal to the public's respect for money and power. Money and power are agreed by society to be desirable, and though they may attract envy and hostility, such hostility will not be personal. This Annabella tells of how she rejected the discouragement of a Welsh uncle, who advised her against trying to write because such efforts were "delusions of grandeur," mere psychological compensation for childhood conflict and physical insignificance. This anecdote originates in Wesker's own experience and reflects the shared reactions he, too, feels when, in reaction to constant criticism, he becomes depressed and cynical: thus Annabella's experiences as a writer are not gender specific.

The last interview is carried out by Annabella alone, without the voiceover, remembering the questions and answering them honestly. She parries the question about "messages" by pointing to the fallacy of thinking that any discourse is message free. The Hollywood producer who joked that "Anyone who wants to send a message uses Western Union" was responsible for supposedly message-free entertainments that were, inevitably, ideologically loaded. As she comments on the producer's joke, she takes off her interview clothes to reveal, the stage directions say, "a vulnerable middle-aged woman in bra and panties" (5:109). There is of course a message in this, a different message from Anna's message of sexual awareness. Male and female nudity or undress always has a different significance, because of the different range of alternatives within which each is seen, but here Annabella's vulnerable appearance not only comments on the stereotype of the underwear pin-up as sexual commodity, her appearance reminding us of the unreality of this stereotype, but also refers more generally to the state of being human and subject to aging, insecurity, and fear. As she says, "Somewhere within us all is a body waiting to give up, don't you think?" (5:111).

Wesker himself was mainly interested in exploring, for the first time in his drama, the experience of a writer and says "I was not writing about marginalization but attempting to recreate the different states most artists go through: false modesty, false arrogance, and finally the genuine terror that they may be mediocre after all…. I was actually attempting to write about real writers and their problems and games."[7] We can see, however, how the games of writers are shaped by the expectations of the dominant society. Of the three women in *Annie Wobbler*, then, all recognize the difficulty of inserting themselves into an uncongenial society, but only Anna focusses on the problems of a relationship with a particular man rather than on the demands of patriarchical society in general.

Wesker's distribution of attention between the difficulties of all marginalized or deviant individuals, as compared with the particular constraints imposed on women, can be seen in comparing the two full-length plays produced in the 1980s, *One More Ride on the Merry-Go-Round* (written 1978, produced 1985) and *When God Wanted a Son* (platform performance 1986). These plays are linked by several themes including the problems of male-female relationships, but their treatment of these problems is very different. In the earlier of the two plays, Wesker depicts a balance of roles between his main characters: the husband and wife Jason and Nita are both out of line with conventional society, she because of her work in raising money for the Third World, he because he has lost all interest or motivation to work at all. They have left each other by mutual agreement, because of either incompatibility or misunderstanding. Each has thought the other dull, dutiful, somehow unsatisfactory: Nita's work has made Jason feel "unworthy"; conversely, for Nita, echoing Beatie Bryant, Jason has "no—no—no urgency, no passion…a wild gaiety, that's what I craved" (6:40).

Though their marriage had lasted for 25 years, she says "I wanted to scream all the time. Walk around and scream and not stop" (6:40). In particular, their sexual relations have been boring and infrequent. This degree of exasperation has driven them apart, but with the younger lovers whom they then find, Monica and Matt, each displays at least temporarily the frivolity, urgency, passion, and everything they had failed to find in each other when together. The subplot brings into the play an illegitimate son of Jason, who is German and a brilliant conjurer and who inspires their morose, unambitious daughter with a suddenly wild enthusiasm for the profession of conjurer's assistant. This subplot seems metaphorically to reflect the quest of both Jason and Nita for the magical element in life, the magic they were unable to find in each other. The significant point here is that the themes are distributed equally between Jason and Nita, and in the circumstances where Nita, Monica and Chris are all working women, controlling their own income and living space, unburdened by maternity or specific female roles, Wesker is able to illustrate a universal desire for what is not, equally pursued by male and female, without having to discuss differential gender roles within the family or society.

Wesker was writing *When God Wanted a Son* while he was involved in the production of *One More Ride on the Merry-Go-Round*, but while the earlier play is a comedy, *When God Wanted a Son* is altogether a darker piece. Again it is about the breakdown of a marriage, but this time there are no younger lovers nor a magical son, only the daughter Connie, who is a stand-up comedian, an unsuccessful one—brief scenes from her act in a night-club punctuate the action. The whole of the first half of the play shows the interaction of Connie and her mother, Martha, with frequent references to the absent father, Joshua. Joshua is Jewish; Martha is not, and their conflict is also a conflict of Martha's antisemitism. She can find numerous reasons for hating Joshua: because he was full of opinions; because he thinks her simple; because he showed no respect for her; because he was "circuitous"; but in the end it is reduced to her hatred of the indefinable total effect of his personality: "he has an air…an air…" and it is useless for him to ask "An air of what? What air? What, what, what, you foolish woman?" (6:166), as she cannot define further. His "air" is connected for her with his Jewishness, but again she will not admit this. As she always refuses to name Joshua, referring to him only as "he" and "him," so she always cuts herself short before saying the word "Jew": "I believe the world is divided into those who are Jer—into those who are 'them' and those who are 'us'" (6:134).

Wesker has called *When God Wanted a Son* "a problematic play, or, more accurately stated, a desperate play" in that its message is that "antisemitism is here to stay."[8] For him, Martha represents antisemitism rather than anything specifically feminine. Yet, as in the case of Annabella's nudity, the effect is different according to whether the antisemite is a man or a woman. Clearly, here Martha does not have the positive role that Nita has, and she is guilty of the labelling of Joshua and all Jews together as the "other," whose ways are an offense to her Englishness. This does not mean that her reaction to him is not painful to her: where Nita says that she had wanted to scream, Martha does scream, and on seeing Joshua, as the stage direction says, she "enters a hysterical outburst which begins, continues and ends at the same high, intense level as though she has become possessed" (6:159).

Joshua is a spokesman for many of Wesker's recurrent themes, such as the need for aspirations, irreverence for a pompous and unworthy establishment, the need to make trouble (the opposite of the first Annabella Wharton's placatory low profile) "because sometimes trouble had to be made" (6:167). He does however also show a lack of sensitivity towards Martha which gives some justification to her frenzied complaints of being overwhelmed by him. One of the ways in which this is shown is, as so often in the plays, through the use of food.

It has often been noted that food is prominent and significant in Wesker's work; he argues that this is natural because food is after all vital to humanity, physically and socially. In her brief but stimulating commentary on Wesker's plays,[9] Micheline Wandor notes that in the *Trilogy*, the domestic space belongs to the women characters, where the women clean the house and make the food, and when they enter that space the men often become ill. In other plays, however, this is not so. Obviously, in *The Kitchen* all the cooking, though commercial not domestic, is done by men, and in *The Four Seasons* it is Adam who makes the amazing apple strudel on stage. In *One More Ride on the Merry-go-round*, Jason and Monica cook one course each of his birthday dinner, and Nita bedevils the dessert by sending a birthday cake full of hash. Joshua tries to placate Martha in *When God Wanted a Son* by offering to cook her a meal. Wesker himself was a trained pastrycook—food preparation for him is not gender specific. So, Martha herself demonstrates her motherly concern for Connie by plying her with unusual sandwiches. It is a game she plays to invite praise and recognition by asking people to guess the ingredients of the food she provides. In the last scene, after all her screaming, Martha tries to effect some kind of reconciliation by offering Joshua a birthday cake, even though it is not his birthday, but this final opportunity for reconciliation in the play is ruined when Joshua characteristically forgets to guess the ingredients in the cake, becoming absorbed in arguing with Connie and ignoring his wife's increasingly desperate calls for attention. The rejection of food is the rejection of the human being, and, as so often in Wesker's plays, the theme of food is connected with the theme of communication.

Though a failure at communicating with his wife, Joshua has a
wild scheme to penetrate beyond both deliberate and accidental verbal deception by inventing a machine to "read" the underlying into-
nation of speech. This theme of the various barriers to communication has always been important to Wesker: in *I'm Talking About Jerusalem*, Ada had said that words were not bridges: "Because language
isn't any use! Because we talk about one thing and you hear another"
(1:164). Joshua hopes to overcome the problem:

> Let me explain. Just as there are only a handful of basic
> plots, so there are only a handful of basic emotions. And
> each basic emotion has its own identifiable melody which
> the voice sings: love, hate, arrogance, modesty, false mod-
> esty, contempt, respect, sanctimony, demagogy, fear, and
> so on. And sometimes people utter words which are mod-
> est but in the melody of arrogance; or they utter words of
> love but in the melody of hate; or they offer words of
> respect but in the melody of contempt. And most people
> can't hear the melody, so they're fooled and misled by the
> words…. So my machine will be sensitive to the melo-
> dies and will show them up as a colour on a screen. (6:168)

Wesker had in 1976 written an essay on *Words as Definitions of Experience*,[10] in which he suggested that a number of key words, related to
key concepts, should be studied as part of the curriculum throughout
secondary education. In both Joshua's machine and the idea of study-
ing words, there is a craving for security and final authority that sits
uneasily with the sliding and ultimately contextual nature of meaning in language. There is a hint of this in some of Martha's ideas: she
works with money, and has a theory about all money, being worth
twice its value, which both Connie and Joshua find meaningless. She
explains that

> The condition of poverty is also the condition of not be-
> ing rich. You're not only a failure, you're also not a suc-
> cess. Unhappiness is more than unhappiness, it's also not
> being happy. Each state is two states. (6:150)

She is, in this suggestion of the binary nature of meaning, proposing
a sharing of significance which overlaps with the idea of the deferral
of significance, and this must undermine the ideal of pinning down
"words as definitions of experience." The different position of the
speaking subject also destabilizes consistency of meaning—when

Martha asks "And why is it, I wonder, that when a Jew tells a Jewish joke it's called Jewish humor but when anyone else tells it it's anti-Semitic?" Joshua replies "Because when a Jew tells a Jewish joke it's Jewish humor but when anyone else tells it it's anti-Semitic" (6:166–67).

In this play then the roles of both characters are ambiguous in their relation to gender and social patterns. According to Wesker, in British society at least, there is a continuing movement towards marginalization of Jews as always regarded with suspicion as different in relation to the dominant gentile society in which they live, but this conflicts with Joshua's embodiment of the theocentric patriarchal nature of Jewish culture—in spite of his attempts to argue that Jews question all authority. Martha offers a reverse image of his position: she is a member of the dominant gentile culture but is oppressed as a woman by elements of the patriarchal position of Joshua. Joshua's refusal to respect authority of any kind is accompanied by his impos-ing—authoritatively—his philosophy of life. Also, at least to her, his view seems to be a refusal to respect her individuality, her nature. He says "I am that I am that I am" but is unable to let her be what she is.

Here the play touches on a major epistemological difficulty, which is also a major liberal dilemma. A woman character is endowed with an irrational, subjective, foolish state of mind in conflict with the male character's well-argued, rational control of the world through language. For example, Martha wants to celebrate the fleeting mo-ment, without introducing anxieties through the need to analyze and discuss, but her appeal for mystery is glossed by Joshua as "medieval darkness," implying the kind of brutal destructiveness perpetrated by the darkness of ignorance. Yet Joshua's faith in making distinctions, of defending one's rights through awareness, knowledge, and reasoned discussion is an ideology that should liberate rather than oppress—and his comments are justifiable in the play, in that we see that Martha's stubborn silence harbors an unpleasant antisemitism. The liberal hu-manist reliance on reason and argument fuses with the prescriptive androcentric pattern of the social order.

There is a useful insight into this conflict in *Roots*, where Beatie is fascinated by but also resentful of the arguments of Ronnie and his friends: "As soon as they start to talk about things I don't know about or I can't understand I get mad" (1:94), in much the same way as Martha is intimidated by Joshua's friends: "Frightening lot they were. Non-stop talkers. Opinions on this, opinions on that" (6:147).

Although she says she "couldn't have any other life now," Beatie also longs to remain in the comfortable torpor of her family, reading comics, constantly eating, questioning nothing, each keeping their own counsel, and refusing to interact with others. Food consumption is the substitute for and evasion of the reasoned discourse of masculine society. Micheline Wandor suggests that Beatie's quoting Ronnie means that she is carrying him around in her head, but that in the final scene she gives birth to her self, not to him.[11] Beatie's experience does not seem however to represent, as Wandor thinks, an exclusively feminine subordinate position, because we see a similar class-based cultural division between for instance Chas and Pip in *Chips*. Rather, Beatie's emergence into reasoning powers and articulacy reflects the child's initial movement from the undifferentiated infantile state, into the social contract and system of discourse.[12] The change is effected through lack, or desire, and for Beatie it has been mediated by her loss of Ronnie. Thus Ronnie has helped to propel Beatie into his world of male rationality and discourse, but she enters it as an independent individual—an individual whose problems are those of any other articulate person, male or female.

Martha's fate is less happy. Joshua ends *When God Wanted a Son* saying that "she will never have any peace," because Martha will not or cannot assert herself or defend herself within the terms of rational social discourse, and her screams of rage and hate are impotent. Martha's attempts to suggest an alternative (female?) discourse of polyvalent attitudes—for instance to like or dislike composers without relating this to rational arguments about their objective worth—are overwhelmed by Joshua's "opinions." His control of the argument is reinforced by his speech behavior, which is consistent with the social characteristics of Western masculine discourse, that is, speaking more, interrupting more, making more assertions, and ignoring others' interventions, etc.,[13] and it fuels her frustrations which she cannot express competitively in his masculine style.

Of course it is a fallacy to believe that she can, in fact, argue about the right not to argue—can rationally justify the right to do without rational justification. It is impossible to step outside social discourse. Here the dilemma remains unresolved and unresolvable.

This dark play, enlivened though it is by the jokes that defy suffering—as Joshua says, "You're not supposed to laugh at the misery they bestow on you. It's unnatural." (6:178)—presents more forcibly and less optimistically the problems displayed in *Roots* and other earlier plays. Characters like Anna, Annabella Wharton, and Nita take their places in the social order by fighting the dominant ideology with its own weapons but without defeatism. For Martha, however, as for Annie Wobbler, an unincorporated life is a beleaguered and unbalanced life.

Wesker is thus suggesting in these plays that the painful efforts to control a place in the social order are experienced by all "different" or marginalized groups, but he chooses to dramatize these efforts through the experience of women, where the conflicts with the social order are so widely felt and supply such a rich range of examples. In the process, however, he includes some specifically female problems with stereotypes such as those affecting Anna and Martha. Wesker shows that rational discourse is the only tool that society has for regulating human interaction for the protection of all but that this discourse is also used as a tool of intimidation and dominance, perhaps unconsciously, by those whose cultural conditioning predisposes them to speaking rather than listening, assertiveness rather than receptiveness, opinion rather than negotiation.

∾

ENDNOTES

1. Arnold Wesker, *Arnold Wesker*. Volume 5 (London: Penguin, 1989), p.7.

2. These plays are *Three Women Talking* (Premiere, Chicago, 1992), *Letter to a Daughter* (Premiere, Seoul, 1992), and *Wild Spring* (1992).

3. Simone de Beauvoir, *The Second Sex*, tr. Parshley (London: Cape, 1953), 273; similarly she asks "Are there women, really?" (13).

4. Quoted in Jacqueline Rose, "Introduction II" in *Jacques Lacan and the Ecole Freudienne*, eds. Juliet Mitchell and Jacqueline Rose (London: Macmillan, 1982), 44. Also see Juliet Mitchell in "Introduction I," claiming that "Lacan dedicated himself to reorienting psychoanalysis to its task of deciphering the ways in which the human subject is constructed—how it comes into being—out of the small human animal.... Lacan's human subject is the obverse of the humanists'. His subject is not an entity with an identity but a being created in the fissure of a radical split." *ibid.*, 5.

5. E.g., in *When God Wanted a Son* (6:165).

6. E.g,. in Arnold Wesker, "Casual Condemnations," *Theatre Quarterly*, I, 2 (1971).

7. Arnold Wesker, in a letter to the present writer, June 8, 1993.

8. Arnold Wesker, in a letter to the present writer, June 8, 1993.

9. Micheline Wandor, *Look Back in Gender* (London: Routledge, 1988).

10. Arnold Wesker, *Words as Definitions of Experience* (London: Readers and Writers, 1976).

11. Micheline Wandor, *ibid*, 23–24.

12. Jacqueline Rose, "Introduction II," in *Jacques Lacan and the Ecole Freudienne*, p.31–32.

13. E.g., a survey cited in Daniel N. Matz and Ruth A Barker, "A Cultural Approach to Male-Female Miscommunication," in *Language and Social Identity*, ed. by John J. Gumperz (Cambridge: Cambridge University Press, 1988), 196–216.

Realistic Directions for Wesker's Stage

Angela Locatelli

I. Premise

Wesker's style has generally been defined as "realistic," an umbrella term loosely applied to widely different aesthetic categories and dramatic strategies, but, in this case, presumably referring to Wesker's gift for social observation and psychological insight.[1]

Discussions of the "realism" of his plays, from the *Trilogy* of the late 50s to the *One Woman Plays* of the 80s, propose a reading of his characters in terms of psychological insight and experiential, if not autobiographical, connoisseurship. "Naturalism" and "socialist realism" are terms which have been used, almost indifferently, to define Wesker's style; and yet, if not antithetical, "naturalism" and "socialist realism" are, at least, epistemically diverging terms. One of my aims here is, therefore, to bring into sharper focus the nature of Wesker's realistic poetics.

Within this aim, special attention will be given to Wesker's use of stage directions, a feature in his plays which has hardly ever been discussed as a topic in itself. This fact is surprising, if one considers that stage directions have a relevant semantic weight in Wesker's scripts, besides being essential to the specificity of his realism.

II. What Sort of Mimesis?

Wesker's irritation at the label "realistic" represents his dissatisfaction with a rather hasty and facile use of this term: "There is no such thing as realistic art. This phrase has been used again and again and is part of the jargon of intellectual discussion, but in fact expresses nothing but a contradiction in terms."[2] And yet, Wesker feels compelled to add: "*But*—all art *deals* with reality, whether it is the reality of conscious experience or the experience of poetic imagination, and some artists express, or re-create, these realities in a naturalistic style, others in a surrealistic style; some re-create what is absurd about reality, others what is lyrical about reality.... The importance of this observation is that we then don't look for imitation, but for interpretation."[3]

As I have suggested, "realism" has often been confused with what should more aptly be termed "naturalism," i.e., with "tranche de vie" techniques in documentary fiction and film. Wesker's style seems to move beyond the photographic aims that characterize naturalism, in the sense that he is aware of the wide context in which his characters belong and he inscribes their behavior into the forces that shape social events.

Significantly, Walter Wager remarked that *Chicken Soup with Barley*, which "was partially autobiographical, as so many first works are, traced the history of the Kahns, an East End Jewish family, from 1936 to 1956. It had a passionately Marxist mother, as did the playwright, and a son who was losing his Communist convictions and political certainty."[4] Wager went on to say that Walter Allen hailed *Roots* as "by far the best and most faithful play about British working-class life that has appeared."[5]

I believe that the Lukacsian definition of "realism"[6] as a form of fiction which is primarily concerned with what is typical, i.e., with what is simultaneously indicative of both the individual character and the general social context, seems to be a suitable term to define Wesker's style. No matter how confined his space may be (and it is usually confined to "a kitchen," "a basement," "a flat," except for the contextually vast spaces of *Their Very Own and Golden City*), the meaning of the action and dialogue has a broad social relevance. In this sense I would say that, despite the fact that Wesker writes plays rather than prose, he stands in the "great tradition" of the English novel[7] with its keen interest in social manners and mores. In fact, Wesker's realism seems be firmly grounded in his preference for a faithful representation of the situational components of everyday life and in an almost instinctive mistrust of ambiguity, be it aesthetic or otherwise. This is perhaps the main reason for the English success of his immensely popular *Trilogy*.

Glenda Leeming and C.W.E. Bigsby are in substantial agreement on Wesker's realistic mimesis. Leeming sees his works in terms of three phases: 1) "the social and family relationships of the *Trilogy*"; 2) "the work-oriented worlds of *The Kitchen*, *Chips with Everything*, and *Their Very Own and Golden City*"; 3) the "interiorizing of his themes" from *The Friends* onwards.[8] Bigsby adds that "The clearest change in

Wesker's work since the mid 1960s, apart from the obvious shift in the class of people he writes about[...] is that his plays have become more self-consciously poetic, that the energy of his work is refracted now through a more precise sensibility."[9]

What I would like to underline is the fact that Wesker's realistic style has changed, while remaining faithful to his belief that "all art deals with reality." In his recent plays (especially in those "for one actress," such as: *Whatever Happened to Betty Lemon?*, *Four Portraits— of Mothers*, *Annie Wobbler*, *Yardsale*) realism has joined hands with a more formal structuring, and the realistic component is situated in a new rhetorical and dramatic context. In the latest works there is much more irony, and a clear "aesthetic" concern as well. In the case of *Betty Lemon*, for instance, the dialogue is "arranged" recursively,[10] not only as a realistic feature in the representation of a senile and therefore repetitive character, but also as a conscious manipulation of dramatic dialogue and as a deliberate creation of "geometric" structures and self-reflective patterns. This text is, in fact, much more highly structured than any organized and repetitive real-life behavior would be.[11]

I believe that we can see a significant continuity in Wesker's poetics from 1960s onwards, and it would be wrong to see his latest phase as an attempt to abandon realism. On the other hand, mimesis has turned into a risky business in the second half of the twentieth century, when the concept of resemblance has become problematic and the idea of representation has reached a greater sophistication, thus displacing entirely the conventional "holding of the mirror up to nature." Photographic rendering of setting, character, and incident has forcefully been questioned, among others, by "stream of consciousness" novelists first, and by playwrights of the Absurd later. This helps to explain the stylistic variations in Wesker's production, clearly noticeable, for example, in the shift from *Roots* to *Annie Wobbler*. It is indeed quite understandable that Wesker, being aware of Beckett, Pinter, and others and being personally interested in cinematic technique, should have come to realize the limitations of traditionally photographic mimesis. And yet, in his "Introduction" to *Mothers*, Wesker elucidates his own recent innovations, within mainstream "realism": "The challenge in these vignettes is to convey an impression of *personalities*, through *timbre*, and *pace of voice*, and through *physical gesture*."[12]

III. Voice and Gesture

The insistence on the relationship between gesture and word is an important and conscious article of poetic faith in Wesker's entire production. From the point of view of compositional strategies, the pillar of Wesker's realism is first and foremost the fact that the life of his characters depends on the relationship between "*voice*" and "*physical action.*" Significant, in this respect, is the great care he takes in choosing and varying the verbs of movement and of gesture in his scripts, often in relation to the development of dramatic dialogue. *The Kitchen* and *Betty Lemon* may well illustrate such a strategy.

In *The Kitchen* the hectic and alienated pace at which orders are shouted and carried out is paralleled by the amazing mixture of accents and languages, which produces almost nonsensical verbal exchanges (for example, between Peter and Kevin or between Hans and Cynthia). Physical discomfort is caused by the terrible speed at which ordinary gestures are to be accomplished, while verbal confusion is both the cause and result of the general alienation. The madness of gesture reinforces the madness of words in an undoubtedly unique dramatic experience. Babel has entered the ordinary world of "a kitchen." The frantic and mechanical movements find a verbal equivalent in the shouting, in the rigid formulas of menus, in the incomprehensible and foreign utterances.

On the contrary, in *Betty Lemon* kinesic and verbal codes are played out alternatively: when gestures recede, words become dominant. Betty's impaired movements and the difficulty with which she accomplishes even the simplest of daily chores (preparing a cup of coffee or making a phone call) are in sharp contrast to her indomitable will, a will which is translated into her torrential eloquence. Every section of Betty's "monologue" is marked by a mixture of linguistic registers: from the colloquial to the vulgar, from the public to the private, from party jargon to highly formal speech. Notable also is the variety of discursive modes, which include quotation, apostrophe, invective, recollection. Betty's gestures and her strange dialogue with inanimate objects are worth noticing as accurate realistic connotations of senile pathologies. However, as symptoms they certainly lack the gratuitous and therefore inexplicable quality of gesture and dialogue which is one of the typical features of the Theatre of the Absurd.[13]

What comes to mind is Wesker's early preoccupation that his characters not be considered caricatures: "My people are not carica-

tures. They are real (though fiction), and if they are portrayed as caricatures the point of all these plays will be lost" (1:7). As I have been
saying, Wesker's realistic art is essentially Lukacsian, and it remains
such, from the earliest works, up to the "one-actress plays" of the 80s
because he remains clearly reluctant to abandon the technique of the
realistic sketch in which he is an unsurpassed master. It would be
wrong to see in recent texts a systematic metalinguistic or metadramatic
structuring (much more visible in the case of Beckett, Pinter, and
Stoppard). It would be equally unnecessary to identify a deconstructive
strategy in Wesker's latest plays exclusively on the ground of the author's
frequent parody of stereotyped bourgeois language or because of his
linguistic and situational irony, sometimes verging on sarcasm.

A comparison between Annie Wobbler and Winnie (in *Happy
Days*) can best illustrate the influence and yet the distance between
the "Theatre of the Absurd" and Wesker's latest productions. In *Annie
Wobbler* (Part 2), the protagonist: "rummages among her skirts and
finds tin plate, tin mug, knife to place on the table. Talks meanwhile"
(1:7). Beckett's Winnie is logorrheic while she extracts from her bag
the most surprising paraphernalia. However, the similarities cease with
the broad analogy of two very talkative female characters, enumerat-
ing personal belongings. The differences, which are far more relevant,
involve the symbolic order of these "actions," the semantic implications of each object, the nature of the linguistic utterances, the incon-
gruity or congruity of gesture in relation to ordinary frames of reference. Annie is perfectly understandable according to the logic of everyday life and also according to the typology of her social class and
her profession (she is "a type" in the Lukacsian sense as much as Sarah
had been "a type" in *Chicken Soup*). Winnie's sense is certainly not
common sense: her referentiality is much more questionable; her in-
congruity (notice the juxtaposition of brush, lipstick, and gun) asks
for a decoding that necessarily transcends the rules of ordinary action
and calls for a radically imaginative effort to move towards a new
mode of signification.

IV. Stage Directions

Aristotle, and a host of theorists after him, have pointed out that
drama is essentially "mimesis," because it consists of unmediated actions and utterances. In this light, and specifically from a semiotic
point of view, stage directions can be considered as crucial diegetic

elements in an otherwise wholly mimetic text. Stage directions have become a relevant topic among semioticians[14] undoubtedly because they determine one of the most noticeable differences between the "dramatic text," i.e., the text on the page, or script, and the "performance text," i.e., the representational event. George Bernard Shaw, the early Osborne, and Wesker himself, all seem to acknowledge, by using them extensively, that stage directions have a central semantic role. Since stage directions are the only direct intervention in the text on the part of the playwright, their function is almost more narratological than dramatic. In fact, they are used in the political, naturalistic and realistic theatre to "fill in" the characterization and to provide elements that are absent or insufficiently given in the dialogue. Their purpose is to add psychological depth and sometimes even supplementary information to the mimetic parts of the text. Stage directions are then often expected to be "translated" into attributes of the various dramatis personae by perceptive directors and actors. They are therefore specially important for a reader of the script who chooses to interpret them as a set of instructions for a performance. Even if this is not our main concern here, I must briefly add that more or even different instructions are provided, in view of the performance by the mimetic sections as well whenever the dialogue contains anaphoric, deictic, and metadramatic elements, i.e., observations on the dramatic setting, the dramatic situation and enunciation itself.[15]

The opening of Wesker's plays usually consists of a long and elaborate set of stage directions, by which the playwright entrusts his script to the virtual director(s) with binding exactness. Wesker's stage directions oscillate between detailed description of set and props and symbolical connotations of the characters' psycho-social dimension, always supporting realistic verisimilitude. Let us sample some of these highly charged beginnings.

The opening of *Chicken Soup* has an almost premonitory significance for the entire Weskerian production: October 4, 1936.

> The basement of the Kahns' house in the East End of London. The room is very warm and lived in. A fire is burning. One door, at the back and left of the room, leads to a bedroom. A window, left, looks up to the street. To the right is another door which leads to a kitchen which is seen. At rear of stage are the stairs leading up into the

> street. [SARAH KAHN is in the kitchen washing up, hum-
> ming to herself. She is a small, fiery woman, aged 37,
> Jewish, and of European origin. Her movements indicate
> great energy and vitality. She is a very warm person. HARRY
> KAHN, HER HUSBAND, comes down the stairs, walks past
> her and into the front room. He is 35 and also an Euro-
> pean Jew. He is the antithesis of Sarah. He is amiable, but
> weak. From outside we hear a band playing a revolution-
> ary song.] (1:13)

This opening stage direction is clearly meant to give an interpretative key to the play. Social and class attributes anticipate its
"Lukacsian style," while the main characters' psychological qualities
and even potential conflicts are expressed as if the first stage direction
were meant to be a miniature of the entire work.

The beginning of *The Kitchen* is emblematic of this same approach, which is prominent, as one would expect, in *Roots* but also in
the recent *Annie Wobbler* and *Betty Lemon*. *The Kitchen* opens with
these indications:

> There is no curtain in this part. The kitchen is always
> there. It is semi-darkness. Nothing happens until the au-
> dience is quite seated (at the appointed time for com-
> mencement, that is). The night porter, Magi, enters. He
> stretches, looks at his watch, and then stands still, realiz-
> ing where he is. It is seven in the morning. Then with a
> taper he lights the ovens. Into the first shoots a flame.
> There is smoke, flame, and soon the oven settles into a
> steady burn, and with it comes its hum. It is the hum of a
> kitchen, a small roar. It is a noise that will stay with us to
> the end. As he lights each oven, the noise grows from a
> small to a loud ferocious roar. There will be this continu-
> ous battle between the dialogue and the noise of the ov-
> ens. The producer must work out his own balance....[16]
> (2:15)

The reader of the script (be it a director, an actor, a critic, a student) has the clear impression that the stage directions are a comple-
ment to the "Introduction and Notes for the Producer" the dramatist
had previously given. Their diegetic nature had allowed the playwright
to elaborate on the typology of his characters and setting. In fact,
Frank, Alfredo, Hans, Peter, Kevin, Gaston, Michael, Bertha,
Mangolis, Anne, Max, Nicholas, Raymond, Paul, the Chef, and Mr.

Marango are all provided with individual "sketches in order of station." With an eye to the performance, their individual tasks are actually "cut out" for them in the paragraphs entitled "The Actions," which precede the stage directions proper (2:13–14).

A truly spectacular use of sight and sound is prescribed in *The Kitchen* and in *Their Very Own and Golden City*. In both plays, in fact, stage directions are meant to convey an insider's view of the professional world they mirror. The typical parable of the draughtsman Andrew Cobham, is aptly set, towards the end, against the "Magnificent abstract set of a building site and its scaffolding" and the "howl of drilling, the whine of machines and the knock of hammers." The "sound and the fury" of Wesker's *Kitchen* undoubtedly speaks of a specific expertise and to a public of equally competent workers.

John Russell Brown, commenting on *The Four Seasons*, has briefly suggested something which I believe could be extended to several other works; for example, "stage directions instruct the performers to create what their words or actions do not necessarily imply."[17] Several stage directions intersperse the script of *The Kitchen* with notes on the characters' emotions which the dialogue "per se" does not convey. For example:

> MAX: [enjoying what he is about to say] (2:37);
> MAGI [unconcerned]:"They nearly killed him" (2:18);
> PETER [following her like the pathetic, jealous lover] (2:30);
> CHEF [as though concerned]: "I don't know. I wasn't there."
> (2:33).

Other stage directions provide specifically or peculiarly expressive gestures:

> PETER [rubbing his thumb and finger together]: "Good
> pay?" (2:24);
> KEVIN [wiping his brow again]: "Yes Sir" (2:28);
> PETER [adopts quixotic stance] (2:26);
> PETER [adopts another quixotic stance] (2:26);
> HANS [makes a movement of his hand to say "Ach, I'm
> fed-up, forget it"] (2:34);
> HANS [Grimace, meaning—'No question of it!'] (2:35).

The relationship between "voice" and "physical action" is always so obviously important to Wesker that it is also often prescribed in the stage directions. In fact, stage directions concerning movement often transpose feelings and emotions that are also expressed through the dialogue. For example, in *Chicken Soup*, after the sympathetic exchange between Ronnie and his father, Harry "shuffles miserably to his room, perceptibly older" (1:56), and in *Betty Lemon*, the protagonist's difficult movements are also meant to show her endurance: "Preparations for making coffee are another of the day's battles" (5:28). We should also notice the rich lexical variety used to express Betty's movements and her different states of mind: she "hobbles," "struggles," "drives," "collapses," "falls forward," "struggles to her feet."

Even if they are in a much shorter form, the stage directions in *Annie Wobbler* (Part 2) still preserve the Lukacsian quality of those in *The Kitchen* and the *Trilogy*: "Student digs. The place is London, the dialect Yorkshire—or anywhere north of Birmingham and south of Carlisle. The time is now" (5:92). Sometimes humor and imagination corroborate the most graphic gesture, as in this stage direction: "Coquettishly accepts an imaginary light to an imaginary cigarette from an imaginary, tall, dark stranger" (5:94).

Wesker's normally elaborate indications of setting are definitely distant from the spare notes of Beckett or Pinter. They do not seem to care particularly for the detailed codification of their settings; their fictional world, especially Beckett's tends to be a "no-where/anywhere"; while, for Wesker the setting is a precise "here and now." His temporal and spatial specifications are hard to ignore as well as the anagraphic attributes of his characters. Sex, age, race, profession are always carefully determined. By prescribing the emotions that are to be expressed, Wesker seems dissatisfied with merely offering a written script. One explanation for his choice might be the lack of confidence in the ability of the words of the dialogue alone to express the required multiple meanings of the play. Another explanation might be that the dramatist believes his own intentions to be "the meaning" of the play; he therefore compels, as far as possible, the director to express the particular range of emotions the dramatist has in mind.

Is the author's attitude due to mistrust of verbal language and to the full knowledge of the fact that words on the page have a million ways of being read and recited? Is it due to his experience of words conveying a multiplicity of meanings, some of which may even be incompatible, and most of which have never been consciously registered by the writer? Or is it a totally different matter: is it a question of rivalry with the director? If this hypothesis is true, why doesn't Wesker direct his own works? Wesker's desire to "control" the performance(s) beyond the range of the script itself has been expressed more than once, also in interviews and formal and informal talks:

"Why should an interpreter demand freedom to explore with his own experience the experience of another, when he himself has not taken the trouble to formulate his own experience into a responsible whole? There is about such ideas an element of *scavenging*."[18] We are reminded here of the intimately twinned roles of playwright and actor-manager and of a long tradition, of both collaboration and conflicts on the stage going back at least as far as Shakespeare.

V. Conclusions

If we consider the series of stage directions we have examined, from the early plays to the latest, we can perceive a substantial continuity in their use and see them as a strong evidence of Wesker's realism. Wesker's stage directions always provide both spatial and temporal coordinates, together with detailed information about the physical features, social background, and psychological traits of the characters. Stage directions are also closely connected with dialogue, as they tend to move in the direction of greater situational specification. It follows that if the Kahns were "typical," Betty Lemon is equally "true to life," in that both are a perfect example of realistic mimesis. Moreover, Wesker has chosen to make his descriptions prescriptive, which, despite the formal innovations of the plays of the 80s, unquestionably proves his deep distrust of any deconstructive undecidability.

Our conclusions would not be complete if we failed to stress the changes in Wesker's realism. I hope to have shown that there is a continuous stylistic innovation in the plays, both at the thematic and semiotic levels and that the novelty is largely determined by the author's deep consciousness of the conventions that make realistic "portraits" dramatically effective at different times. Wesker clearly knows that characters, precisely when they aspire to typicality, have to change in order to remain convincing for an ever-changing audience.

His latest style displays a closer perception, not only of the nuances of the characters' individual psychology (there is a significant increase in the use of the monologue) but also of the extra-textual and even extra-literary realities shaping contemporary culture. The predominantly female characterization of the one-act plays, for example, may be a way of acknowledging the growing significance of women in culture and society. In this respect, we could say that if "class" was a fundamental theme of the early plays and of the decade in which they were written, "women" have become a correspondingly relevant theme of the latest plays.[19] Moreover, Pinter and Beckett leave their mark on Wesker, in the growing self-conscious organization and concomitant stylization of plot and dialogue, so that, to put it in a nutshell, the Wesker one-act plays have become more of a "play" and less of a "photograph" or vignette. I would define these changes "rhetorical," not in the narrow sense of "decorative" but in a full stylistic sense. Wesker is truly at home in a sound and variably complex Lukasian type of verisimilitude. His poetics constantly reflect a valuable subtlety within mainstream realism.

∾

ENDNOTES

1. Ronald Hayman, *Arnold Wesker* (London: Heinemann, 1970); A.R. Jones, "The Theatre of Arnold Wesker," *Critical Quarterly*, II (1960): 366–70; Jacqueline Latham, "*Roots*: A Reassessment," *Modern Drama* VIII (1965): 192–97; John Mander, "Art and Anger," in *The Writer and Commitment* (London: Secker, 1962): 179–211; George E. Wellwarth, "Arnold Wesker: Awake and Sing in Whitechapel" in *The Theatre of Protest and Paradox* (New York: New York University Press, 1964): 234–43; Walter Wager (ed.), *The Playwrights Speak* (London: Longmans, 1967): 213–30; Glenda Leeming and Simon Trussler, *The Plays of Arnold Wesker: An Assessment* (London: Victor Gollancz Ltd., 1971); John Russell Brown *Theatre Language: A Study of Arden, Osborne, Pinter and Wesker* (London: Allen Lane The Penguin Press, 1972): 158–89; Glenda Leeming. *Wesker the Playwright* (London: Methuen, 1983).

2. Arnold Wesker, *Fears of Fragmentation* (London: Jonathan Cape, 1970): 98.

3. Arnold Wesker, *Fears of Fragmentation*, 98.

4. Wager, *op. cit.*, 216.

5. Wager, *op. cit.*, 217.

6. G. Lukacs, *Teoria del romanzo*, Roma, 1972 and *Saggi sul realismo*, Torino, 1950.

7. F.R. Leavis, *The Great Tradition*, London, 1948.

8. Glenda Leeming, "Articulacy and Awareness: The Modulation of Familiar Themes in Wesker's Plays in the Seventies" in C.W.E. Bigsby, *Contemporary English Drama*. London: Edward Arnolds, 1981: 65.

9.   Bigsby, 21.

10. Angela Locatelli. "Recursivita' dialogica e dell'azione in *Whatever Happened to Betty Lemon*," in *Quaderni del Dipartimento di Linguistica e Letterature Comparate* (Bergamo: Universita' di Bergamo, 1988): 29–35.

11. Erving Goffman, *The Presentation of Self in Everyday Life*. New York: Doubleday, 1959; *Interaction Ritual*. New York: Doubleday, 1967; *Replies and Responses*. Working Papers Urbino: del CISL, 1975.

12. Emphases mine.

13. Angela Locatelli, *Coping with the Inexplicable: Language and Situation in Pinter's Early Plays* (Milano: Coopli-IULM, 1983).

14. P. Bogatyrev, "Les signes du theatre," *Poetique* no.8, 1971; Jansen Steen, *Appunti per l'analisi dello spettacolo* Working Paper no. 68 (Urbino: Centro Internazionale di Semiotica e Linguistica, 1977); Elam Keir, *The Semiotics of Theatre and Drama* (London: Methuen, 1980); De Marinas Macro, *Semiotic del teatro* (Milano: Bompiani, 1982); De Marinas Macro, *Al limite del teatro* (Firenze: Edizioni Usher, 1983).

15. Serpieri Alessandro. "Ipotesi teorica di segmentazione del testo teatrale." in A.A.V.V. *Come comunica il teatro*. Milano: Il Formichiere, 1978.

16. John Russell Brown, 185.

17. Arnold Wesker, *Distinctions* (London: Jonathan Cape, 1985): 25.

18. The near exclusively "female" characterization of the latest plays may be irritating, if taken as one of the numerous instances of male writers appropriating women's voices and creating male projections of female identity. However, it may also be a sign of Wesker's ability to grasp and foreground shifting contemporary issues.

Chips with Everything
A Snob's Progress?

Martin Priestman

Wesker's most immediately popular play, *Chips with Everything*, ostensibly deals with the national conscription which continued to be an everyday feature of postwar British life until 1963. Though written in 1960 and first staged at the Royal Court Theatre in 1962, it draws on Wesker's own two years' service in the Royal Air Force in 1950–52, whose details he had pinned down at the time in lengthy letters home and an attempted novel. Part of the play's strong impact derives from its precision about such details, particularly in the long, grinding parade-ground drills. To ensure accuracy, the first director John Dexter consulted a retired sergeant major, RSM Brittain.

The play starts with the breaking-in of a raw squad of R.A.F. conscripts, first by the corporal, Hill, and then by the commissioned officers. One of the conscripts, Smiler, is singled out for an apparently cheeky smile which is actually congenital; another, the upper-class Pip Thompson;, singles himself out by leading the others into insubordinate gestures culminating in the singing of revolutionary folk songs at a Christmas party and then in a meticulously executed theft from a guarded coke-yard. In the second act, despite the humanity increasingly glimpsed earlier, Hill victimizes Smiler in ways which finally lead the rest of the squad to near-mutiny. Meanwhile, the officers wrestle to bring Pip over to their side and finally do so by persuading him that he is only seeking a different kind of power. After submitting to the soul-destroying bayonet drill he has previously refused, Pip dons an officer's uniform in time to diffuse the potential mutiny over Smiler's treatment. In an ironic final parade, the officers confirm that the squad has "turned out well, as we expected, nothing else would have done."

In an introduction to the play, Wesker wrote, "*Chips* is not about the troubles of national servicemen in the R.A.F. It is about the subtle methods employed in this country for debilitating the spirit of rebellion" (Marland 69). Nonetheless, the troubles of servicemen as a theme was in itself well calculated for the exploration of some strong national tensions, because it served as a microcosm of the broader state of the nation as witness its recurrence in many powerful plays of the time from John Arden's *Serjeant Musgrave's Dance* (1959) to John McGrath's *Events While Guarding the Bofors Gun* (1966) and much of the output of Charles Wood.

For many in Britain, the shared struggle of the Second World War had promised a significant erosion of class differences. In the late 1940s and early 1950s, this promise found political expression in the Attlee Labour government's establishment of general rights to government-funded education, welfare, and health provision. As time progressed, however, it became increasingly clear that less of the old pattern of class privilege had been dismantled than expected. By 1960 the government had long been back in the hands of Eden's and then Macmillan's very old-school-tie Conservative administrations, and Britain's role on the international stage had reverted to attempts to sustain vestiges of imperial dominance in Suez, Aden, and Cyprus. Hence the armed forces, earlier a vital focus for much left-wing idealism, now seemed increasingly to represent a belated attempt to reimpose right-wing values not only overseas but at home. Through "national service" a generation of young men could be systematically reintroduced to the class division between officers and troops, with the NCO's hard-earned power to bully those below in the name of those above as the upper limit of working-class aspiration.

It was also often claimed that conscription was essential to channel the anti-social energies of the newly-discovered "teenager," an American-inspired phenomenon prone to jiving, relative financial autonomy, and general juvenile delinquency. Hence national service could in general be seen as a kind of national marching-on-the-spot, devoted in equal parts to teaching young men the rules of the world in which they would have to live, keeping them out of trouble, and making the occasional foray into such outposts of empire as the Malta, Cyprus, and Aden to which Pip ends up dispatching three of his former messmates.

Thus Wesker's remark about *Chips* could easily be rephrased: "It *is* a play about the troubles of national servicemen in the R.A.F. *And hence* it is about the subtle methods employed in this country for debilitating the spirit of rebellion." But that isn't actually quite what he is saying. Superimposed on the vivid depiction of the ways in which the agents of the system finally grind their raw material down to "just as we expected" is the much more resistant and/or personal issue of the grinding-down of a single highly idiosyncratic bag of problems: Pip. By embodying the "spirit of rebellion" chiefly in the shape of this wealthy general's son whose motive for joining the ranks rather than the officers remains problematic throughout, Wesker opens up a gap between the oppressed and the "spirit of rebellion" which is itself problematic.

Wesker's own relationship with the working class was specific but complex like most such relationships unless denied altogether: on the one hand, very much "one of them" (raised in the East End, a manual worker until 24), on the other "enlightened" from the start (Jewish, socialist, articulate). It's possible that the exaggerated space between Pip's class and his mates allows Wesker to explore the ambivalences of his own involvement with more freedom than anything more tuggingly autobiographical; in particular, it enables him to re-create that involvement throughout as a matter of choice. And this element of choice also enables a very straight route through to the likely ambivalences of the left-inclined but largely middle-class theatergoing audience.

In many British plays and novels of the 1950s and 1960s, the tension between hopes for a less class-ridden society and the need to get along within the older structure is focused through the inner conflicts of an uprooted thinker torn between allegiance to the workers and the middle-class identity temptingly held out as a reward for talent. Most such protagonists (including many of Wesker's own) are themselves working class or, like Jimmy Porter in John Osborne's *Look Back in Anger*, at least project themselves as such. Some, such as Osborne's Luther, Arden's Musgrave, and Wesker's own Ronnie Kahn, become (like Brecht's Galileo on whom they are perhaps all distantly based) tragic lost leaders, leaving their tattered banners to be taken up by betrayed disciples and ultimately—it is implied—the audience itself. In the possibility his class gives him to opt out from the fray completely, Pip's role sharply intensifies one common function of such figures: to offer the spectator a self-reflexive glimpse of the potential hypocrisy involved in what may prove only a temporary, voyeuristic celebration of working-class causes.

But this strategy does raise the classic question: is Pip part of the solution or part of the problem? Here it is arguable that Wesker tries to have it several ways at once.

One possible reading might be that Pip rightly finds his own personal solution through denying the problem altogether and recognizing that "it is not necessarily wrong to Belong" to the officer class of "born leaders." This was the response of the *New York Herald Tribune* critic Walter Kerr to the first Broadway production in 1963 (see Marland 78–79). Such a writing-off of the whole idea of solidarity with oppressed classes as a mistaken side-issue, assuming the purpose of drama to be a simple one-to-one empathy with the hero, is not, however, really conceivable within the 1960s British context Wesker is actually addressing.

But Wesker does give some color to this approach in apparently building Pip's "spirit of rebellion" up as the *only* solution to the problem which clearly is being described. We (the middle-class audience) are strongly tempted to the view that what he finds hopeless *is* hopeless. Here it is important to consider the credentials by which Pip is built up in the first place. His first major introduction is through a long speech in the second scene describing an unaccustomed foray into a working-class East End café: his sense of shock is conveyed in the repeated refrain "I don't know why I should have been surprised" and his conclusion in the dismissal which gives the play its title: "You breed babies and you eat chips with everything" (3:16-17). From this basis it might indeed be possible to describe a trajectory in which Pip, at first a little intrigued by the new form of animal life he has discovered, finally decides the investigation isn't worth the candle.

Wesker is, however, ringing much subtler changes. In presenting a hero who doesn't "mind being a snob" (as Smiler remarks half-admiringly), he brings many British fears and miseries into sharp focus. The word "snob" originally meant "cobbler," then "someone with social pretensions," and only finally "someone who looks down on others." The word's history thus encapsulates the quaint British delusion that lords and laborers get on fine and it's only the bustling middle classes who have problems, although in fact much effort is wasted by all classes in trying to tiptoe around its embarrassing nuances. In ignoring these nuances (though he does describe his family's progression through some of them) and telling Wilfe who challenges his accent to "put your working-class halo away," Pip presents himself as a

fresh, disinterested eye on this national sport. He also rubs the nose
of the spectator, who may have come to the theater expecting to see
the latest Royal Court lefty polish his own working-class halo, into
the fact that there's nothing particularly glamorous *per se* in being
deprived.

Having established his authenticity of response in this arresting
way (though one critic remarked that in his own R.A.F. experience
such a performance would probably have been "laughed at, sworn at
or ignored," see Marland 77), Pip goes on to establish his credentials
with deeds rather than words. He organizes the first chief insurrec-
tion—the subversive folk singing—through a few terse suggestions
to the musicians, and the second—the robbing of the coke-store—
silently after a few reminded instructions. These two show-stealing
events in fact owe a great deal of their force to their being "pure theatre," in which the *ensemble* orchestration of sounds and voices in the
first instance and disciplined physical actions in the second magically
aligns Pip's role with that of the director of the play we, as the audience, are actually watching. Our trust in the exciting new *ensemble*
theatrical style reinforces our trust in Pip as backstage director, and
vice versa.

Much of the strength of the party scene (Act 1, Scene 7) in which
the squad breaks free of the officers' contemptuous expectation that it
only needs rock 'n' roll to keep it happy lies in the exhilarating beauty
of hearing first one and then many hitherto disregarded voices singing to the "different drummer" of shared, potentially radical purpose
embodied in "The Lyke-Wake Dirge's" curse on the cold-hearted rich,
and "The Cutty Wren's" encoded Peasants' Revolt promise to give the
dismembered Richard II's goods "to the poor" (3:38). In the context
of barked commands and mechanical square-bashing, even as punc-
tuated by Hill's melancholy solo harmonica and Wilfe's obscene ren-
ditions of "Eskimo Nell," the sense here of controlled but also spontaneous outpouring strongly ratifies the economy of means by which
Pip—no singer himself—has brought it all about.

With hindsight over the folk-rock fusions which helped to define
1960s radicalism, the staged style-war between rock 'n' roll and folk
music on which this scene depends can easily look topsy-turvy, given
the roots of rock in oppressed black experience and the transmission
of the British folk tradition through literati such as the eighteenth-
century Bishop Percy. Wesker's misattribution of the anonymous

"Lyke-Wake Dirge" to the more canonical Robert Burns doesn't help either. But in 1960 it was easier to see rock as a callous invasion from the commercial powers-that-be and British folk music as a vitalizing rediscovery of far more precise regional and politically conscious identities, absorbing as it did much new input from such figures as Ewan McColl, a formidable folk-ballad singer as well as the founder of the radical Theatre Workshop. While it is realistically unlikely that the whole squad would in fact know the obscure "Cutty Wren" as if taught it at their mother's knee or through some instinctive folk-memory, it is a bit more possible that the guitarist of the rock group, who leads the singing, would have a foot in both musical camps. In any case the rendition is perhaps best seen as a brief, non-naturalistic utopian vision of the common culture of the future for which Wesker was to fight so hard with Centre 42, taking a similar backstage directive role to Pip's here.

The coke-stealing scene (Act 1, Scene 10) is a chiefly silent one in which a piece of wire-netting across the stage represents the barrier between the squad and the coke-store patrolled by a guard who appears and disappears regularly. To keep time with these brief disappearances, Wesker plots a hilariously precise series of moves involving the rapid placing and removal of chairs enabling Pip to enter the store, pass filled buckets back to the others, then escape—all only just in time. As originally written, the audience looks chiefly at the teamwork of the squad, with Pip, after giving precise instructions, removed beyond the fence. In a joint interview with Wesker, the original director John Dexter explained how he switched the audience's point of view through 180 degrees: they were to look chiefly at the coke and Pip's solo performance while the others "looked better on the other side" (Hayman 1973, 66). Whether or not this "purely physical decision" reflected Dexter's unconscious need to wrest his own directorial powers back from Wesker/Pip, the dispute admirably summarizes the ambiguity of Pip's role throughout: is he chiefly the liberator of the squad's dormant abilities, or is he chiefly using them as a backdrop to his own starring performance?

This returns us to the question asked earlier: how far is Pip also part of the problem? The second act deals with this head-on through the scenes (4 and 7) in which he is "turned round" by the Pilot Officer. These bear similarities to other classic temptation scenes in which the hero is made to doubt his or her own motives for taking an unpopular stand, a particularly close model being T.S. Eliot's *Murder in the Cathedral* (still seen in 1960 as one of the classics of modern theater). Like the four tempters who try to undermine Thomas à Becket's principled resistance to his natural ally Henry II, the Pilot Officer appeals first to class solidarity, then to Pip's moral obligation to resume his natural role to keep out worse "bastards," then (like Eliot's third tempter—a baron proposing an alliance) he argues that "the best of revolutionaries" can choose to undermine the system from within, and finally, most insidiously, that Pip is only seeking a different type of power as a martyr. Becket's cry—"Can sinful pride be driven out/ Only by more sinful?" (Eliot 295)—perhaps lies somewhere behind Pip's climactic "Oh, God—," on which the Officer pounces with "Are you his son?... Messiah to the masses!" (3:60).

Pip's crumbling before this final accusation (in the next scene he performs the humiliating bayonet charge marking his re-entry into the system) lends credence to the Officer's triumphant if logically dubious claim that "No man survives whose motive is discovered, no man." Down this road lies the argument that all commitment is corrupt at source, an argument Wesker himself firmly reversed in a letter quoted by Ronald Hayman:

> [The Pilot Officer] is corrupting Pip and I employ my own special definition of "corrupt" in this sense, i.e., to corrupt is to present sensitive people with motives that they *could* have had but haven't really, but which they are *persuaded* to have and in this way their confidence is undermined and they are argued out of action. In other words Pip was not really concerned with power but he is tricked into believing he was. (Hayman 1970, 58)

But, arguably, drama is about representatively significant choices, not just psychologically possible ones. Becket, like Shaw's Saint Joan, Sophocles's and Anouilh's Antigone and Christ in the wilderness (again, Brecht's Galileo is an important intermediate case), *doesn't* finally buckle, and as an audience we need a clearer understanding of why Pip does. The easiest assumption becomes that temporary upper-class fellow travellers can't be trusted, in which case what are we supposed to make of all the credentials he has built up so far?

Two of the later scenes try to tackle this problem by showing Pip's attempts to pass the struggle on to his chief disciples in the very act of rebuffing them. Act 2, Scene 6 involves a rather inconclusive debate with Andrew to which I shall return. In the much longer Scene 9, Pip instructs his more acknowledged disciple Charles in the pronunciation of "economics" but then stonewalls his further requests for enlightenment with "Ask someone else." Arguably, this desertion stands for the "fortunate fall" of the teacher which enables the pupil to carry the lesson forward, as with Beatie in *Roots*; it is only now that Charles leads the silent mass protest over Smiler's treatment. Pip's final "Swop masters? You're a fool, Charles, the kind of fool my parents fed on, you're a fool, a fool—" is, at any rate, deliberately segued into the corporals' taunts "You're a slob," etc., which ironically drive the victim Smiler into assuming the sacrificial Christ-like role Pip himself has refused, from the mocking in the temple to the footwashing by a Magdalenian Charles (3:63). The "working-class halo" Pip began by rejecting so bracingly now returns as a reality with Pip as its Judas.

The answer to some of the problems noted above would seem to be that Pip's final suppression of the very "spirit of rebellion" he was supposed to represent is vital to the mock-closure backed up by the playing of the national anthem just a decisive moment or two before the end, when it would have been guaranteed to bring any well-trained British audience to its feet (see Hayman 1973, 66). Within this mock closure, the audience is to consider its own various *trahisons des clercs*: of voyeuristically enjoying scenes of oppression without doing anything about them; of entertaining hopes that an enlightened compromise between rulers, agitators, and ruled is already in hand; of simplistically (like Walter Kerr) rooting for the hero; or (almost to the end) hoping the ruled can sustain the "spirit of rebellion" even when their mentor proves either inherently corrupt by his class or "corrupted" by similar fears of *trahisons des clercs* on his own part. The last point is arguably the clincher, since our mistaken identification with Pip now drives us back around the whole track with a greatly enhanced sense of personal guilt.

For the actor playing Pip, however, these complexities do not so much reinforce as cancel each other out. How, for instance, can he show in the last scenes that he was not seeking power but only "corrupted" into thinking so? The screaming bayonet-charge (a scream of confused grief or a catharsis of hitherto-hidden aggressions?) and the stonewalling of Charles are both constructed so as to convey either message equally. A kind of Cheshire-cat withdrawal into inscrutability is the only real option. The very name Pip—perhaps influenced by Dickens's similar confluence of potentials for growth in *Great Expectations*—evokes chiefly the "seed" of equal sets of possibilities towards snobbery or egalitarianism.

Hence, unlike Osborne's Jimmy Porter, Pinter's Davies or Wesker's own Beatie, Pip is not an actor's dream. By contrast, the roles of Smiler and Hill seem to have attracted more attention from the start as powerful "actorly" parts in production, perhaps because they combine considerable complexity with relatively clear overall through-lines as victim and oppressor respectively. Smiler's complexity relates chiefly to the symbolic load he has to carry, not only the Christ symbolism already discussed but also the permanent smile which can be read variously as: a) a sign of imbecility; b) the smile of ingrained acquiescence which no mistreatment can remove; c) the "cheeky grin" which drives the authorities to fury because it *might* denote a subversive inner self-confidence.

Ronald Lacey's account of playing the original Smiler highlights the importance of working against the apparent grain of these readings: "As he has been conditioned to people asking 'Why are you smiling?' his answers are bored." He describes how he had to maneuver the audience slowly into the reality of his repeated "I'm not smiling," particularly in the punishment scene where he is sadistically taunted with questions about his mother: "I decided that Smiler had loved his mother deeply, and that she had died when he was still a boy. His answer to the question 'Is your mother pretty?' has to carry the weight of this when he answers 'Yes. She was.'" (Marland 73). Lacey goes into most detail describing the precise changes of pace and emphasis in the "running away" soliloquy of Act 2, Scene 10, a scene with which John Dexter wrote "Arnold and I seemed powerless to help him…he only finally solved [it] for himself 24 hours before the first night" (Leeming 64). Here and throughout, Lacey writes, "I had to be careful of two things: to avoid sentimentality and to keep smiling." Lacey's account describes a good naturalistic job of work which supports rather than detracts from the pre-arranged symbolism of the smile. To work against the three class stereotypes of stupidity, cheery acceptance, and permanent insolence is really to continue the symbolism at another level, one which asserts that people can't just be written off although authority constantly tries to do so.

Frank Finlay's Corporal Hill, as groomed by ex-RSM Brittain, was the other performance that attracted most comment. Some of the play's most exhilarating—and even wittily poetic—language appears in his ritualized diatribes, every word and gear change honed to maximum effect by years of practice:

> My name is Corporal Hill. I'm not a very happy man. I don't know why. I never smile and I never joke—you'll soon see that. Perhaps it's my nature, perhaps it's the way I've been brought up—I don't know....But I will tear the scorching daylights out of anyone who smarts the alec with me—and we've got some 'ere. I can see them, you can tell them. I count three already, you can tell them, by their faces, who know it all, the boys who think they're GOOD. (*Whispered.*) It'll be unmerciful and scorching murder for them—all. (3:14)

The rhythmic effects are beautifully calculated, with each idea repeated through a kind of antithetical balance to give it time to sink in and then lead deliberately to the next point, and the final menacing switch from yell to whisper. There is also the constant play of subtext, whereby the elaborate self-portrait as a non-joker is itself a sardonic joke designed to upstage any rival "smart alecs." The complexities extend further when we discover later that behind the mordant sarcasm of such set pieces there actually *does* lurk a sensitive soul whose mournful harmonica accompanies the growing intimacy of the squad hut where the smart alecs have it increasingly their own way, at least in Act 1. But these touches of humanity—like the against-the-grain aspects of Smiler—only reinforce the character's overall meaning at another level: the idea of the worker who has sold his soul for his stripes is reinforced, not weakened, by showing us that he has a soul to sell.

The context of performance is likely to make clearer than in reading an element of patterning among the large cast of characters which also contains a degree of complexity within strong, clear outlines. Most of the characters interact in pairs: among the conscripts, Dodger and Ginger ponder job prospects, Cannibal and Dickey repeatedly clash over the latter's penchant for long words, Wilfe is the butt of constant needling from Smiler, and Charles addresses Pip almost exclusively. Among the officers, the bellicose Wing Commander is repeatedly restrained by the Squadron Leader. Apart from Corporal

Hill with his solo diatribes, the only two important characters not clearly anchored in such a pair are the sinister Pilot Officer and the intelligent Scots conscript Andrew.

Interestingly, these two share a single but significant early scene (Act 1, Scene 5) in which, outsmarted by Andrew's ironic mask of Schweyk-like stupidity, the Pilot Officer collapses first into personal confession and then into what in the semiotics of the time (a hand on the knee) could be a homosexual pass. On being rebuffed, he makes the thematic-sounding pronouncement "don't ever trust me to be your friend...we slum for our own convenience," a moment subliminally recalled later when he insinuates that Pip's behavior is "a little— revealing....You enjoy mixing with men from another class...do you enjoy your slumming?" (3:25, 55) Though Pip smartly turns the suggestion back on the Officer, the sexual implication of "slumming" possibly contributes to the "corruption" of his self-belief—followed as it is by a rejection first of Andrew and then of Charles which echoes the Officer's own warning to Andrew: "don't ever trust me to be your friend."

If the Pilot Officer represents a possibility in Pip which the play can only hint at (especially given the rigid censorship still exercised by the Lord Chamberlain), Andrew arguably represents a working-class potential which the play seems equally unwilling to follow through. Shown at times to be Pip's equal in intelligence and subversive spirit (it is his recitation of the vengeful Scots ballad that starts off the Christmas party revolt), at others Andrew has to alternate rather uneasily with Charles as Pip's chief disciple and is cleared out of the way in the brief scene (Act 2, Scene 6) in which his cogent critique of Pip's "heroic gestures" is somewhat awkwardly rebuffed by Pip's "I will die of good, well-meaning, intelligent people who have never made a decision in their life" (3:58). We wonder who is really most likely to "die" from Pip's decision-making abilities. Hereafter Andrew asks only two lame one-of-the-gang questions in the general rallying around Smiler and is then one of the three whom Pip dispatches to imperial trouble-spots, though the only one honored with a place in the typing pool. His potential to carry on the fight in different terms from Pip's is thus dodged in favor of the much longer scene in which it is Pip's rejection of the dependent Charles that is made to "stand for" his break with the working class in general.

The two rejection-scenes encapsulate the two possibilities which the play repeatedly raises but finally fails to reconcile. Are the workers passively dependent on middle-class educators, or have they strengths which those educators must, in turn, come to respect? Despite his brief and abortive leadership of the silent protest over Smiler, Charles pre-eminently represents the first model—as do Smiler and the others, whose energies are neutralized by the bickering and point-scoring through which their characters are largely revealed. Andrew, by contrast, usually speaks either for himself or the group as a whole: as well as conveying the collective judgment on Pip's agonizings, it is he who says at one point "I like us. All of us here, now," an "us" Pip would be incapable of (3:44). As such he constitutes at least a gesture to the second model in which the workers do prove able to survive communally without middle-class teachers (or "slumming" officers). That this model needs to be at first invoked and then suppressed to secure the required ironic closure constitutes perhaps one of those fissures through which we glimpse the tensions of high-cultural socialist engagement in the early 1960s.

℘

WORKS CITED

Eliot, T.S. *The Complete Poems and Plays*. London: Faber and Faber, 1969.

Hayman, Ronald. *Arnold Wesker*. London: Heinemann, 1970.

——, ed. *Playback 2*. London: Davis-Poynter, 1973.

Leeming, Glenda. *Wesker the Playwright*. London and New York: Methuen, 1983.

Marland, Michael., ed. *Chips with Everything, by Arnold Wesker*. London and Glasgow: Blackie, 1967.

Wesker, A. *Arnold Wesker*, Vol. 3. Harmondsworth: Penguin, 1980.

Wisdom in Fragments
The Old Ones

Robert Gross

> The absolute fragment is a tease, more or less invented in
> its modern form when millions of people were being frag-
> mented, warmed therefore by a rather desperate gaiety
> that was founded on the disparity between the world as
> officially presented and the facts of the battlefield.
> (Kermode 143)

Like many artists of this century, Arnold Wesker has been fascinated
by the fragment. This fascination puts him in unusual company.
Wesker and *Woyzeck*? The *Cantos* of Ezra Pound? The collages of
Braque, Picasso, and Ernst? The photomontages of John Heartfield,
the *merzbau* of Kurt Schwitters, the assemblages of Louise Nevelson?
"The fragment has become one of the calling cards of the modernist
movement" (Tytell 3).[1] What are we to think when we see Wesker
with that card? It seems too avant-garde for Wesker, too incoherent.
By labeling him a "realist" (a label Wesker himself has grown to de-
test), critics have pigeonholed Wesker into a pre-modernist tradition;
Lillo, Galsworthy, and Odets may easily seem to be closer kin to Wesker
than Tzara, Brecht, and Howard Barker.[2] And yet there is value to
investigating to what extent Wesker's interest in the fragment places
him in company of modernist (and postmodernist) artists of
fragmentation and to what extent his particular treatment of the fragment places him outside that company.

Wesker's thoughts about fragments are articulated most straightforwardly in his discursive rather than dramatic writings. In one journal entry, associated with the writing of *The Friends* (pf. 1970, pub.
1970), Wesker begins with the assumption of a chaotic and meaningless universe:

> I believe that the universe, the cosmos, all that is known
> and guessed at externally, all—is chaos...that chaos is the
> nature of all existence...and that man's task is the

> constant effort of creating order and in this lies his
> richness of spirit and its fulfillment (quoted in
> Mannheimer 36).

Human beings hold a privileged and separate station in this universe, since they are the sole creators of meaning and order. Not believing in a divine creator (*Distinctions* 252), Wesker shapes a human demiurge to impose order on the primal chaos. Wesker sees the human artist working like the demiurge—not *ab vacuuo* but out of pre-existing fragments. The artist arranges, rather than creates: "the arrangement of fragments is the artist's purpose in life" (*Fears* 106), he writes. The basis on which the arrangement is to be made, however, remains shadowy:

> The major distinction which must be made is between
> the process which elevates a fragment to being the whole
> truth, and the process of collecting fragments together
> which hint at the truth. (*Fears* 112)

This explanation of the artistic process raises more questions than it answers. How, in the universe of chaos, is the truth known? Is it a Platonic schema, like that used by the Demiurge in the *Timaeus*, or is it some Divine Spark of Imagination in a godless world? To elevate any part of it to the status of "the whole truth" is clearly a form of idolatry, but what would "the whole truth" be, anyway, and how many and what kinds of fragments would one have to collect to be able even to hint at it?

Pondering questions such as these, we soon realize that Wesker's aesthetics are founded less on a system of rational analysis than on a creation myth. An investigation of *The Old Ones* (pf. 1972, pub. 1973), Wesker's most ambitious dramatic study of fragmentation to date, however, reveals that the myth is less one of creation than of restoration: the reconstruction of Osiris' dismembered body from the waters of the Nile; the revival of the torn and devoured Dionysus; or, most appropriately, the Fall and the coming of the Messianic kingdom to the dispersed tribes of Israel. As Heiner Zimmermann has pointed out, Wesker's utopian thinking is strongly shaped by Messianic images:

> Although he [Wesker] is not a believing Jew, elements of
> the Messianic dream of the millennium, which brings
> salvation on earth, appear everywhere in his plays with
> humanistic and socialist conceptions. The essential field
> of reference for the author's dream is formed by the exo-

dus and the return to the Promised Land, and also by the
expectation of the Messiah, who will bring peace and
happiness, abolish injustice, and establish the kingdom
of God for the Chosen People with Jerusalem at its centre. (14)

In *The Old Ones*, there is little discussion of utopia. In fact, Wesker
may never have written a play in which the possibility of utopia was
more remote. In the play's aesthetic concern with the meaningful re-
integration of fragments into a whole, however, Wesker's utopian
imagination can still be felt.

   The Old Ones began, in part, as an experiment in form, in which
Wesker tried to build a play out of more loosely related elements than
ever before in his career. Whereas *Chips with Everything* (pf. 1962,
pub. 1962) and *Their Very Own and Golden City* (pf. 1965, pub. 1966)
both experimented with episodic form, the scenes were united by the
story of their protagonist. In *The Kitchen* (pf. 1959, pub. 1960) and
The Friends, the focus was more diffuse, in that the plays look at a
group of individuals, rather than a protagonist, but this diffusion of
focus is bounded by strong unity of place and action. *The Old Ones*
combines the broader focus of *The Kitchen* and *The Friends* with the
episodic structure of *Chips with Everything* and *Their Very Own and
Golden City*. Wesker somewhat anxiously described his formal intention with the play:

> What I wanted—and I don't know whether it's even pos-
> sible but this touches upon the relationship between di-
> rector and writer—was to be able simply to present a se-
> ries of scenes which had nothing more to connect them
> than the fact that some of the characters were related or
> were friends. (Hayman 94)

This description is obviously something of an oversimplification. The
scenes in *The Old Ones* are linked in a number of ways, atmospheri-
cally, imagistically, and thematically. It is clear from this description,
however, that Wesker wanted to make the structure of the play less
reliant on plot and causality than he had attempted before. Wesker's
fragments in *The Old Ones* are, most obviously, fragmented actions.
Rather than a unified, Aristotelian plot with a beginning, middle,
and end, we have a collage of actions: Rudi discussing his paintings;
Rosa trying to lecture an audience of unruly adolescents; Teressa trying to translate a Polish poem into English; Martin quarreling with

his father, etc. Although the relationships among the characters often seem complex, Wesker devotes little time to exposition that would clarify them. The only major speech that deals with family relationships at length, as Wesker has pointed out, is Boomy's explanation as to why he and his brother Manny have been at odds throughout their adult lives (*Distinctions* 336). This speech is central to understanding the myth of fragmentation in Wesker's work.

As Boomy tells the story, Manny, as the elder of the two sons, was entrusted by their father with a bag of diamonds, which was to pay for their education. One day, after their father's death, the two sons went for a walk around London that ended on Westminster Bridge. "And we stood on the bridge and talked and talked about the future" Boomy recollects (3:163).[3] But then

> ...suddenly Manny says: "But Boomy," he says, "everything we do must come from our own hands. You agree?" And of course I agree, 'cos I thought he was only talking about the efforts we would have to make in our studies. "Good," he says, and he embraces me and we cry and before I know it he's thrown the bag of diamonds into the river. (3:163)

Since that time, the brothers have lived under the same roof but in opposition. This opposition has taken on a ritual form: Manny finds quotations that support an optimistic view of life, and Boomy counters them with pessimistic quotations.

This narrative is reminiscent of the biblical tale of Jacob and Esau (Genesis 25:19–27:40) but with an important difference; this is not a story of one brother tricking the other out of his patrimony but of a brother who discards the entire patrimony. The diamonds are an image of great wealth, and in this story, they are linked to the metaphorical riches of knowledge and education. They are thrown away, ironically, at the moment when the brothers are embracing each other, incorrectly believing that they each agree with the other. Boomy assents to Manny's proposition that "everything we do must come from our own hands," not understanding what Manny actually means by this. Whether Manny acts upon an innocent misunderstanding or a rhetorical manipulation remains unclear, but what is clear is that the enmity of the brothers is based on different understandings of Manny's proposition. This moment of linguistic confusion leads to a loss of patrimony and establishes a rivalry between the brothers. After this moment, one speaks only the language of optimism; the other, of pessimism. Dialogue is replaced by opposing monologues. These monologues are, moreover, nothing but pastiche; the brothers do not speak in their own voices, but quote passages from Yeats, Carlyle, Ruskin, and Martin Buber. In one, particularly comic exchange, both quote from the writings of Voltaire to prove their opposing viewpoints (3:28–29). Each one of these literary fragments is supposed to be the final word in the search for the meaning of life, and each one fails. In this duel of quotations, learning ceases to illuminate the complexities of life but merely deepens entrenched positions. Language ceases to facilitate dialogue.

This fall from a common tongue into uncommunicative speech echoes the Biblical myth of the Tower of Babel, in which a single language is replaced by a multiplicity of tongues (Genesis 11: 1–9). George Steiner has traced the influence of that myth on certain branches of occult Jewish thought such as the Kabbalah. Thus tradition

> holds that a single primal language, an Ursprache lies behind our present discord, behind the abrupt tumult of warring tongues which followed on the collapse of Nimrod's ziggurat. (Steiner 59–60)

This loss of an original, common tongue becomes a second Fall of Mankind, and the plurality of tongues becomes a sign of our postlapsarian condition.[4] Linguistic distance is further dramatized by Teressa's vain attempt to render four lines of a Polish poem into English (3:157–58). We learn that she has been working on this verse for two months and still has not found a satisfactory English equivalent to the original (3:158). Rosa's inability to communicate successfully with the working-class counselees is another example. Those youths, identified with the silent, violent street toughs who mock Millie (3:158) and attack Gerda (3:165), are the furthest remove from language. Indeed, the historical vision of *The Old Ones* is one of a progressive loss of meaning. The world degenerates from the prelapsarian state of the patriarch whose wealth and the access to education that went with it have been irrevocably lost. We then go to the "old ones" of the title, who still value art and learning (Teressa, Manny, Boomy) and social bonds but are largely incapable of taking meaningful action: Teressa cannot finish her translations; Manny refuses to go to the police when his wife is mugged; Boomy refuses to keep his son out of prison. In the next generation, we see Martin and Rosa, neither of whom are happy in their marriages or successful in their attempts at social change, and Rudi, whose attempts at artistic expression are woefully inadequate. The youngest characters are the thugs—nameless, dumb and violent. This historical trajectory is the same as Lindemann has found in other plays of Wesker's, in which a utopia is projected into the past (171–72).

Critical interpretations of *The Old Ones* have tended to see the play structured by the opposition of Manny and Boomy. Leeming, for example, argues that "*all* the scenes are tangentially relevant to the conflict between optimism and pessimism" (3:110) and that the play fails to the extent that it comes to favor Manny's view over Boomy's (3:114–15). Wilcher disagrees with Leeming's conclusion, "The debate is by no means over," he asserts (103), but he agrees with her that the war of quotations between the brothers establishes the fundamental structure of the play (95). Both of these readings miss the absurdity and pathos of this dramatic motif. "We don't even scream like we used to," Boomy explains to Gerda. "It's only a ritual that's left. Funny, even" (3:163). Both brothers have made the mistake of taking a fragment of text and raising it to the status of a totalizing statement about life. To identify Wesker's purpose in the play with this ultimately naive battle of fragments is to present the playwright as naive himself. The Boomy/Manny feud is an important part of the play, not because it establishes a thoughtful dialectic between two valid views of the world but because it shows the degeneration of intellectual life when parts are mistaken for wholes and dialogue degenerates into stubborn opposition.

The critical tendency to see the play structured through the opposition of Manny as the optimist to Boomy the pessimist also ignores the fact that Wesker gives Manny a tortured, despairing side as well, making the division between the brothers less clearcut than the critics would have it. The play begins with Manny screaming in the dark, a motif that is repeated at the beginning of Scene 1 (3:133). Both screams are followed by desperate fragments of speech, such as "There should be an echo, a coming back of something"(3:133). In both scenes, Gerda tries to comfort him, telling Manny he's torturing himself. "All the time we've been married you've never given yourself a moment's happiness," she tells him (3:149). This nighttime self of Manny is every bit as pessimistic as his brother's gloomiest aspect. All of his hopeful daytime pronouncements must be interpreted against the background of these nocturnal episodes. Rather than weighing the argument in favor of Manny's optimism, as Leeming argues (114–15), Wesker admits a strain of fundamental terror and alienation even in the most determinedly sunny individual. Manny, as well as Boomy, feels the horror that comes from living in a fallen world, but he refuses to share it with his brother. All of his optimism may be tinged with desperation, even marked by bad faith.

II

JACK: It wobbles.
SARAH: I know it wobbles. (3:159)

The deterioration of language in *The Old Ones* is paralleled in the deterioration of cultural heritage and ritual. This is most fully dramatized through the preparations for the Jewish feast of Succoth. These preparations were a late addition to the play and came from director John Dexter's belief that Wesker's succession of dramatic fragments needed a stronger frame to contain them. Wesker agreed to the revisions but noted that the emphasis on Succoth made *The Old Ones* far more a play about the Diaspora than he had intended (Hayman 94). Regardless of Wesker's original intention, it is clear that the building of the Succah and Rosa's attempts to revive the Succoth rituals strongly link the play's themes of disintegration to an explicitly Jewish frame of cultural references.

The motivations for building the Succah at Sarah's are somewhat obscure. Sarah admits that she does not believe in it, but is doing it to remember her father and please "Aunty Gerda who likes these things"(3:137). It, however, fails to please Gerda, who arrives at the Succoth celebration bandaged and recovering from the assault on her, and the other guests are ill at ease with it. "It was only meant to be a gesture," Rosa explains, but the meaning of the gesture is hazy, since no one remembers enough about the feast to make sense of it:

TERESSA: It's sacrilegious. I mean, we don't even remember.
RUDI: Doesn't anyone remember?
SARAH: Who can remember? We were children. (3:179)

Their awareness of their cultural heritage has been eroded over time, and their attempts to re-enact the rituals are self-conscious and intermittent (3:181–82). The Succah, we are told repeatedly, is not strongly built (3:137, 159, 169, 170). All of their preparations depend on a book from which Rosa reads at length, Isaac Fabricant's *A Guide to*

Succoth (3:136). Like her uncles, Rosa becomes a reader of quotations drawn from a complex cultural tradition and reduced to incompletely understood and unintegrated fragments.

Rosa's reliance on Fabricant's *Guide* testifies to a loss of memory within the community. This loss is most fully dramatized in the character of Millie, who has serious lapses of memory, in which she forgets where people live (3:158–59) and that her brothers are dead (3:145–46), but also in the character of Teressa, who cannot remember why she wants contact with other human beings (3:169). Teressa's forgetfulness suggests an extreme of alienation, in which human beings are so isolated that the desirability of human contact becomes a foreign notion.

As memory and cultural continuity disintegrate, books increasingly become the vehicle of cultural transmission or, to put it more accurately, the idea of the Book as the foundation of cultural identity over time. Yet, the Book serves merely as an artifact in a culture that has begun to forget. The way in which Wesker links the Book to forgetfulness in *The Old Ones* resonates with Socrates' condemnation of writing in the *Phaedrus*, in which the god Ammon tells Theuth, the inventor of writing, that his invention will not be good for humans, since it encourages people to rely on texts rather than their memories. It will not give wisdom, he explains, but only the semblance of wisdom (Plato, *Phaedrus* 275 a–b). So, too, *The Guide to the Succoth* transmits information about the feast that has been forgotten by the community, but that information in itself is insufficient to revive the feast as a meaningful action. Writing, explains Jacques Derrida, is figured in the Western tradition as an orphan, language that exists in the absence of the speaking Father (77). Without a clear patriarchal voice speaking, one is left with a Babel of written texts, all cut off from their speakers. In *The Old Ones*, we are similarly confronted with a welter of texts, none of which offer certain knowledge—Yeats, Carlyle, Wilczynski, Voltaire, Buber, Fabricant, d'Epinay, and Ecclesiastes. It is an indication of the literary confusion in this dramatic universe that Rosa does not offer her hostile and recalcitrant students a particular book that will speak to their problems. All she can offer them is "Books!" (3:178–79), plural and undifferentiated. The best she can do is offer them these disordered fragments, and she finally assesses her efforts as "So feeble. So bloody feeble" (3:179).[5]

Yet Rosa's efforts are not completely in vain. Her tirade to the students holds their attention this time, if only through its anger and brutal realism. Her attempts to revive the Feast of Succoth, though not ultimately successful, do bring members of the community together and present it with pieces of its past that have otherwise been forgotten. Rather than use fragments as weapons as her uncles do, Rosa becomes a collector of fragments for the community. In *Fears of Fragmentation,* Wesker compares workers in social projects to artists:

> a project, like a work of art, must contain as many fragments as possible in order to confront a community constantly not only with what is happening to it now, but why it is happening and what happened before and what can happen again. (Wesker, *Fears* 122)

The Succoth celebration, no matter how incomplete, still represents an attempt to combat the forces of forgetfulness and alienation.

III

> So I turned my attention to the nature of wisdom and knowledge [on the one hand], and of foolish behavior and vulgarity [on the other]. I learned that this too was grasping at the wind. For with more wisdom comes more worry, and he who adds to his knowledge adds to his pain. (Ecclesiastes, i, 17–18)[6]

Among the many quotations in *The Old Ones,* the reader will search in vain for a single citation from the Torah. That text, most closely identified with the Word of the Father, seems to have been forgotten—like the language spoken before the Tower of Babel, or lost, like the sack of diamonds. Instead, the only biblical text cited is Ecclesiastes, and that, no fewer than ten times. The choice of Ecclesiastes is certainly appropriate for a play that treats Succoth, since it is the text read on the seventh and eighth days of that festival (Fabricant 29). Wesker himself points out the identification of Ecclesiastes with the feast: "You know what book belongs to 'Succous' [sic]? Ecclesiastes!" Boomy observes (3:180). Yet the importance of Ecclesiastes as an intertext for *The Old Ones* goes far beyond this realistic detail. This biblical book poses some of the same questions that Wesker's play does and presents some of the same problems of interpretation.

"The Bible's strangest book" is how biblical scholar James Crenshaw describes Ecclesiastes (23), not only echoing R.B.Y Scott's

"Ecclesiastes is the strangest book in the Bible," (191) but also centuries of earlier commentary.[7] Indeed, there have been those who argued that it should not be included in the Bible at all, and commentators still feel the need to justify its place there (Fabricant 29; Scott 194–96). It has been seen as the product of a counterculture, voicing doubts and dissents that were suppressed in the official literature (Fox 262) or were completely outside the Judaic tradition altogether—"Ecclesiastes has no known antecedents or spiritual posterity in Jewish thought" writes one commentator (Bickerman 142)—an expression of Greek, Babylonian, or Egyptian thought (Ellul 13–15). Ecclesiastes is a scandal within the canon, a work that sits uncomfortably amongst its more orthodox neighbors.

There are two reasons for this scandal. First of all, Ecclesiastes is a particularly difficult work to interpret, because it is filled with contradictions (Wright 245; Ellul 39). How can one reconcile:

> [So] the thoughts of the wise turn to the house of mourning, but the thoughts of fools to the place of amusement. (7:4)

with:

> what is satisfying and suitable is to eat and drink and enjoy oneself in all one's struggle under the sun (5:18)?

Or reconcile:

> For with more wisdom comes more worry, and he who adds to his knowledge adds to his pain. (1:18)

with:

> A man's wisdom lights up his face, and the hardness of his countenance is transformed (8:1)?

Scholars have tried to explain away these contradictions by finding a structural progression in the work, but the work resists such systematization (Crenshaw 47). Qoheleth, the pseudonymous sage and author of the book, a scribe comments at the book's conclusion, "instructed the people in what he had learned, pondering and examining the composition of many wise sayings" (12:9). Qoheleth, in other words, was a collector of and commentator on proverbs. We see this manner of instruction most clearly in 7:1–14, in which he cites a series of traditional proverbs and comments on them. He, like Wesker's artist, is a collector and arranger of fragments, and no one of these fragments is placed beyond the possibility of contradiction. Indeed,

Jacques Ellul has concluded that the meaning of Ecclesiastes resides in its strategy of contradiction:

> We must get to the point where we understand that con-
> tradiction alone can enable us to move ahead. The prin-
> ciple of noncontradiction relates to death. (Ellul 40–41)

Wesker is certainly aware of the use of contradictions in Ecclesiastes. He even calls attention to it with Manny and Boomy quoting philo-sophically opposed passages from it in the final scene of the play (65). Like Qoheleth, Wesker is not interested in making any single charac-ter his mouthpiece in *The Old Ones*, nor is he trying to vindicate one insight at the expense of another. Each point of view is a fragment and can therefore only be understood by reference to other, some-times contradictory, fragments.

Both Qoheleth and Wesker rely on fragments because they see no way that human beings can know the whole and absolute truth. It is this philosophical skepticism that has made religiously orthodox readers of Ecclesiastes uncomfortable. This skepticism is far more scan-dalous than mere contradiction, which can be found in more than one book of the Bible. The God of Ecclesiastes is unknown and un-knowable; not the God of revelation and Covenant found in the other books (Scott 192). "Man cannot discover what is going on in this world," writes Qoheleth, "however hard he may search he will not find it out" (8:17). One can collect precepts that have a limited valid-ity, but that is all. Qoheleth moves between moments of despondency, in which all life is nothing but *hébel* (a breath, a vapor), and moments of hedonism, in which these fleeting pleasures are to be enjoyed. There is no way to move beyond the contradiction. The contradiction must be lived.

So it is in *The Old Ones*. The characters repeatedly draw generali-zations from their experience that are quickly countered by other char-acters. Teressa, for example, uses the young thugs as proof of the prob-lems of the working class (3:39), which provokes Sarah into an ode to the working class (3:160). This relationship between specific cases and generalizations is foregrounded when Sarah and Martin argue about his politics. He tells her about a friend of his who died in police custody and uses this as an example of injustice; Sarah discounts this as an exception from which no generalization can be drawn (3:177). Rosa is aware of how she irrationally draws generalizations from experience:

> I read about the terrible things men do to each other—
> wars for gain or prestige, massacres for religious principles,
> cruelty to children, indifference to poverty—and then,
> one morning, one person, one, does something beautiful
> and I say, "See! people are good!" (3:174)

For Qoheleth and Wesker, all generalizations are drawn from experience, and are therefore, partial. Their responses to this limitation of human thought, however, differ. Qoheleth remains the solitary scholar, drawing conclusions from his own experience. Wesker points toward a social dimension, in which the limited insights of one person are compensated for by the insights of others. Manny expresses this notion in a quotation from Thomas Carlyle:

> Great is the combined voice of men; the utterance of their
> instincts, which are truer than their thoughts: it is the
> greatest a man encounters among the sounds and shad-
> ows which make up this World of Time.[8]

This idea of Carlyle's articulates on the most universal level what Wesker sees in the work of the artist and worker in society—a drawing together of fragments into an arrangement that can hint at the higher truth.

IV

> I love to see full cupboards. Got it from you. I used to
> love unpacking your shopping bags. (3:173)

Thus far, I have concentrated on the relationship of the two feuding sons to the patriarchal tradition and have largely painted that tradition as a lost one. It would be a distortion of the play, however, not to consider the role of their sister, Sarah, in that tradition. Sarah is the one who wants to build the Succah in her father's honor, even though she no longer shares his belief (3:138). Rosa is bothered by this gesture:

> ROSA: It's not logical.
> SARAH: It's not logical. (Stubborn pause.)
> ROSA: Actually, maybe it is logical. After all, I suppose
>   it's very human to want to remember your
>   father. (3:138)

For a moment, Rosa and Sarah seem as irrevocably opposed as Manny and Boomy. What stands between them is the idea of "logic," with its connotations of rationality and proof. Their difference of opinion is resolved, however, as Rosa works her way from impersonal logic as the basis for action to common humanity. The intellectual question of consistent belief fades in the light of familial affection. Affection, in this dramatic context, leads to an act of memory, a bulwark against the forces of forgetfulness. This opposition between logic and a love of humanity parallels Carlyle's belief that human instincts are truer than human thoughts. For all the talk about learning in *The Old Ones*, Wesker ultimately puts his faith in a benign vision of the instinctual.

Sarah stands for a mode of connection that is neither intellectual nor rational but instinctive and immediate. She is the one who can make plants grow, rather than her son-in-law who is an expert in soils (3:155). Every speaking character in the play is connected through their relationship to Sarah. While one of her brothers has no children, and the other repudiates his, Sarah has a daughter who sees herself as the continuation of her mother's values, thoughts, and moods:

> My laughter, my ups, my downs, my patience, my impatience, my love of music, mountains, flowers, knowledge—a reverence for all things living? You! You, you, you! (3:174–75)

Even though much of their heritage has been forgotten, Sarah and Rosa know, without recourse to books, how to perform a "delicate Hasidic dance" together (3:190, 193). That dance, testifying to the seemingly unconscious, bodily, continuation of tradition, contrasts with the simultaneous verbal duel of Manny and Boomy. In *The Old Ones*, fragmentation is a symptom, first and foremost, of the disintegration of a male, written culture as opposed to a female, oral one. The brothers' lost diamonds are set in contrast to Sarah's full cupboards; both are images of richness and abundance, but the first is romantic, inorganic, and irretrievably lost, while the other is immediate, organic, and present. The hopes for a Messianic restoration of meaning in *The Old Ones* become embodied in the relationship between mother and daughter.[9] Indeed, one could go so far as to say that, in the dance of Sarah and Rosa, that the Fall has never occurred.

In this respect, *The Old Ones* articulates two seemingly incompatible myths. The first charts the progressive fragmentation of language and intellect to the level of violent, speechless youths. The other celebrates the continuation of a prelapsarian state of mutual sympathy. The first derives from the Judaeo-Christian tradition. The second is rooted in romanticism. Manny quotes Carlyle, but he could just as well have quoted from William Wordsworth's "Ode: Intimations of Immortality," with its reliance on "the primal sympathy/Which having been must ever be"(181–82). The intellect has fallen, but the *instincts* (to use Carlyle's term) have not. This may get us out of the impasse we found ourselves in earlier when considering Wesker's aesthetic pronouncements about chaos and order. It may well be the instincts that guide the artist in the collection and arrangement of fragments that hint at the higher truth. This is consistent with Wesker's skepticism concerning theories of art as opposed to the play of the imagination (Wesker, "Nature" 364). Although Wesker's statements about fragmentation and chaos may sound postmodern, even existentialist at times, his reliance on terms such as "imagination," "instinct" and "human" to connote primal integrative forces places him more comfortably in the Romantic tradition.

The Romantic poetry of Wordsworth even makes its appearance in a key moment of *The Old Ones*. The walk of the two brothers through London leads them to Westminster Bridge:

> You ever stood on that bridge and looked at London?
> Wordsworth wrote a poem from it, the river bends, a wide
> sweep, you can look up and down—beautiful! (Pause.)
> And we talked. (Pause.) (3:163)

Boomy invokes Wordsworth's experience of calm and beauty in his sonnet, "Composed upon Westminster Bridge, September 3, 1802," as an indication of his own serenely exalted feelings while standing on the bridge with his brother. This moment of aesthetic vision is suddenly cut short as Boomy moves from contemplation to speech—"and we talked." This clause, set off with pauses, indicates the beginning of a turn in the narrative, from understanding to misunderstanding, from a moment of harmonious silence to a lifetime of mutual antagonism. For a playwright who often places such a strong positive value on the uses of language, *The Old Ones* shows Wesker exploring the possibility that language may be potentially divisive and that more noble sentiments lie somewhere outside of speech. Though Zimmermann may well be correct when he accuses Wesker's writings of the 1960s as "overestimating the possibilities and means of enlightenment" (191), his works of the 1970s, particularly *The Old Ones*, are less optimistic about the unifying potential of speech, education, and rational discourse.

V

> The arrangement of fragments is the artist's purpose in
> life; and yet, paradoxically, the fear of fragmentation is
> the subject of this artist's lecture. (Wesker, *Fears* 106)

Wesker's writing is marked with a longing for wholeness. The fragment is feared, taken as a sign as a fall from a mythic unity. Artistic
creation attempts to move beyond the fragmentary, through acts of
arrangement. This leads to an approach to the fragment that is largely
opposed to that of the modernists. This difference can most easily be
seen by contrasting Wesker to a modernist like Russian formalist critic
Victor Shklovsky. Shklovsky argues that the purpose of an art work is
to challenge the deadliness of habitual perception. It does so by making familiar objects unfamiliar: "to make forms difficult, to increase
the difficulty and length of perception because the process of perception is an aesthetic end in itself and must be prolonged" (12). The
aesthetic value of the fragment, then, resides in how its removal from
its usual context forces us to look at it anew. The modernist wrenches
the fragment loose from its place in a deadening and specious unity
to release otherwise invisible aesthetic qualities, while Wesker gathers
up the fragments in hopes of creating a whole. Wesker's approach to
the fragment is ultimately anti-modern. What the Dadaist celebrates,
Wesker deplores.

These fundamentally conservative aesthetic values of Wesker's
made themselves felt in his revision of *The Old Ones* prior to its premiere at the Royal Court Theatre. Wesker had misgivings about the
looseness of the work's dramatic structure. "I don't know whether it's
even possible," he remarked in an interview (Hayman 96). John Dexter, the director of the production, felt that the work needed tighten-
ing. In the same interview, Dexter spoke of the need of a "thread," or
"container" to hold the scenes (Hayman 95). Dexter wondered if the
preparations for a Friday night supper might work; Wesker responded
with the idea of preparations for Succoth, thus providing a sequence
of actions that Robert Wilcher has identified as the narrative line of
the play (94). By revising the play so that the celebration at Sarah's is
its climax, Wesker and Dexter chose to close *The Old Ones* in a more
strongly festive comic atmosphere and mute somewhat the vision of
radical fragmentation that has characterized the play up to that point.

This final scene stands apart from the earlier ones in several ways. First of all, while the other scenes are quite short, ranging from less than a page to five pages in length, the final scene runs to seventeen pages in the printed version. It replaces the episodic, fragmentary structure of the play with something far more coherent. Secondly, while seven of the earlier scenes were monologues and the rest have two or three speaking parts, the final scene includes nine characters—all the speaking roles except Martin. The immediate effect of this is to give an impression of liveliness and conviviality, especially since Wesker stresses that this scene "must be full of energy" (3:179). The loneliness and isolation of the earlier scenes is replaced by a vigorous social milieu. The dominant atmosphere is comic and festive.

This is not to say that there are no difficult or painful moments. There are a number of them. Gerda, still recovering from the attack on her, lies bandaged and separate from the others (3:179). Boomy refers to the Holocaust and brings the festivities to an momentary halt (3:181). Rudi asks why both Rosa's husband and Martin are absent, and causes further embarrassment (3:185–86). Boomy delivers a tirade on violence that reveals the depths of his own self-hatred (3:168). None of these incidents, however, deal a permanent blow to the festivities. Even Boomy's diatribe is immediately countered by Sarah's comic understatement, "Boomy, you're a very depressing man" (3:188). In fact, these more somber moments testify to the elasticity and tolerance of the comic gathering that has been constituted in the play's final scene. The limits of that tolerance, however, are indicated by the limits of Sarah's sympathies. Rosa's husband, the soil expert who cannot grow things, is absent, though his exclusion carries very little weight, since we have never seen him onstage. The absence of the street thugs is easily explained both realistically and thematically: speechless and violent, they are presented as the embodiment of the anti-social. The absence of Martin is more subtle and significant. The last time we saw him, he was reprimanded by Sarah for not being able to tolerate his father's curmudgeonly ways: "You must have strength to ignore Boomy's weaknesses and leave him a little bit of useless old peace," she admonished him (3:177). Ultimately, the one thing that the comic society of *The Old Ones* cannot tolerate is the lack of tolerance. Martin has not simply been excluded from this company; he has chosen to exclude himself when he walked out of Sarah's apartment rather than stay and talk with his father. Although we first saw him helping erect the Succah, Martin's anger and intolerance have steadily moved him away from the festive community.[10]

The final scene reaches its climax as Manny finally meets his brother's quotations, not with another quotation but with a thought expressed in his own words. Although Wesker has written that he did not want the audience to accept Manny's speech as true, calling it "a desperately charitable definition of evil" (*Distinctions* 337), it carries a strongly positive theatrical charge that tends to weigh the speech in Manny's favor. First of all, rather than his usual, simple, unprepared statement, Manny's original speech is both the climax of the scene and the high point of a four-page sequence, which begins with Manny's entering the festivities clothed only in a bath towel and ends with his "mooning" the guests—a earthy comic gesture that can easily insure a quick laugh. Secondly, it tends to resolve the stalemate between the brothers in Manny's favor, since Manny is able to find his own voice rather than relying on quoted fragments, a comic echo of Beatie's discovery of her own voice in Wesker's *Roots* (Leeming 111). Manny's energy, the verbal excitement generated by his own discovery, its bawdy punctuation, and the fact that no one onstage specifically calls attention to the weaknesses in Manny's argument, all work to counter the hitherto loose, open form of the play, in which no single fragment is to be raised to the level of the whole. Although Wesker has accused Dexter of upsetting the play's delicate balance of thoughts and moods by staging the last moments of the play in terms too upbeat and reminiscent of *Fiddler on the Roof* (*Distinctions* 113), it is also important to note that Wesker's own writing in the final scene works toward a traditional sense of comic closure that endangers the balance established in the earlier scenes. The climax of *The Old Ones* shows Wesker's fear of fragmentation leading him toward a more traditional closure than the early scenes might lead us to expect. At the same time, it demonstrates Wesker's impulse to embrace structure and wholeness as the requisites for a civilized life. Like critic Frank Kermode, Wesker regards the fragment as something that relies on the whole for meaning: "…without routine, without inherited structures, carnival loses its point; without social totalities there are no anti-social fragments" (143). Wesker does not present his plays as fragments but as wholes that work to transcend the fragmentary nature of their raw material.

ↄ৲

ENDNOTES

1. Critical literature on the fragment and its place in modernism and postmodern is extensive. Two particularly useful and succinct treatments can be found in Tytell, and in Kermode 128–46.

2. For Wesker's unhappiness with the term "realist," see *Distinctions* 138–40 and "The Nature of Theatre Dialogue," 367.

3. All quotations from *The Old Ones*, unless otherwise noted, are taken from the 1990 edition of Wesker's *Plays* (Harmondsworth: Penguin), Vol. 3.

4. For an interesting investigation of this tradition and its manifestation in the writings of another twentieth-century Jewish author, Walter Benjamin, see Wolin 37–43.

5. Wesker's 1980 revision of the text, printed in Vol. 3 of his *Plays*, emphasizes Rosa's awareness of how futile her speech is by adding the following stage directions to her speech: "*Softly, without hope*" and "*Forlorn, weary*" (Wesker, *Plays* 179). The 1973 edition published by Jonathan Cape does not contain these lines.

6. All quotations from Ecclesiastes are taken from Proverbs. Ecclesiastes ed. R.B.Y. Scott.

7. For useful summaries of critical approaches to Ecclesiastes, see Bergant 57–64 and Crenshaw.

8. This quotation from Thomas Carlyle only appears in the 1972 version of *The Old Ones*, published by Jonathan Cape in 1973.

9. Wesker has said that the role of Rosa was originally written for a man and was changed at the suggestion of John Dexter, who felt the play needed another female voice for contrast. Although he followed this revision in the Munich production and the revised version of the play, he has said he thought it was a mistake (*Distinctions* 113). It remains unclear how much of the role Wesker changed to accommodate this shift of gender; certainly, Rosa's description of herself as the continuation of her mother would be more unusual, arresting, and subversive if it crossed gender lines. One could argue that Rosa's gender is not terribly important in itself; what is important is that the tradition is carried on through Sarah, not Boomy or Manny. Yet the fact remains that Sarah's offspring remains female in both printed versions of the play and that this choice of Wesker's resonates through the gendered structure of *The Old Ones*. Wesker's ambivalence about this character's gender might well

be an interesting subject for investigation in itself.

10. For a discussion of this vision of comedy, see Frye 164–69.

Works Cited

Bergant, Dianne. *What Are They Saying About Wisdom Literature?* New York: Ramsey, 1984.

Bickerman, Elias. *Four Strange Books of the Bible: Jonah, Daniel, Koheleth, Esther.* New York: Schocken Books, 1967.

Crenshaw, James L. *Ecclesiastes.* Philadelphia: Westminster Press, 1987.

Derrida, Jacques. *Dissemination.* Tr. and ed. Barbara Johnson. Chicago: University of Chicago Press, 1981.

Ellul, Jacques. *Reason for Being: A Meditation on Ecclesiastes.* Tr. Joyce Main Hanks. Grand Rapids, MI: William B. Eerdmans, 1990.

Fabricant, Isaac A. *A Guide to Succoth.* London: Jewish Chronicle Publications, 1958.

Fox, Michael. "The Voices of Ecclesiastes." *College Literature* 15 (September 1988): 262–68.

Frye, Northrop. *Anatomy of Criticism: Four Essays.* Princeton, NJ: Princeton University Press, 1971.

Hayman, Ronald. "Arnold Wesker and John Dexter." *Transatlantic Review* 48 (December 1973): 89–99.

Jones, Alexander, ed. *The Jerusalem Bible.* Garden City, New York: 1968.

Kermode, Frank. *History and Value: The Clarendon Lectures and the Northcliffe Lectures 1987.* Oxford: Oxford University Press, 1988.

Leeming, Glenda. *Wesker the Playwright.* London: Methuen, 1983.

Lindemann, Valeska. "Raum und Zeit in ihrer Beziehung zur sozialer und psychologischen Thematik in Arnold Wesker's Werk." *Literatur in Wissenschaft und Unterricht 11* (1978): 161–77.

Mannheimer, Monica. "Ordering Chaos: The Genesis of Arnold Wesker's *The Friends.*" *English Studies* 56 (February 1975): 34–44.

Plato. "Phaedrus." Tr. R. Hackforth. In *The Collected Dialogues.* Eds. Edith Hamilton and Huntington Cairns. Princeton, NJ: Princeton University Press, 1961, 475–525.

Ronsand, David. "Composition/Decomposition/Recomposition: Notes on the Fragmentary and the Artistic Process." *New York Literary Forum* 8–9 (1981): 17–38.

Scott, R.B.Y., ed. Proverbs. Ecclesiastes. *The Anchor Bible*. Garden City, New York: Doubleday, 1965.

Shklovsky, Victor. "Art as Technique." In *Russian Formalist Criticism: Four Essays*. Trs. Lee T. Lemon and Marion J. Reis. Lincoln, NE: University of Nebraska Press, 1965, 3–24.

Tytell, John. "Epiphany in Chaos: Fragmentation in Modernism." *New York Literary Forum* 8–9 (1981): 3–16.

Wesker, Arnold. *Distinctions*. London: Jonathan Cape, 1985.

———. *Fears of Fragmentation*. London: Jonathan Cape, 1970.

———. "The Nature of Theatre Dialogue." *New Theatre Quarterly* 8 (1986): 364–68.

———. *The Old Ones*. London: Jonathan Cape, 1973.

———. *Plays*. Vol. 3. [*Chips with Everything, The Friends, The Old Ones, Love Letters on Blue Paper*.] London: Penguin, 1980 and 1990.

Wilcher, Robert. *Understanding Arnold Wesker*. Columbia, South Carolina: University of South Carolina Press, 1991.

Williams, James G. "What Does It Profit a Man? The Wisdom of Koheleth." In *Studies in Ancient Israelite Wisdom*. Ed. James Crenshaw. New York: KTAV Publishing House, 1976: 375–89.

Wolin, Richard. *Walter Benjamin: An Aesthetic of Redemption*. New York: Columbia University Press, 1982.

Wordsworth, William. "Ode: Intimations of Immortality from Recollections of Early Childhood." In *English Romantic Writers*. Ed. David Perkins. New York: Harcourt, Brace and World, 1967: 279–82.

Wright, Addison G. "The Riddle of the Sphinx: The Structure of the Book of Qoheleth." In *Studies in Ancient Israelite Wisdom*. Ed. James Crenshaw. New York: KTAV Publishing House, 1976: 245–66.

Zimmermann, Heiner. "Wesker and Utopia in the Sixties." *Modern Drama* 29 (1986): 185–206.

V. The Critical Response

The Four Seasons
Robert Wilcher

I

In an interview with Arnold Wesker taped in July 1977, Robert Skloot confided that he was drawn to *The Four Seasons* as a director because of the challenges offered by "its austerity and its lyricism" and confessed that he was disconcerted by "the discontinuity" between "the play itself" and its dedication to Cuban revolutionaries.[1] He was in effect, identifying the two features of the play which had alienated many of the early reviewers and which have to a large extent blighted its reputation ever since.[2] Those who had admired Wesker's naturalistic dialogue in *The Kitchen* and the *Trilogy* were unprepared for the highly stylized prose in which Adam and Beatrice meditated on their past lives and negotiated their relationship with each other. And those who had cast Wesker in the mould of Clifford Odets—as a socialist dramatist whose "people live politics, idealism, and reform in an everyday world"[3]—were disappointed by the intensely introspective emphasis of a psychological drama which, in the words of one review, "totally excludes the outside world."[4] The dedication of the printed text "to the romantic revolution" of Cuba was, perhaps, the dramatist's act of compensation for turning away from the issues of economic and cultural exploitation and the theme of political idealism that had been at the center of his vision in the works of the late 1950s.

The hostile reception accorded to *The Four Seasons* provoked Wesker into formulating a considered defense of the play, which was subsequently published as an epilogue to the Penguin edition of the text.[5] With regard to style, his determination to move on from "the words and rhythms of everyday speech" which had served him well in his first six plays meant that he had to "avoid the trap of creating a pseudo-poetic dialogue" (2:112). With regard to his stated project of exploring "only the essentials of a relationship with deliberately little recourse to explanation or background," he had to solve the artistic problem of how much information could be willfully withheld from an audience without sending them off in pursuit of "irrelevant questions," and he had to confront the political argument "which says that individual or private pain can have no relevance in a society where man's real tragedies are bound inextricably with his social environment" (2:112–13). Experience had taught him that critics were all too eager to supply interpretation where information was lacking, and he protested against a symbolic or allegorical reading of the play: "Adam does not represent 'man' nor Beatrice 'woman,' nor is the deserted house a womb....the scenes and sequences of events are nothing more than they seem" (2:112). And as for the argument about political relevance, he made this reply:

> If compassion and teaching the possibility of change are
> two of the many effects of art, a third is this: to remind
> and reassure people that they are not alone not only in
> their attempts to make a better world but in their private
> pains and confusions also....*The Four Seasons* was writ-
> ten because I believe the absence of love diminishes and
> distorts all action. (2:113–14)

Nevertheless, these protestations have not done much for the reputation of *The Four Seasons* and the place it has been assigned in the context of Wesker's development as an artist was recently summed up by Christopher Innes: "His alienation from the Labour movement led to a more introverted and symbolic drama in *The Four Seasons* (1965) or *The Old Ones* (1972), which verges on abstraction in *Caritas*" (1981).[6]

II

Any attempt at reappraisal of what one critic has called "almost a prose poem"[7] must begin with its consciously "heightened and lyrical language" (2:113). Part of Wesker's success in the early plays lay in his ability to create distinctive speech rhythms for characters from different social backgrounds like the Kahns and the Bryants in the *Trilogy*, and control of rhythm is fundamental to the more formally patterned mode of expression he devised for *The Four Seasons*. In the following passage, from Adam's long reverie about the woman he once loved, the rhythmic effects depend upon repetition and variation—of words, and of the structure of phrases and sentences:

> And I? I rummage about the world looking for bits and
> pieces of old passions, past enthusiasms, and echoes of

old laughter. But it's a feeble search, really. I see things
wanting her to see them. I visit places wanting her to be
with me. I think thoughts wanting her to share them,
crying out for her praise. (2:94)

Such devices are not confined to the longer set speeches but also reinforce the dramatic tension generated by dialogue. As summer is about
to give way to autumn, the lovers confront qualities in themselves
and each other that will eventually drive them apart—Beatrice's pos-
sessiveness and Adam's distrust:

BEATRICE: It's your laughter. I can't bear your laughter,
          it's unnatural. It casts everybody out.
ADAM: Everybody?
BEATRICE: Well me, then.
ADAM: You resent my laughter?
BEATRICE: Every second. Every touch, every thought,
          every feeling, every second you should give
          to me.
ADAM: And then there would come a moment when
          every touch would be flinched from, every
          thought sneered at and every feeling abused.
BEATRICE: And that's the moment you're afraid of?
ADAM: Yes. (2:104)

The pointed repetitions of the word "laughter," the questioning and
revising of the word "everybody," and the heavy rhetorical patterning
of "every touch...every thought...every feeling" constitute a poetic
crystallization rather than a naturalistic representation of this crisis in
their relationship.

Stylistic effects of this kind are fraught with dangers, and Wesker
was well aware of the challenge he had set himself. He was still busy
eradicating poeticisms from the script during rehearsals and has gone
on revising the diction and improving the rhythms in successive printed
editions.[8] For example, the "Spring" sequence begins with Beatrice
decorating the sleeping figure of Adam with bluebells. In the 1966
text, the following dialogue ensues:

ADAM: I've not had such a beautiful thing done to
          me since—
BEATRICE: See what we give to the people we comfort?
          The tested gestures of love.
ADAM: You garlanded your lover with bluebells?

> BEATRICE: Every morning.[9]

Both of Adam's speeches have been changed in the 1990 text:

> ADAM: Woken with flowers? Not since—
> BEATRICE: See what we give to the people we comfort?
>   The tested gestures of love.
> ADAM: You woke your lover with bluebells?
> BEATRICE: Every morning. (2:80)

Adam's clumsy commentary on his own surprise at Beatrice's extravagantly romantic gesture is replaced by a more dynamic question—"Woken with flowers?"—which both registers his startled delight and contributes to the symbolism of life reasserting itself after the inertia of winter. The revisions enhance the dramatic force of the dialogue by replacing the descriptive past participle "garlanded" with the active verb "woke," by highlighting the event itself rather than Adam's wordy gloss upon it (enough of which survives to make the point in "Not since—"), and by forging a link (woken/woke) between Adam's two responses—first to the implications of what Beatrice has *done* and then to what she has *said.* Beatrice's opening speech in both versions of the text repeats exactly the remarks made by Adam when he is brushing her hair towards the end of "Winter." Repetitions of this kind serve a dual function as poetic refrains which distill the "essentials" of the relationship into verbal form and as dramatic events which mark significant developments in the action. These are the first words uttered by Beatrice in the play, after her prolonged period of recuperation from the collapse of both a marriage and an adulterous affair. The phrases themselves—particularly the stylization through internal rhyme of "tested gestures"—acknowledge the limited repertoire of signs available to human beings for the *expression* of their feelings for each other. Adam's previous use of the same words to introduce the confession that *his* marriage had failed through infidelity and jealousy was a signal to the silent Beatrice about his readiness to love again and also a warning that the past must inevitably cast its shadow over any relationship that develops between them. The fact that she repeats his earlier speech indicates that she, in turn, is prepared to risk a new commitment on the understanding that both of them will carry the memory of former loves—and the gestures in which they were made manifest—into their future together.

III

The structure of the play, charting the rise and fall of a love affair through the symbolic course of four seasons, is as stylized as the language. Adam's announcement near the beginning that he intends to "commit a whole year" to Beatrice dispels any expectations of naturalistic plausibility in the unfolding of the action, and the unavoidable process though which the lovers are passing is underlined from time to time by the spoken text: "Do you think the winter will ever pass?" (2:79); "Spring comes and it's time to repair the damages of winter" (2:81); "You can smell the days getting shorter" (2:100); "Autumn leaves. Dead. What did you expect?" (2:111). But even in this most deliberately lyrical of his works, Wesker does not forget his early dictum "that the theatre is a place where one wants to *see* things happening."[10] The seasons supply him with activities as well as images— fetching wood and lighting a fire in "Winter," the bluebell episode in "Spring," a walk in the fields in "Summer"—and even the symbolism of "the damages of winter" and the deadness of autumn is secondary to the simple realities of a broken drainpipe that needs mending and damp leaves that will not burn.

The title of *The Four Seasons* invokes not only the natural cycle of growth and decay but also the artistic analogy of Vivaldi's famous concerto for violin, strings, and continuo. While this may not have provided Wesker with an exact structural model, his management of dramatic materials in this play certainly owes something to the sister art of music.[11] Each of the four movements is constructed from dialogues and monologues which are essentially duets and arias, with minor transitions marked by the repeated stage-direction, "*The days pass, the weeks, even,*" and with major alterations of key clearly indicated in the text: "*When* BEATRICE *turns to him she is a changed woman. The venom of her words is matched by the hardness in her eyes*" (2:95); "*Complete change to exuberant mood*" (2:100); "*The cry ends abruptly. Both realize that the year has ended.* BEATRICE *moves to the chest of drawers and meticulously brings out the clothes to fold them ready for packing. Her calm is chilling*" (2:109). As we have seen already, repeated motifs like "the tested gestures of love" are woven into the verbal pattern of the text, and themes are developed in a way reminiscent of musical variation—"You hear what you want to hear, you understand what you need to understand" (2:95) being echoed later in "You saw in me what you needed to see in me" (2:108).

The first movement is scored for the single voice of Adam as he tends the desolate Beatrice through the winter, but even here subtle changes of mood and tempo are introduced in his attempts to coax, shame, and tease her into life. This solo performance is full of imperatives and questions that enact one side of a desired dialogue— "Won't you even say you like it? Say 'I like it.' Just those three words" (2:75); "What colour is the wind, do you think?" (2:78)—and culminates in a long monologue about his failed marriage, spoken as much to ease his own pain as to engage Beatrice's attention. Nor does this opening movement lack dramatic suspense, since a reaction from the silent antagonist is always expected, and on three occasions she does exert her presence positively by weeping, breathing in the woodsmoke, and smiling until the impasse is resolved in the final moments when she slowly raises her hand to stroke Adam's head. The "Spring" movement is devoted largely to the first tentative reachings toward genuine dialogue. These are accompanied by the sharing of a meal and the joint activity of painting the house that is turning into a home. In an extended aria, Beatrice confesses her failure in love, and this leads directly to the climax of the first embrace and the ceremonial decking of Beatrice in the golden cloth that will be the symbol of high summer in their relationship.

"Summer" itself is the longest and most complex of the four movements. After a silent sequence, in which Beatrice pulls Adam gently round the room *"in order to see him in different lights"* (2:90), the set flies away and the lovers' new-found freedom in each other's company is expressed in the gaiety of their exclamations of amazement at the everyday phenomena of nature. At the climax of this playful dialogue, Beatrice turns away from Adam to face the sun with a speech of exhilarated self-absorption: "I'm a flower, Adam see me? See me opening, watch me, I'm blossoming, watch me, watch meeeee" (2:93). The sun sets, Adam moves away from her, and the walls of the house return to enclose them. Days and weeks pass, and the light-hearted mood gives way to a somber meditation by Adam on the kind of woman whose love "is an oppressive sun burning the air around you till you can't breathe" and who has "a passion no part of which relates to any living man nor any living man could share" (2:93). The first quarrel follows, but the decline of the relationship is temporarily checked by Adam's sickness. In a monologue that covers the weeks spent nursing him, Beatrice meditates on the disappointment she has experienced in her quest for the qualities of peace, majesty, and great courage in a man. A recovered Adam tries to revive their fading love by performing for Beatrice's benefit the theatrical set-piece of the play—the preparation of an apple strudel on stage. But his delight in the artistry of this feat serves only to irritate and frighten Beatrice, who feels shut out by his self-absorbed laughter. "Autumn" begins with another external scene, this time by starlight. Faltering attempts at dialogue break down with the questions, "Why didn't you love your wife?" "Why didn't you love your husband?" (2:105). Adam recalls his first sexual betrayal of a girl he loved as an adolescent, and a bout of bitter recriminations ends with a moment of physical violence. As the walls close in again, the play moves into its final rituals: the parting lovers agree that "there was nothing between us really, was there?" (2:109); they recall good moments from earlier love affairs, and they prepare to abandon the house, while damp leaves smolder in the grate where Adam had kindled their first fire.

IV

Interpretation of *The Four Seasons* must begin with the effects created by Wesker's decision to focus "on the relationship alone" and to omit the kind of contextual details (social, economic, political) characteristic of naturalism.[12] Such an approach courts the danger that Adam and Beatrice will be dismissed as "neither fully individualized nor quintessential Man and Woman."[13] And furthermore, the prominence that the exclusion of other contexts gives to the seasonal framework has led to charges of predictability and determinism.[14] There is no evading the fact that some of Adam's speeches tend to derive universal judgments from his own particular experiences—on the nature of women ("How I recognize that look. The female dismissing the male" [2:77]); and on the inescapable consequences of past mistakes and failures ("We never recover, do we?...We never really recover" [2:94-95]). Since Wesker has explicitly rejected attempts to allegorize his text, however, it may be more profitable to read Adam not as "man" but as a specific example of the kind of self-absorbed human being who converts personal disillusionment into philosophical principle—a habit of mind that gets short shrift elsewhere in this writer's work.[15] Beatrice, lamenting the bitter disappointment she has encountered in her search for someone to match her ideal of manhood, has her own deterministic refrain: "My husband always said I expected too much from people" (2:95). Both lovers may thus be seen as living out self-fulfilling prophecies of disaster derived from their individual pasts, and for such a story, to enter the cycle of the seasons at a point which will lead to completion amid the dead leaves of autumn provides an apt metaphorical structure.

The literary effect is not unlike that of a sixteenth-century sonnet sequence, in which there is an intense focus on various states of mind and emotion within the highly formalized framework of a courtship but little direct reference to the implied narrative circumstances. Wesker's quasi-musical design, with its carefully marked transitions, breaks the text into units similar to the individual sonnets in a sequence, each devoted to the expression or analysis of an "essential" phase of the relationship. Particular stretches of dialogue show us the characters interacting dynamically in a variety of ways—testing each other's responses, sharing a moment of communion, inflicting pain, breaking into open abuse or recrimination. Occasionally the dialogue will be interrupted by a glimpse of earlier experience presented in narrative form. Beatrice, for example, suddenly broaches the subject of her marriage during the celebratory meal:

> Do you know what my husband once said to me? "You're like a queen," he said, "without a country. I hate queens without their country." *He* felt nothing and *I* felt nothing.... We spent the last years living a cold courteous lie. (2:83)

Any function such a passage may fulfill as exposition for the audience is secondary to the purpose it serves within the dramatic situation, as one speaker entrusts the other with a precious confidence, appeals for comfort, provokes resentment, or withdraws into the separateness of an identity sanctioned by the past. The more elaborate monologues that stand as individual units within the overall structure have been condemned as mere "rhapsodies," which cause the action to be suspended "for the sake of verbal flourishes."[16] But this is to misunderstand the distinctive nature of Adam and Beatrice, whose tendency to be preoccupied by their own needs and their own failures—given formal expression in these periodic retreats into extended reverie—is the destructive element in the doomed relationship that Wesker is exploring. They reach towards each other, knowing that "without love" there is neither "appetite" nor "desire" and that "nothing should be held back, ever" (2:88–89), but they cannot break free of the morbid obsession with the past that poisons their attempts to forge a lasting relationship in the present. It is characteristic of their damaged personalities that they bring their year together to a close by ritually relinquishing each other into the possession of their respective memories: "Beatrice, what do you remember most about him?...And you? Tell me what you remember about her" (2:110).

Like all Wesker's plays, *The Four Seasons* requires, in the words of advice he gave to Robert Skloot, "to be played straight."[17] A production which sought to emphasize the vulnerable individuality of Adam and Beatrice—to accept them as "nothing more than they seem"— might discover in this neglected text a moving distillation of "the private pains and confusions" that are as important a part of human experience as the more public disillusionments dramatized in its companion-piece of the mid-1960s, *Their Very Own and Golden City*.[18]

ひ

Endnotes

1. Robert Skloot," Arnold Wesker: On Playwriting," *Performing Arts Journal* 2 (1978): 46.

2. *The Four Seasons* was first performed at the Belgrade Theatre in Coventry on August 24, 1965. An account of the reviews can be found in Glenda Leeming, *Wesker the Playwright* (London, 1983): 78–82.

3. Henry Goodman, "The New Dramatists: 2 Arnold Wesker," *Drama Survey* 1 (1961): 216.

4. Review in *The Times*, September 11, 1965, quoted in Glenda Leeming, *Wesker on File* (London, 1985): 28.

5. The play was first published by Jonathan Cape in 1966. It was reprinted in the same Penguin volume as *The Kitchen*, and *Their Very Own and Golden City* in 1966. Quotations in this essay are taken from the revised text in *Arnold Wesker*, Vol. 2 (Harmondsworth, 1990).

6. Christopher Innes, *Modern British Drama: 1890–1990* (Cambridge: Cambridge UP, 1992): 114.

7. Malcolm Page, "Whatever Happened to Arnold Wesker?: His Recent Plays," *Modern Drama* 11 (1968): 321.

8. Wesker records in the Epilogue that he deleted the phrase "autumn soft skin" from the rehearsal script, when it was suggested to him that it called up not "the image of walks through the wind and soft rich colours

of autumn landscapes," but an advertisement for a well-known brand of soap (2:113).

9. This is the version in the edition published by Jonathan Cape, p. 9.

10. Arnold Wesker, "Art Is Not Enough," *The Twentieth Century* 169 (1961): 192.

11. *The Four Seasons* by Antonio Vivaldi begins with "Spring" and concludes with "Winter." In an interview with Giles Gordon (*The Transatlantic Review*, No. 21 (Summer 1966), Wesker acknowledged that the thought of setting the text to music had occurred to him but added, "I wanted the play to stand up on its own music" (17). He was to say of a later play, "I wanted to write it like a symphony." See Garry O'Connor, "Production Casebook No. 2: Arnold Wesker's 'The Friends'," *Theatre Quarterly* 2 (1971): 78.

12. In a note to the Epilogue in the 1990 edition, Wesker admits that by 1981 he had changed his mind about omitting all reference to the ownership of the house to which Adam brings Beatrice: "I made the house belong to Adam's uncle to whom I also gave a fleeting personality which I hoped would immediately set the play in a real rather than abstract world" (2:112).

13. Malcolm Page, 321.

14. See comments made by Martin Esslin, cited in Glenda Leeming, *Wesker the Playwright*, and by Leeming herself, pp. 79-80.

15. Wesker speaks of the danger of building universal theories upon the basis of partial truths derived from individual experience in *Fears of Fragmentation* (London, 1970): 107, and he dramatizes the effects of this habit of mind in Gerda's pessimistic reaction to an encounter with three young thugs in *The Old Ones* (3: 183).

16. Ronald Hayman, *Arnold Wesker* (London: Heinemann, 1970): 77.

17. Interview with Robert Skloot, p. 46.

18. In an interview with Ronald Hayman, Wesker made the connection between the two plays explicit: "You could say that *The Four Seasons* was the story of a Kate and Andrew Cobham taking a year's sabbatical off from building the Golden City and spending it in a deserted house" (*Arnold Wesker*, 112).

Wesker: Searching the Oneness Time
Robert Skloot

Arnold Wesker's career, spanning more than a third of a century, is a study in contrasts. It is marked by adulation and critical success, dogged by disappointment and even worse, public rejection. Since the late 1960s, critics have worried about his fate and his legacy, and most admit to a combination of grudging praise amid continuing irritation. The long winding down after the heady years of the 1960s finds him as contentious as ever in the 1990s, determined still to give as good as he gets in the continuing evaluation of his place in post-war British theatre.

Never possessed of the vituperative energy of Osborne nor the paranoid ambiguity of Pinter, Wesker, nonetheless, has made his own unique, substantial contribution to English playwriting. His flaws are easy to dislike and his gifts easy to overlook now that his "time" has passed. Striking a critical balance seems to be a permanent part of the writing about him as exemplified in Benedict Nightingale's summary from the early 1980s:

> Wesker may not always have communicated his passion-
> ate beliefs effectively. But he has felt that passion, held
> those beliefs, and kept those ideals alive, if only as distant
> markers for people tempted to be satisfied with the here
> and now. Again and again he has resisted human practice
> and reminded us of human potential. It is an honorable
> achievement.[1]

As he enters the middle of his seventh decade (he was born in 1932), less prominent at the center of theatrical activity or criticism, Wesker has been several times displaced by younger colleagues whose "revolutions" seem to have receded also from a fashionable public consciousness, too out of date or out of touch with the cultural velocity of contemporary times. Yet, a sustained reading of all the work cannot help but impress with its prodigality and consistency. In addition, the totality of his literary and theatrical contribution reveals a variety of expression exceptional in a writer in any age. (He is an accomplished essayist, journalist, librettist, short story writer, director, and reader of his own work in addition to being a playwright.) In the following essay, I would like to call attention to some of the qualities that brought Wesker his early triumphs and then to place them in a context useful for a brief retrospective assessment.[2]

At the center of Wesker's work is the tension between the individual and the collective or larger, surrounding society. Beginning with his first play *The Kitchen* (pf. 1959), he has returned obsessively to this inherently dramatic situation, defining the many layers (social, political, psychological) of the conflict. In *The Kitchen*, Wesker describes the workplace under intense pressure and wonders if the enduring dream of a more just and compassionate society (or brotherhood) can be created and sustained within an environment that crushes both energy and spirit from even its most idealistic representatives. Here, we remember the credo of one of Wesker's philosophical inspirations, the Victorian socialist William Morris: "Fellowship is life, lack of fellowship is death."

Over his long career, Wesker expands this theme, shifting his attention often to a more considered first cause: the need for self-definition that must precede the great commitment to communal improvement and social harmony. Thus, many of Wesker's protagonists who seek to acquire standing and justice also search for the oneness of both self and time that the anchoress Christine yearns for in *Caritas* (pf. 1981); most fail miserably in their attempt.

The record of Wesker's early stage characters is the record of the great failures and smaller triumphs to achieve a sense of community and, concurrently, to reconcile the demands of the community with the needs for individual expression and fulfillment. The usefulness of this theme to Wesker lies in the fact that it establishes a dynamic opportunity for his characters to confront the challenge of a life of *engagement*. His major plays define the options possible in an engaged life, establish the terms of the struggle, and assert the high probability of failure. And the better plays advance the idea, with greater or lesser certainty, that the struggle is worth the existential candle in the fight to subdue doubt and despair (the private struggle) or compromise and drift (the public struggle). Activism is the true mission of the pained (private) and aware (public) person. But life seems to take more than it gives: Beatie Bryant finds her voice in *Roots* (pf.

1959), but Dave and Ada Simmonds lose their dream in *I'm Talking About Jerusalem* (pf. 1959). Andrew Cobham in *Their Very Own and Golden City* (pf. 1966) finds his combination of artistic and social improvement broken on the rubble of political compromise. And immigrant factory owner Louis Litvanov, at odds with his English workers and at war with himself, suffers humiliation in *The Wedding Feast* (pf. 1974).

Persons familiar with the record of Wesker's civic involvement as a writer will recognize immediately the relevance of these themes to his own sense of citizenship (itself an old-fashioned term) and will have discerned the relationship between the conflicts in the plays and the public conflicts surrounding his life. Whether fighting to establish and maintain the alliance between Labor and the arts in Centre 42 or to prevent nuclear holocaust in the 60s (an event increasingly unlikely now with the fragmentation of the Soviet Union), riding the giddy victory of the Cuban Revolution (see the Dedication to *The Four Seasons*) or taking up the cause of the embattled State of Israel or (more recently and controversially) the endangered Salman Rushdie, he hasn't avoided what he instinctively sees as the evil of tyranny in any and all of its multifarious guises. Lately, it can be argued, he has retreated, increasingly embattled and reactive, unwilling to capitulate to forces whose victory he accepted over a generation ago. In refusing to desist, however, he articulates in his recent work an ever-narrower pitch, both vocally and scenically.[3]

One of Wesker's most insightful and sympathetic observers, Glenda Leeming, began her study of his work trying to identify Wesker's "voice" and argued correctly for the complicated interrelationship between the public and the private man.[4] In a distinct way, Wesker's work may be seen increasingly as the struggle for precision of statement and advocacy, his own as well as his characters'. A self-confessed lover of language as well as a writer thematically committed to a discussion of the claims and uses of language, hardly an effort goes by without his acknowledgment of linguistic corruption or misinterpretation.

The unhappy divorced couple of *One More Ride on the Merry-Go-Round* (pf. 1985) spent their marriage in a contest of "besting": who will have the last, annihilating word. The first words of Joshua, a cashiered philosophy professor in *When God Wanted a Son* (pf. 1989) are "It seems to me we reveal our true meaning through the musicality of what we say rather than the words we use. Each word is carried on a note. The words add up to meaning. The notes add up to meaning." Joshua is planning a voice machine that can "distinguish between what's honestly intended and what's dishonestly intended." In the long view, at his weakest, Wesker's words sound fussy and self-indulgent, lacking the *dramatic* substance for all their weighty or sometimes purposefully "jokey" content. At his best, when brimming with feeling, as in Beatie's verbal triumph in *Roots* or a Shylock meditation in *The Merchant,* now called *Shylock* (pf. 1976), Wesker provides both drama *and* revelation.

This attachment to words and the sounds they make, discussed in prose, for example, in his 1976 essay "Words—as the Definition of Experience," is a direct and crucial part of his Jewishness, his Talmudic inheritance. Traditionally, in working with biblical texts, commentary allows for opportunity for individual creation, *but there is no end to it either.* As many critics over a generation have noted, Wesker's people are gifted talkers and story tellers, and an important issue of many of his plays lies in the conflict between talking and doing, for though words may define experience, they can also defer action by turning purpose onto itself.

Thus, characters are urged to *do*, to make their words more than *mere* expression by acting on them lest they drift into paralysis (the lower-class Bryants of *Roots*, criticized by Beatie) or self-loathing (the middle-class shop owners of *The Friends*, castigated by Simone). In his recent plays, there is a not always admirable tendency to offer words as a substitute for deeds. Making strudel or furniture, decidedly purposeful behavior Wesker (and we) once applauded, appears lately to be subordinated to discussion of wine vintages and the aesthetic discrimination of obscure ingredients of sandwich fillings. When this happens, the struggle with society and within the self becomes a pale skirmish, and articulateness turns to chatter.

In fact, Wesker's Eastern European Jewish legacy takes a number of crucial forms, including the "eternal fatalism" noted by Leeming and Trussler that deprives characters of victory. Of course, Jewishness also reveals itself as a dimension of Wesker's continual grappling with the outsider/insider conundrum, noted above. To this issue, Wesker's Shylock brings his prodigious intellect and learning, contending with a society plagued by competition, ignorance, envy, and injustice. In

The Old Ones (pf. 1972), Sarah and Manny, though advanced in age, are still determined to be life's masters.

Wesker's Jewishness also involves love of learning, continuous questioning of doctrine, attachment to causes of social justice, anguished self-doubting at war with pride in achievement, refusal to become a victim of sloth or circumstance for ethical reasons, and the seemingly permanent status of outsider within a hostile social environment. Yet, these traits can have uncomfortable, even dire consequences for those who inherit them, and, for Wesker, they are most certainly inherited along with one's Jewishness. Education can lead to pretentiousness. Clarification of ideology can issue forth in nit-picking sectarianism. The search for social equality may result in self-righteousness as well as social ostracism. And the love for humanity may degenerate into a sour or sententious condescension. These cultural tensions were identified early in Wesker's career,[5] and he doesn't always escape their artistic pitfalls. (Of course, it must be remarked that these perils are found in other cultures too.) Connie in *When God Wanted a Son* tells "Jewish jokes" in her stand-up comedy act but fails at making them funny. For Wesker, as the years move him on, asserting the triumph of hope over experience is ever harder to maintain or even imagine, though the struggle of the one against the many, and the one against the self remains visible. Connie, for example, fails with her "audience," her family and her half-Jewish, divided self.

Despite the early plays' social orientation (establishing a viable and nurturing community), the concerns Wesker's people confront have evolved into something more personal and individual. Nonetheless, over the course of a generation, the variety of human experience Wesker displays is quite extraordinary. In the scope and duration of his output, the fidelity to a psychological realism and in his concern with revisiting moral issues in a social context (and some might even add, in his creation of substantial women characters), Wesker's career bears a resemblance to the long middle years of Ibsen's, say, from *Brand* through *Hedda Gabler*. And like Ibsen, Wesker has long adhered to a traditional foundation on which to build the edifice of his (once) revolutionary art. Wesker's is a conservative perspective expressed as early as the 1960s. His belief in objective standards, historical consciousness, and the positive social impact of artistic endeavor, articulated in early essays collected under the title *Fears of Fragmentation* (1970), attest to his orthodox understanding of the world. Although his belief comes permeated by the rhetoric of social activism and governmental policies taken from humanistic socialism elaborated in the 1950s and 60s, Wesker's activism was and remains influenced by the politics of the 1930s just as his artistic vision was shaped by revolutionary Victorians.[6]

In his 60s, Wesker continues to insist on his right to speak his mind in *exactly* the way he wishes; the act of creation, in newspaper articles no less than in full-length plays, is truly an act of precise description. Leeming remarks how the playwright's *tone* dominates the field of Wesker's expression, a condition that demands for the author centrality and maintenance of control. Wesker's disgust has been lavished recently in dismissive condemnation of directors whose efforts have succeeded, he resolutely believes, only in mangling the intention and shape of his and others' dramatic art. *Working mightily against* the current critical and popular belief which perceives "intention" as outdated and irrelevant (another manifestation of the one against the many), Wesker predicts the triumph of the playwright over the depredations of the director, that is, of his conscience over their authority.[7] In *When God Wanted a Son*, the condescending egotism of Joshua Mankowitz, passionately reviled by his estranged wife Martha, finds self-justification in adversarial existence: "I screamed at the pompous, the complacent, the tyrannical, the opportunistic—I screamed and I stirred and I made trouble because sometimes trouble had to be made." It is a familiar posture in Wesker's life and work.

Wesker has directed productions of his own plays since *The Friends* in 1970. A casebook of the production is a seminal document for a number of reasons, one of which is the description of Wesker's heroic attempt to develop a *community* of actors devoted to a non-authoritarian process in the production of his play.[8] The attempt was willfully sabotaged by the destructiveness of one actor, resulting in the collapse of the production's internal harmony and, perhaps, a warped presentation of the essential text. Here again, Wesker's life and art resonate together to the bitter, intractable lesson of human meanspiritedness. First seen in Alfredo, *The Kitchen's* roast chef and in the nay-saying of Libby Dobson (*I'm Talking About Jerusalem*, pf. 1960), this human trait frustrates and baffles Wesker in its imperviousness to correction. It surfaces again as a "poisonous human need to cut better men down to our size," as he describes it in the Introduction to *The Journalists* (pb. 1975). The need provokes the individual's conflict with society as in the spectacle of the tamed "free-spirit" of biblio-phile Shylock; it is also a source of the individual's conflict in more intimate, personal experience, as in the sad breakdown of love in *The Four Seasons* (pf. 1965). This need "corrupts such necessary or serious human activities as government, love, revolution or journalism," he writes; in short, all aspects of human endeavor, including the search for oneness.

After a distinguished artistic career spanning more than a genera-tion, how best can we evaluate the sum of Wesker's work and how may we assess the artistic change his own maturity has settled upon him?[9] As so many have noted, *people confronting change* is a crucial issue of his playwriting. I would argue for the unchangeable contra-dictoriness of Wesker's writing and for applying to him the standards he has set for others in his writing, standards that presuppose certain principles of humanism: generosity of spirit, clarity of thought, genu-ine emotional insight that rings true to human experience. I believe that Wesker's work suffers most when it lacks these qualities and when it displays a constriction of vision and a self-consciousness of "voice." The problem, alluded to earlier, is manifested all too clearly in the "set speeches" (frequently "jokes") around which scenes in later plays appear to be constructed, as, for example, the "football story" of *Three Women Talking* (pf. 1991). There is little doubt that the plays since the mid-1980s are less capacious and outer-directed, the action more pinched and "busy," the language more brittle. In these plays, the theme of infidelity predominates, and the struggles his characters face involve patrimony as much as social justice. In his 60s, Wesker ap-pears very concerned with his legacy.

Nonetheless, Wesker's "oneness" search continues. A determined striving for community and self-understanding, and a continuous concern to purge himself and the world of doubt and fear are the essential features of his work. In my own striving for a balanced as-sessment of Wesker's career, I am reminded of one written about his admired, contradictory mentor, John Ruskin:

> The cross-grained moralist and petulant theorist was also
> a poetic visionary with a passionate instinctive love of life,
> deeply enamoured of the beauty of the visible world and
> capable of translating that passion into superbly expres-
> sive and melodious language.[10]

∽

ENDNOTES

1. *A Reader's Guide to Fifty Modern British Plays* (London: Heinemann, 1982), p. 316.

2. Wesker's prolific career has produced numerous, and remarkably similar, identifications. Thus, separated by twenty years and a differently sized body of work, Henry Goodman and Glenda Leeming can agree without difficulty about what comprises Wesker's major thematic concerns. Cf. Henry Goodman, "Arnold Wesker," *Drama Survey* 1:2 (October, 1961): 215–22, and Glenda Leeming, "Articulacy and Awareness: The Modulation of Familiar Themes in Wesker's Plays of the Seventies," in *Contemporary English Drama*, ed. C.W.E. Bigsby (London: Edward Arnold, 1982), pp. 64–77. The latest full treatment (1993) of Wesker's career is Reade Dornan's *Arnold Wesker Revisited*.

3. Never a playwright of expansive spatial interests (*Their Very Own and Golden City* [pf. 1966] is a notable exception), the dominant stage image in his plays tends toward a communal, frequently domestic enclosure, a place of security and occasional serenity that is shattered by the explosive force of rampaging ideology or unchecked passion. In *Chicken Soup with Barley*, the fascists demonstrate outside the Kahns' house; in *Caritas*, the enclosing cell remains though ideology and passion are shown to destroy both normalcy and, equally important, order.

4. Glenda Leeming, *Wesker, The Playwright* (London: Methuen, 1983), pp. 1–13.

5. See John Garforth, "Arnold Wesker's Mission," in *The Encore Reader*, eds. Charles Marowitz, Tom Milne, and Owen Hale (London: Eyre Methuen, 1965), pp. 223–30.

6. See, for example, "Theatre, Why?" in *Fears* (London: Jonathan Cape, 1970), pp. 83–101. Thus, if "the artist's purpose in life" is the "arrangement of fragments," the order and utility of the arrangement becomes crucial, p. 106.

7. See "Interpretation: To Impose or Explain," in *Performing Arts Journal* 32:11, 2, pp. 62–76. Another (post)modern enemy is the ambiguity (not to say indeterminacy) of language itself, with which Wesker hopes to strike at least a truce. Taking refuge in the continual struggle for authorial clarity, he argues with pride that *Their Very Own and Golden City* went through thirteen drafts, and *The Merchant/Shylock* no fewer than nine as if the essential "truth" or "vision" of the plays became more perfect as it was more refined.

8. Garry O'Connor, "Production Casebook No. 2: Arnold Wesker's *The Friends*," *Theatre Quarterly* 1:2 (1971): 78–92. Glenda Leeming and Simon Trussler assess negatively Wesker's first directing assignment while praising his work as the author. In *The Plays of Arnold Wesker* (London: Gollancz, 1971), p. 186.

9. Certainly, he has changed, in small ways and large. In a 1978 interview, he remarked that there is no sex in his work. Subsequently, the two parts of *Merry-Go-Round* begin with couples copulating, and *Lady Othello* (1987) contains an erotic striptease. See interview with Robert Skloot, "On Playwriting," *Performing Arts Journal* 2:3 (Winter 1978): 45.

10. Peter Quennell, *John Ruskin* (London: Longmans, Green, 1956), p. 7.

Contributors

KEVIN ASMAN is a Ph.D. candidate at Michigan State University. His previous publications include an article on Richard Wright's *Native Son* and book reviews in *Nature Society and Thought* and the British monthly *Socialism Today*. He is currently writing a dissertation on British working-class literature.

CLIVE BARKER has pursued a parallel career in the theatre and the university. He was Festivals Organiser for the Centre 42 project, taught at the University of Warwick and authored *Theatre Games*. Today, he is joint editor of *New Theatre Quarterly* and travels the world, running training classes for actors.

ROSSANA BONADEI teaches English literature at the Faculty of Foreign Language of the University of Bergamo (Italy). She is a specialist in the poetics of the nineteenth and twentieth centuries, especially Victorian and modernist literature, and has devoted a steady interest to translation studies and activities. She has recently published a monograph on Dickens (*Paesaggio con figure. Intorno all'Inghilterra di Dickens*, [1996]).

READE W. DORNAN is the author of *Arnold Wesker Revisited* (1994) and co-author of *Multiple Voices, Multiple Texts* (1997). She has also published articles on John McGrath, Caryl Churchill, and the Omaha Magic Theatre. She teaches in the English Department at Michigan State University.

MARGARET DRABBLE was born in Sheffield in 1939 and educated at the Mount School, York, and Newnham College, Cambridge. She is a novelist, critic, and biographer, author of fourteen novels and editor of the fifth edition of *The Oxford Companion to English Literature* (1985). Her most recently published novel is *The Witch of Exmoor* (1997).

KEITH GORE is a Fellow of Worcester College, Oxford. Although his main area of activity is French literature and thought, his interest in the theatre has led him to translate a number of English authors into French; they include Alan Bennett, Edward Bond, Richard Crane, and of course, Arnold Wesker. His translation of Wesker's revised version of *The Kitchen* has recently been presented at the Théâtre du Soleil, and published by Editions Gallimard (1997).

ROBERT F. GROSS is Director of Theatre and Professor of English and Comparative Literature at Hobart and William Smith Colleges. He is the author of *Words Heard and Overheard* and *S.N. Behrman: A Research and Production Sourcebook*. He has published essays on a variety of modern dramatists from Henrik Ibsen and August Strindberg to John Guare and Harry Kondoleon.

KIMBALL KING is professor of English at the University of North Carolina. Author of the reference work, *Twenty Modern Dramatists*, he is currently General Editor of the Casebooks on Modern Dramatists series and has edited *Sam Shepard: A Casebook* as part of this series. He has currently completed an edited collection on stage plays about Hollywood, *Hollywood on Stage: Playwrights Evaluate the Culture Industry*.

GLENDA LEEMING is a graduate of the University of London where she also took her M.Phil and Ph.D. degrees. She has written widely on the nineteenth century novel and modern drama, and her most recent books include *Wesker the Playwright, Poetic Drama*, and *The Plays of Christopher Fry*. She currently teaches part time for the Open University and the University of Southampton Language Centre.

PAUL LEVITT, a longtime contributor to BBC radio drama, has written numerous articles and books on topics ranging from medicine and law to literary criticism as well as fiction for children. He teaches at the University of Colorado at Boulder and has recently completed a historical novel set in the 1920s.

ANGELA LOCATELLI is professor of English Literature at the University of Bergamo (Italy) and Adjunct Professor at the University of Pennsylvania. She has written books on Shakespeare, the Stream of Consciousness novel, and Harold Pinter. She has written several articles on semiotics and literary theory.

ALESSANDRA MARZOLA teaches English literature at the Faculty of Foreign Languages of the University of Bergamo (Italy).

KLAUS PETER MÜLLER holds a doctorate in philosophy from the University of Bonn and a postdoctoral degree in English philology from the University of Düsseldorf. He has taught English literature and British cultures at the universities of Berlin (Humboldt), Chemnitz, Dresden, and Düsseldorf. His chief research areas are British literature and the relationships between literature and epistemology, anthropology, and culture.

MEENAKSHI PONNUSWAMI is Assistant Professor of English at Bucknell University, where she teaches dramatic literature and theatre history. She has recently completed a study of the uses of history in postwar British socialist drama, *Performing Museums: Alternative History in Contemporary British Theatre, 1956-1989*. Ponnuswami is also editing *Contemporary British Theatre: The New Left and After*, a collection of new approaches to the study of postwar theatre and performance art.

MARTIN PRIESTMAN is currently a Reader in English at Roehampton Institute, London, where he has taught both English and drama. Books published include *Cowper's 'Task': Structure and Influence* and *Detective Fiction and Literature: The Figure in the Carpet*. Previous articles on drama include "A Critical Stage: Drama in the 1960s" and "Up against the Wall: Drama in the 1970s."

MARGARET ROSE teaches English Literature and Theatre Studies at Milan State University. She has published widely in the area of nineteenth-and twentieth-century theatre (*The Symbolist Theatre Tradition from Maeterlinck and Yeats to Beckett and Pinter* and *Monologue Plays for Female Voices*). Her most recent study is *Political Satire and Reforming Vision in the Works of Eliza Haywood*.

ROBERT SKLOOT has published numerous articles on modern drama and theatre, has won several teaching awards, and has been the recipient of Fulbright Lectureships to Israel, Austria and Chile. His research interests deal with plays of political and social importance. He holds a joint appointment with the Jewish Studies Program and serves as an associate vice chancellor for academic affairs at the University of Wisconsin–Madison.

ROBERT WILCHER is currently a Senior Lecturer in English the University of Birmingham, where he teaches Renaissance literature and modern drama. His publications include *Andrew Marvell, Andrew Marvell: Selected Poetry and Prose, Understanding Arnold Wesker,* chapters on Beckett's radio plays, Stoppard, Howard Barker, Rudkin and other dramatists.

HEINER ZIMMERMANN is an Akademischer Oberrat at the Anglistische Seminar of Heidelberg University, where he has taught mainly drama (medieval to contemporary) and literary theory. He has published a monograph on Shakespeare and about twenty articles on Shakespeare, Fielding, Yeats, Pinter, Stoppard, and Howard Barker in books and periodicals.